THE REAL PRESENCE THROUGH THE AGES

the Real Presence
through the ages

Jesus Adored in the Sacrament of the Altar

Compiled and Edited by

MICHAEL L. GAUDOIN-PARKER

ALBA · HOUSE alba house NEW · YORK

SOCIETY OF ST. PAUL, 2187 VICTORY BLVD., STATEN ISLAND, NY 10314

Library of Congress Cataloging-in-Publication Data

The real presence through the ages : Jesus adored in the sacrament of
    the altar / compiled and edited by Michael L. Gaudoin-Parker.
        p.   cm.
    ISBN 0-8189-0662-6
    1. Transubstantiation.   2. Catholic Church — Doctrines.
    I. Gaudoin-Parker, Michael L.
    BX2220.R43   1993
    234'.163 — dc20   92-42274
                                                            CIP

Produced and designed in the United States of America by the
Fathers and Brothers of the Society of St. Paul,
2187 Victory Boulevard, Staten Island, New York 10314,
as part of their communications apostolate.

ISBN: 0-8189-0662-6

Printing Information:

Current Printing - first digit   2   3   4   5   6   7   8   9   10

Year of Current Printing - first year shown

                                                            1998

For
My Parents and Sister,
Brethren in the Ministry,
the Congregation of the Blessed Sacrament,
and
All whom the Sacrament of Friendship
has given me the joy of meeting.

Is there not that in all Catholic Churches which goes beyond any written devotion, whatever its force or its pathos? Do we not believe in a presence in the sacred tabernacle, not as a form of words, or as a notion, but as an object as real as we are real? And... before that presence we need neither profession of faith nor even manual of devotion.

— *John Henry Cardinal Newman*

Seeing, touching, tasting are in thee deceived;
How says trusty hearing? That shall be believed;
What God's Son hath told me, take for truth I do;
Truth himself speaks truly, or there's nothing true.

— *St. Thomas Aquinas*

Acknowledgments

Excerpt from Hans Urs von Balthasar, *The Glory of the Lord: A Theological Aesthetics*, Vol. I, *Seeing the Form*, edited by Joseph Fessio and John Riches, translated by Erasmo Leiva-Merikakis, © copyright 1982 by Ignatius Press, 2515 McAllister Street, San Francisco, California 94118. Used by permission of Ignatius Press.

Excerpt from Adrienne von Speyr, *Farewell Discourses: Meditations on St. John 13-17*, translated by E.A. Nelson, © copyright 1987 by Ignatius Press, 2515 McAllister Street, San Francisco, California 94118. Used by permission of Ignatius Press.

Excerpt from *Catherine of Siena: The Dialogue*, translated and introduced by Suzanne Noffke, O.P., © copyright 1980 by Paulist Press, 997 Macarthur Boulevard, Mahwah, New Jersey 07430. Used by permission of Paulist Press.

Excerpt from *Francis and Clare: The Complete Works*, Regis Armstrong, O.F.M. Cap. and Ignatius C. Brady, O.F.M., © copyright 1982 by Paulist Press, 997 Macarthur Boulevard, Mahwah, New Jersey 07430. Used by permission of Paulist Press.

Excerpt from *Hildegard of Bingen: Scivias*, translated by Mother Columba Hart and Jane Bishop, © copyright 1990 by Paulist Press, 997 Macarthur Boulevard, Mahwah, New Jersey 07430. Used by permission of Paulist Press.

Excerpt from *Maximus the Confessor*, edited by Rev. George C. Berthold, © copyright 1985 by Paulist Press, 997 Macarthur Boulevard, Mahwah, New Jersey 07430. Used by permission of Paulist Press.

Excerpt from *Meister Eckhart: The Essential Sermons, Commentaries, Treatises and Defense*, translated and introduced by Edmund Colledge and Bernard McGinn, © copyright 1981 by Paulist Press, 997 Macarthur Boulevard, Mahwah, New Jersey 07430. Used by permission of Paulist Press.

Excerpt from *Pseudo Dionysius: The Complete Works*, translated by Colm Luibheid and Paul Rorem, © copyright 1987 by Paulist Press, 997 Macarthur Boulevard, Mahwah, New Jersey 07430. Used by permission of Paulist Press.

Contents

FOREWORD XV

ABBREVIATIONS XVIII

INTRODUCTION XIX

    The Triumph of the Eucharist XIX
    Joy in Proclaiming the Whole Mystery of Christ XXI
    The Beauty of the Eucharist XXIV
    All Enfolded in Love's Presence XXVI
    Transubstantiation — The Mystery of Being Converted ... XXVIII
    Christ — Our Neighbor XXXII
    Eucharistic Worship Reveals Human Worth XXXIV
    The Word — Basis of Belief.. XXXVIII
    The "Voices" of History XLII

BIBLICAL ABBREVIATIONS XLVI

SHORT READING LIST XLVII

THE HEART OF THE CHURCH'S PROCLAMATION
OF THE MYSTERY OF FAITH 1

    From the Anaphora of Hippolytus (c. 215): 3
    From the First Eucharistic Prayer ("Roman Canon") 4

"THE ROCK WAS CHRIST" 7

    Monuments in Stone 7
    Epitaph of Abercius (late 2nd Century) 7
    Epitaph of Pectorius (2nd Century?) 9

EARLY WITNESSES 11

    St. Ignatius of Antioch (c. 35 - c. 107) 11
    The Didache
        (The Teaching of the Twelve Apostles, c. 2nd Century?) ... 13
    St. Justin Martyr (c. 100 - c. 165) 14
    St. Melito of Sardis (mid 2nd Century; d. c. 190) 16
    St. Irenaeus of Lyons (c. 130 - c. 200) 18

ALEXANDRIAN CATECHISTS 21

    Clement of Alexandria (c. 150 - c. 215) 21
    Origen (c. 185 - c. 254) 24

CHURCH OF MARTYRS 27

    Tertullian (c. 160 - c. 225) 27
    St. Cyprian (d. 258) 29

A GOLDEN AGE OF CATECHESIS 33

    Eastern Fathers 33

    St. Ephraem (c. 306-373) 33
    St. Cyril of Jerusalem (c. 313-387) 34
    St. Basil the Great (c. 330-379) 36
    St. Gregory of Nyssa (c. 330 - c. 395) 38
    St. John Chrysostom (c. 347 - 407) 40

    Western Fathers 43

    St. Hilary of Poitiers (c. 315 - 367) 43
    St. Ambrose (c. 339 - 397) 44
    St. Gaudentius of Brescia (4th - 5th Century) 47
    St. Augustine of Hippo (354 - 430) 49
    St. Leo the Great (d. 461) 53

BYZANTINE MYSTAGOGY 55

    Dionysius the Areopagite (End of the 5th Century?) 55
    St. Maximus the Confessor (c. 580 - 662) 57
    St. John Damascene (c. 675 - c. 749) 59

Contents

GREGORIAN COUNSEL TO ENJOY THE LORD'S SUPPER 61

St. Gregory Agrigentinus (late 6th Century) 61
St. Gregory the Great (c. 540-604) 62

CELTIC AND ANGLO-SAXON FAITH 65

St. Columbanus (543-615) 65
St. Bede the Venerable (673-735) 66
The Oldest Eucharistic Hymn (Compiled 680-691) 69

CONTROVERSY, BUT FIRM IN FAITH 71

St. Paschasius Radbertus (c. 790-865) 71
Ratramnus (+ 868) 73

THE CAROLINGIAN RENAISSANCE:
TEXTS OF PERSONAL DEVOTION 75

Carolingian Texts (9th Century) 75

FAITH SEEKING UNDERSTANDING 77

Lanfranc (1010-1089) 77
St. Anselm (1033-1109) 78

MONASTIC MYSTICAL THEOLOGY 81

William of St. Thierry (1085-1148) 81
St. Bernard of Clairvaux (1090-1153) 83
St. Aelred of Rievaulx (1109-1167) 85
St. Hildegard of Bingen (1098-1179) 88
Baldwin of Ford (+ 1190) 90

THE RENEWAL OF THE CHURCH 93

The Ancrene Riwle or Wisse (c. 1220) 93
St. Francis of Assisi (1182-1226) 94

SCHOOLED IN FAITH 97

St. Albert the Great (1206-1280) 97
St. Thomas Aquinas (1225-1274) 98

A Mirror for Simple Souls (13th Century) 102
Meister Eckhart (c. 1260-1327) 104

MEDIEVAL GEMS 109

St. Catherine of Siena (1347-1380) 109
Pearl (Late 14th Century) 111
Julian of Norwich (c. 1343-after 1413?) 112
Thomas à Kempis (c. 1380-1471) 113
St. Ignatius of Loyola (1491-1556) 115

ENGLISH WILLS AND WITNESSES 117

Raynolds' Decree (1325) 117
Henry VII (1457-1509) 119
St. Thomas More (1478-1535) 119
St. John Fisher (1469-1535) 121

MYSTICISM AND DEVOTION 123

St. Teresa of Avila (1515-1582) 123
St. John of the Cross (1542-1591) 125
St. Francis de Sales (1567-1622) 128

THE BAROQUE AGE 131

Blaise Pascal (1623-1662) 131
Jacques Benigne Bossuet (1627-1704) 131
St. Margaret Mary Alacoque (1647-1690) 133
Brother Lawrence (c. 1605-1691) 134

PASTORAL MISSIONS 137

St. Alphonsus de Liguori (1696-1787) 137
St. Elizabeth Ann Seton (1774-1821) 139

THE AGE OF NEWMAN 143

Nicholas Cardinal Wiseman (1802-1865) 143
St. Peter Julian Eymard (1811-1868) 145
Matthias Joseph Scheeben (1835-1888) 149
Gerard Manley Hopkins, S.J. (1844-1889) 150

Contents

John Henry Cardinal Newman (1801-1890) 152
St. Therese of Lisieux (1873-1897) 155
Charles de Foucauld (1858-1916) 157

POST-MODERNISM: A REAFFIRMATION 159

Maurice de la Taille, S.J. (1872-1933) 159
Gilbert Keith Chesterton (1874-1936) 160
Anscar Vonier, O.S.B. (1875-1938) 161
François Mauriac (1885-1970) 162
Ronald Knox (1888-1957) 165
Emile Mersch, S.J. (1890-1940) 167
Julien Green (1900-) 169

VISIONARIES 171

Paul Claudel (1868-1955) 171
Pierre Teilhard de Chardin, S.J. (1881-1955) 172
Caryll Houselander (1901-1954) 176
Gerald Vann, O.P. (1906-1963) 177
Adrienne von Speyr (1902-1967) 179

THEOLOGIANS OF VATICAN II 183

Charles Journet (1891-1975) 183
Karl Rahner, S.J. (1904-1984) 184
Hans Urs von Balthasar (1905-1988) 186
Yves Congar, O.P. (1904-) 188
François-Xavier Durrwell, C.SS.R. (1912-) 190
Francis Clark (19??-) 193

ADORERS IN SPIRIT AND TRUTH 195

James Alberione, S.S.P. (1884-1971) 195
Carlo Carretto (1910-1988) 196
René Voillaume (1905-) 198
Bishop Fulton J. Sheen (1895-1979) 201
Mother Teresa of Calcutta (1910-) 204
Sister Briege McKenna (19??-) 205

EPILOGUE 207
    Towards the Love Banquet 207

NOTES 209
INDEX OF ENTRIES 221

Foreword

Recently a friend disclosed to me that his nephew at Oxford was embarrassed before his materialistic-minded peers who chided him for clinging to such "a medieval superstition" as belief in Christ's Real Presence in the Eucharist. This made me recall a similar experience about twenty years ago when someone asked me: "Prove that your God is present in the specious wafer that Catholics bow down before."

At such moments one may feel lost and somewhat foolish in the aloneness of one's faith. For, the truth is there is no *proof* for such mysteries! Faith resists ridicule, however, and baffles its opponents not by rational arguments or a flood of words, but mainly by the overall consistency between what we profess externally, are reputed to believe, and our tolerant attitude and patient endeavor in understanding and accepting the lives of others. I am convinced that we are first and foremost evangelical not by outright proselytizing nor by taking up the cudgels of polemics or apologetics, but by gratefully seeking to live what we are called to be: faithful to and in Love. This is a greater challenge than that of defending the faith, for an attitude of deep gratitude for so great a gift as the *mystery of faith* plunges us into the mystery of Christ's love which the Holy Eucharist contains and communicates. Fidelity to our Lord's command to "go and make disciples of all" presupposes that we are faithful to his invitation to celebrate and live the eucharistic mystery: "Do this in memory of me."

The silent "voices" recorded in the pages of this book, I hope, will offer some comfort that one does not stand alone. These witnesses, who span nearly two thousand years, strengthen us in realizing that we share in the richest tradition of belief in the reality at the heart of Christianity. Such a tradition of faith sprang from and develops Israel's greatest glory, namely, the mystery of the nearness of God's transcendent presence to humanity.

Life would be dull and, indeed, worthless without presence! A sense of presence is an essential characteristic of being fully human. Through a sense of presence we reflect the image of God in us: all our communication expresses in some way a response to the mystery of God's communion of Three Persons, which is revealed through our capacity for seeing, forming and deepening relationships. A sense of presence puts us in touch with realities which are not accessible to the feelings of our senses. It opens us to a higher quality of awareness — a consciousness in faith, in hope, in the tender responsibility of loving.

"Faith comes from hearing..." The presentation of this reality of traditional faith, I trust, will enable us to learn from the witnesses of faith in the Real Presence to appreciate this delightful truth of God's immense love which they — a *Eucharist-hearted people* — recognized and reverenced in Christ's sacrament *par excellence* of charity. By listening to these witnesses and reflecting on their fidelity to Christ's sacrament I am certain that there is everything to be gained: a sense of communion whose significance permeates and transcends history as an invisible light.

Christ Light of the Nations — the theme of the Forty-fifth International Eucharistic Congress at Seville, Spain in June 1993 — appropriately expresses the significance of the Decade of Evangelization. This theme also captures symbolically the significance of light spreading from East to West insofar as the preceding Congress took place in the Far East at Seoul, South Korea in October of 1989 — a significance towards which Teilhard de Chardin's poetic and mystical faith looked forward. In a letter, written near the end of his first journey to China, he reveals his conviction about humanity's future, which he sees as intrinsically linked to its growth in unity and peace being realized only through the spread of the knowledge of Christ, our "real science." He ends his letter by describing a vision which he experienced when considering what there is to be learned from history and archeology's investigation into the ancient civilizations of the East:

> Perhaps it was on the eve of my departure that I heard the hidden message I was waiting for China to utter, as I leaned over the battlements of the small fortified Christian community of Belgacoum and watched the sun set in the fiery sky of

the steppe.... This evening, as I watch the flight of wild geese showing black against the play of gold and red clouds above the river, I repeat to myself again and again: if we want to understand the Far East, we must not look at it at dawn, nor at high noon; we must look at it at dusk when the sun bearing the spoils of Asia with it in its glory, rises in triumph over the skies of Europe.[1]

Though we might hesitate to claim or recognize this vision as being prophetic, we can hardly deny that it witnesses to deep faith in Christ, the inner Light of the world. Without proclaiming and witnessing to Christ's presence in the depths of the Church's mystery, as the 1976 Synod of Bishops emphasized, there is no true evangelization.[2] The Christian task in bearing living witness to the good news of God's revelation draws its inspiration from Christ whose light plays through the often deceptive "faces" or appearances of all things of this world: bread, wine, human conversations, and even written words seeking to witness to what cannot be caught between the covers of all the books of the world!

Feast of Corpus Christi
June 13, 1993

Abbreviations

AAS	Acta Apostolicae Sedis
ACW	Ancient Christian Writers
ANF	Ante-Nicene Fathers
CC	Corpus Christianorum
CSEL	Corpus Scriptorum Christianorum Latinorum
CTS	Catholic Truth Society
CWS	Classics of Western Spirituality
DO	Divine Office
DS	Denzinger-Schönmetzer
FC	The Fathers of the Church
ICEL	International Committee on English in the Liturgy
PG	Patrologia Graeca
PL	Patrologia Latina
SC	Sources Chretiennes
ST	Summa Theologiae

Introduction

The Triumph of the Eucharist

All life is from God. The seventeenth century Anglican author, Sir Thomas Browne, put it this way, "All things are *art*ificial, for nature is the *art* of God."[1] Our life is rooted in the deepest possible mystery — the mystery of God's own inner life which is a communion of love. The revelation of the Father's creative love is communicated to us through Jesus Christ, the "Light of the Nations."[2] By the "working of the Holy Spirit" (cf. Eucharistic Prayer III), the Christian Church constantly proclaims the revelation of our gift of life from God in celebrating the Eucharist. The Eucharist reveals the heart of the Church's mission to spread the Gospel, the "good news" of the Kingdom of God on earth.

Since the Holy Eucharist is thus the focal point and fulcrum of all evangelization, it is the well-spring of delight to the human mind and heart.

> There is a sacrament whose principal effect consists in the enjoyment of the Godhead — it is the Blessed Eucharist. Hence we can understand the statement of St. Thomas in which he endorses the words of the pseudo-Areopagite (*Eccles. Hist.*, III): "The Eucharist perfects the other sacraments."[3]

Raphael celebrates this perspective in his famous fresco in the Vatican *Stanze*. The central subject of this painting is the life-absorbing, thought-stimulating, heart-warming theme of all human endeavor in art and discussion: *communion*. Raphael depicts this communion in the varied gathering of artisans, scholars and saints who seem to be intently engaged in divine discussion. Such discussion focuses on the *Triumph of the Eucharist* (which is the proper name of this fresco, not "The Dispute" [*Disputa*] as Vasari later mistakenly named it). All discussion, following life, turns about the way God has enabled us to experience, indeed "taste," his design in the gift of the Holy Eucharist. In the light of faith we already behold a glimpse of the glory of the saints' beatific vision of God. The Eucharist challenges us to respond in faith to our Lord's gift of himself, who is the Light of the world, for the Eucharist is the "mystery of faith" radiating the light of God's presence "on earth as it is in heaven."

The Eucharist is *the* sacrament of faith, the faith of the Church, as we recall at every Mass in the embolism on the Lord's Prayer just before approaching Holy Communion. Raphael seems to grasp the nub of the issue in calling his fresco the "Triumph of the Eucharist" for this sacrament is at the center of the Christian perspective in which we too share the saints' delight already enjoying the same reality: the presence of Love divine which is communicated to us in the "*res sancta*" (the "holy things" or "sacrament") of the altar. This is the original sense of the phrase we affirm in the Creed: "I believe... in the *communion* of *saints*." That is, I believe in that communion realized by becoming at-one with the "holy things" or "sacrament" of the Lord's body and blood.[4] The Creed implies faith in the Eucharist. Indeed, would it be possible to profess our faith without proclaiming the *mystery of faith*?

In presenting the *mystery of faith*, Raphael seems to provide in the fresco of the Triumph of the Eucharist a perspective of hope, confidence, and joy regarding the fulfillment of God's best design to save all humankind through this sacred *sign* or *sacrament* of his love. Unlike his older contemporary, Michelangelo, Raphael did not depict a terrifying scene of the Last Judgment. Instead, in the light of the Eucharist, he shows God's will to save all humanity: Christ's presence in this mystery reveals to the world God's ultimate judgment of love.

There is no dispute about the way the Eucharist has been and continues to be the focus of real delight for myriads of persons from the dawn of Christian times to our own day. This way, truth and life is manifest in Jesus Christ whose desire and gift for our integral well-being is through this sacrament which signifies, communicates, and contains the essence of all true and eternal delight: the "*fountain of all holiness*" (cf. Eucharistic Prayer II), the very presence of the giver of eternal life and beatitude. Quite simply, that is why this is the "*Blessed Sacrament.*"

The Second Vatican Council sought to refocus and manifest this deep faith of Christians. In its first statement, which significantly concerned the Sacred Liturgy, the Church's central reality of worship, this Council cited the words of the Council of Trent:

> ... the Church has never failed to come together to celebrate the paschal mystery, reading those things "which were in all the Scriptures concerning him" (Lk 24:27), celebrating the Eucharist in which "*the victory and triumph* of his death are again made present," and at the same time "giving thanks to God for his inexpressible gift" (2 Cor 9:15) in Christ Jesus, "in praise of his glory" (Ep 1:12) through the power of the Holy Spirit.[5]

This Council, however, broadened and deepened the appreciation of the understanding of Christ's triumph and victory insofar as it saw this not only in terms of exposition and processions of the Blessed Sacrament — as the Council of Trent's words indicate — but in regard to the Mass as the central sacramental act of celebrating Christ's paschal mystery.

Joy in Proclaiming the Whole Mystery of Christ

The expression, "the *mystery* of Christ," which pervades St. Paul's entire proclamation, points to the deepest nature of the Church which, as the Second Vatican Council emphasized, is the visible fellowship or communion (*koinonia*) of mystical oneness with God. The Church's task thus consists in preparing even here in this world the eternal communion of life in the "Kingdom of God/Heaven." High on the agenda in realizing this task is the responsibility to prepare the human heart for conversion so that it may be capable of the quality of enjoyment which befits communion with God.

The Church prepares the ground in the human heart by untiringly repeating St. Paul's exhortation to "*rejoice in the Lord always*" since it is convinced, no less than the Apostle, that "*the Lord is at hand*" (Ph 4:4 ff.). It would hardly be straining the sense of this passage to find in it an allusion to the Eucharist since the following verse speaks of offering "*prayer and supplication with thanksgiving.*"[6] This exhortation to rejoice sounds a call to celebrate! Such a call strengthens us to enter into the joy of the Lord; it encourages us to look forward to the wedding banquet of the Mystic Lamb as depicted in Van Dyck's famous triptych in Bruges.

The Blessed Eucharist is the source and heart-warming fullness of all human conversation, for without the reality of God's presence, how empty our discussion would be! how sterile and inconclusive! how loveless our arguments, debates, and wrangling over mere words! As C.S. Lewis so truly remarked:

> I do not know and can't imagine what the disciples understood our Lord to mean when, His body still unbroken and His blood unshed, He handed them the bread and wine, saying *they* were His body and blood.... I find no difficulty in believing that the veil between the worlds, nowhere else (for me) so opaque to the intellect, is nowhere else so thin and permeable to divine operation. Here a hand from the hidden country touches not only my soul but my body. Here the prig, the don, the modern in me have no privilege over the savage or the child. Here is big medicine and strong magic... The command, after all, is "Take, eat," not "Take, understand..."[7]

The sheer simplicity of Our Lord's command, or rather, invitation to experience God's gift of joy takes some believing — as real goodness and truth also do in a world soured and embittered by so much hostility, meanness, deception and by so much uncertainty and insecurity. Yet, without divine assurance of God's interest and presence in our life-situations, how pointless, how hopeless, how unreal our very lives would be!

Faith in Christ — that is, obedience to his invitation to love the world as he did — offers an alternative lifestyle. This faith, focused on Jesus Christ in the Eucharist, is the finest response which the world longs to see truly lived. Nothing can better awaken and enliven a sense of responsibility than awareness of Christ's Real Presence, which transforms our materialistic attitudes when we are confronted by the poverty in the world. Because of our poverty and darkness Christ the Light of the world calls and enables us to discern our vocation to know, love, serve and enjoy God here and forever.

The Eucharist — the Real Presence of Christ in this sacrament of love and unity — throws light on our human situation which stands in need of hearing his Good News today. It reveals how the Church must be involved in cultivating a sense of responsibility for this world, how it must teach respect for those values effecting a deeper human quality in living, and foster among people freedom and harmony based on justice. But, above all, the Eucharist reveals that the Church is a community of service for reconciliation and love. This is what the Founder of Christianity commanded in defining the characterizing feature of his followers: "All will know by this that you are my disciples, if you have love for one another" (Jn 13:34-35).

This love of Christ is the uniquely creative force in the world! It is the art of God the creator who cannot be thwarted in his wonderful design for his world by any of the destructive forces of pride or selfishness. The *"abundant life"* which Christ communicates to his followers — *eternal life* — is the Church's primary task to proclaim: "Eternal life is this, to *know* You the One, True, God and him whom You have sent" (Jn 17:3). This means to know God by experience. To claim this experience entails a love that is responsible, selfless, genuinely liberating and permanent. All else flows from this *knowing Christ by experience.* In a word, it is to *live "the mystery* of Christ." The Eucharist is the basis of Christian belief, morality and, moreover, mysticism. The implications of love — Christ's gift of love in the mystery of the Eucharist — are immense! His love commands our complete respect; it covers all situations of our lives: "Do this in memory of me."

Joy is discovered not in moralism, but in a challenge to genuine Christian *mysticism* — an awareness-in-love of Christ's Real Presence. This reality is the *joy of man's desiring*! It is the basis of the Christian life and the reason for the Church's existence and mission: "I've come that you might have life and have it abundantly" (Jn 10:10). In preparing for the advent of the third Christian millennium, the Church, therefore, sees its essential task of evangelization afresh in the light of the Eucharist in which it beholds the hope and joy of a new humanity — an abundance of life in this dawn of *the new creation,* Christ, the world's Light.

The early Church rang out with joy while singing the psalmist's invitation in approaching the *holy things* of Communion: "Taste and see how good the Lord is!" (Ps 34:9). This call needs to be heard again today in all its freshness, with its heart-warming and life-transforming directness. The utterly authoritative, but gentle, clarity of the Lord and Savior himself is enough to affirm our worth and change the entire course of our lives — as his presence once inspired the disciples in Galilee. It is to this refreshing, personal presence of Christ who lives through the experience of the Church that Georges Bernanos' Monsieur le Curé de Torcy refers in speaking of the Church's mission to spread joy.[8]

But let us be quite clear about it: this joy is no tawdry, ephemeral emotion. It is joy of quite a unique kind. The nearest comparison to this delightful truth of communion through, with, and in the eucharistic Christ is that sense of harmony with the universe which is experienced by those who are in love or who are deeply moved by beauty.[9] Such joy would be inconceivable, insubstantial, and have no real significance without the presence of the Beloved, whose beauty delights the whole person — heart, soul, and spirit — in such a way that he or she discovers both the freedom to respond in love and the deep worth of being faithful in a consistent and persevering manner of living. This deep and intimate response to Christ's presence in the world is the joy and beauty of the Eucharist.

The Beauty of the Eucharist

If Francis Thompson's phrase, "the many-splendoured thing," can be applied to anything at all, it certainly can to the mystery of the Eucharist. For this mystery's rich texture, integral significance, various aspects, and breadth of its implications paradoxically present so sublime and, at the same time, so simple a reality that human intelligence is utterly dazzled by it so as to be either rendered restless in seeking to grapple with its intensity or reduced to a sense of awe and the silence of adoring love in worship. The manner in which the crucified and risen Lord Jesus transforms our lives defies human comprehension (cf. 1 Cor 2:9; Jn 1:9-11). The mystery of the Eucharist is the way Christ extended his passover — the whole mystery of the cross, resurrection, ascension, and sending of his Spirit — into time in order to manifest the presence of God's total availability to human need. The Fathers of the Church were deeply imbued with a sense of the reality of Christ's presence in the *holy things* of the *mysteries* or *sacraments* which they handled and passed on to others: "Christ has now passed into the sacraments... we meet you, O Christ, in your sacraments."[10]

Both the simplicity and the sublimity of this mystery consist in the way God's *Being-in-love* touches and transforms not only "the fruit of the earth and the work of human hands," but the very substance of our personal and communal existence. This mystery draws everything of human experience — our joys, sufferings, and hopes from birth to our dying itself — into the eternal embrace of God who is love (cf. 1 Jn 4:16). By coming among us as a man and walking our ways, his beloved Son, the second Adam, reversed humankind's selfishness and desire to clasp to itself what God created to be shared in love. St. Augustine describes this tendency in the poignant phrase, "lust to dominate."[11] This tendency he found is contradicted in the light of Love's truth, which struck him at the time of his conversion:

> Your light shone upon me in its brilliance, and I thrilled with love and dread alike. I realized that I was far away from you. It was as though I were in a land where all is different from your own and I heard your voice calling from on high saying, "I am the food of full-grown men. Grow and you shall feed on me. But you shall not change me into your own substance, as you do with the food of your body. Instead, you shall be changed into me."[12]

The stark simplicity of the eucharistic mystery converts us from being *consumers* into being consumed by Love. Christ's presence among us casts a new light on our situation in the material world. He imbues us with a new sense of purpose and spirit of creative hope as he reveals the inner goodness of creation by taking into his hands and sharing the everyday stuff of our food and drink — a sharing that was the gift of himself. He proclaims that this manner of caring for all is Life-giving. He thus reveals that living the Eucharist is a *many-splendoured thing*. His proclamation that bread and wine were his — indeed, to become his own substance — took place only insofar as this act of claiming lordship over created realities was verified by his total gift of himself — his self-emptying (*kenosis*) in his sigh of consecratory love on the cross: "All has been fulfilled" (Jn 19:30). The Fathers of the Church saw in this breath of Love "to the end" (cf. Jn 13:1) nothing less than the new creation of the Mystical Body, imbued with the life-breath of God's Spirit renewing the face of the earth in the sacraments of salvation (cf. Ps 104:30).[13] Such is the transforming power of the Creator-Savior's love which is re-presented in the eucharistic mystery of the Church's sacrifice.

There can be nothing more powerfully persuasive in attracting us to turn from evil and become converted, as Dostoevsky remarked, than beauty. But, much more beautiful than the harmony of nature or some abstract truth is the beauty of this person, Jesus Christ. For by giving himself up he demonstrates in the most moving and concrete way his loving presence and desire to remain among us for all time. This gift vividly demonstrates the tangible reality of God's beauty, which is all love. The presence of Christ in this gift stirs a response in the heart of every believer, who "inflamed with love of God burns to contemplate his beauty."[14]

All Enfolded in Love's Presence

One aspect of the eucharistic mystery — the most central or most divine! — is the Real Presence of Christ in the forms of bread and wine. The truth of this aspect, however, must never be "dislocated" from its integral and organic relation to the other aspects of the eucharistic mystery — especially the celebration of sacrifice and communion.[15] It would be a distortion of the truth of the Real Presence itself to try to separate or isolate it from the Church's understanding of it within the perspective of the endeavor to live the whole eucharistic mystery. Furthermore, it is likewise the misleading source of many errors in doctrine and devotion to fail to relate this expression of his presence to the context of God's nearness to his people in the overall sacramental economy of salvation, which today we might even call a *divine ecology of human hope.*

At the Second Vatican Council great care was exercised in describing the arc of the manifold ways in which Christ is present during the divine liturgy, when the Church gathers in worship to celebrate its mystery of being united with the Father through Christ in his Holy Spirit:

> To accomplish so great a work Christ is always present in his Church, especially in her liturgical celebrations. He is present in the Sacrifice of the Mass not only in the person of his minister, "the same now offering through the ministry of priests, who formerly offered himself on the cross," but especially in the eucharistic species. By his power he is present in the sacraments so that when anybody baptizes it is really Christ himself who baptizes. He is present in his word since it is he himself who speaks when the Holy Scriptures are read in the Church. Lastly, he is present when the Church prays and sings, for he has promised "where two or three are gathered in my name, I am there among them" (Mt 18:20).[16]

The Council goes on to express how our supreme value or worth of being human derives from being created and called by God to be worshippers — a worth and wholeness revealed by Christ in uniting us to himself in his Mystical Body:

> Christ, indeed, always associates the Church with himself in this great work in which God is perfectly glorified and men are sanctified. The Church is his beloved Bride who calls to her Lord, and through him offers worship to the eternal Father.

Pope Paul VI amplified this statement in his teaching on the truth of the manifold ways in which Christ is present in the Church.[17] This truth concerns not merely our intellectual grasp or assent of the mind, but penetrates and converts our hearts, our inner attitudes and our whole lives, because it relates us to the person of Christ in the "supreme form" of his presence in the sacrament of the Eucharist. Because it manifests the fullness of Christ's presence, the Eucharist is frequently called by the Vatican Council the "source and summit" of Christian worship and life.[18] To borrow an analogy from architecture, as St. Paul does, Christ's presence in the Eucharist is the keystone at the center and high point of the arch of all the sacraments, which are all, as it were, held in place and receive their strength to be the doorway through which we may pass into the Kingdom of God's dwelling place precisely because their "line of force" comes from him (cf. Ep 2:20; 1 P 2:6; Jn 10:1 ff.).

The sacrament of the Eucharist, thus, shows the "supreme form" of presence as Pope Paul VI states, because

> ... its content is Christ himself and it is "the perfection, as it were of the spiritual life and the term of all the sacraments." It is called the "real" presence, not in an exclusive sense as though the other forms were not "real," but by reason of its excellence. It is the substantial presence by which Christ is made present without doubt, whole and entire, God and man.[19]

Not only does this sacrament contain the "supreme form" of Christ's reality or express it in a "special manner," but it also, as it were, "signs" ultimate Reality insofar as it both offers the most specific means which both points us to God's inner life of communion and also communicates this communion of the Father, Son and Holy Spirit.

Transubstantiation — The Mystery of Being Converted

It is for our wholeness that Christ came. The Eucharist is the sacramental mystery *par excellence* since it challenges our complete conversion, which is our deepest and best "love story" through the thickets of time in which we are gradually guaranteed personal growth in be-coming towards the wholeness of love — a wholeness in which our feelings, our sensitivities, our imagination, processes of thought and self-determination, dynamism and discernment about significant and lasting values all have their due part.

This is the *mystery of faith* proclaimed in the Eucharist! Nothing less will do than the integration of all our energies, experiences and levels of conscious (and even unconscious) awareness. Such an "integration" — a "gathering-in" or "recollection" — intensifies in the most profound sense our capacities for living in an awareness of tenderness which is greater than our habitual tendency to possessiveness so that we surrender the core of individualistic feelings and gladly discover our true personal quality of intimacy in communion with Otherness: "God all in all," as St. Paul says in more than one place. Though this has been described in the categories of "I-Thou" becoming "we," the description of St. Paul cannot be bettered: "I live now; no, not I, but Christ lives in me" (Gal 2:19-20).

Love alone can create integration, while guaranteeing discovery of true personal (as distinct from individuated or individual) being. This is the mystery of the Incarnation which is extended to our experience through the Eucharist, the "source and summit" (*fons et culmen*) of our desired delight (nct mere "happiness"!) — namely, the "communion" of God's beatitude: *"Blessed* (not just "happy"!) *are those called to his supper."*

The process of "our reversion to God" expresses in a new way the inner reality of "conversion," to which Christ invites our participation in the sacramental form of "dying to self" celebrated in offering his sacrifice and ours in the Eucharist. This "conversion" of mind, heart and spirit — even more than sense-experience of the "elements" of bread and wine — is not a matter of cultivating our motivation or willing. This smacks of the "voluntarist" mentality familiar to a "muscular" Christian moralist response, which is neither "Christian," "moral," nor "response," since it is in-focused on ourselves; it is pride clawing us back to self-glorification. But conversion means entirely "grace" (*charis*), that is, God attracting or drawing and transforming us (cf. Jn 6:44).

"Metanoia" or "conversion" is at the heart of what is called in the language of the Schoolmen "transubstantiation": the revelation of the substratum of Love's Being in our experience — a revelation of the Word's presence through the *"epiclesis"* or transforming prayer of

praise and thanksgiving to the Father in the power (*dynamis*) of the Holy Spirit. Only in this sense — the sacrificial sacramentality of the Eucharist — are we "spiritual," that is, discover ourselves as "relational beings." For here we are becoming the Mystical Body in-Love through the pilgrim route of becoming "Church," the "sacramental mystery of salvation." Here there is hope, because "love (charity) is poured forth into our hearts by the Holy Spirit" (Rm 5:5). Here, in the *mystery of faith*, there is only Love which enables us to identify with him in pronouncing: "This is my body/blood... flesh of my flesh, bone of my bone." The *mystery of faith*, namely, the presence of Love, "pronounces" the reality we are to become and which we are already although it has not yet become fully manifest (cf. 1 Jn 3:2). Here that deepest desire to claim to be "I am," which too often is experienced merely in a superficial way instead of as our God-etched capacity for being, is fulfilled and justified in God's eternal and new Covenant.

We are converted — as experience richly shows — not through and to doctrines or dogmas, but essentially through and to the person of Christ. The doctrine of transubstantiation would be a mere refinement of subtle scholastic thought and of academic interest unless it led us to be united in deeper love for the presence of Christ our Savior, through whom we experience the joy of being in communion with his Mystical Body.

The grace and beauty of this presence may at times seem too much for us to accept — baffling to our ordinary experiences, too "mystical" and far removed from our everyday concerns and preoccupations. Yet, the core message of Christ's whole Gospel concerns the everyday realities of doing justice to the way we share food and drink, and of discovering the joy of friendship through this sharing. Moreover, his Gospel announces the nearness of God's presence, which transforms every detail of our ephemeral experience. The reason for our Lord's choosing bread and wine — fruits of the earth and human toiling with or, at times, seemingly against the forces of nature — must be that he desires us to "feel" him in the ordinary things of experience: his presence cannot be divorced from our daily chores, he cannot and will not be different from our being! Presence, that most wonderful of all our experiences — as friendship deliciously reveals! — is not "superimposed" on the ordinary, the boring, the tiring, the backbreaking or on the occasionally joyful surprises either of sharing a meal and the wine of laughter; Presence is in and through precisely all of this! His Presence is grace running with us all the way. It is the *Most Real* meeting us in more than bread and wine!

We frequently use the darkness of our concepts, "meanings," words to block out the sheer brilliance of the Word's silent light playing through all created realities — that brilliance challenging a total commitment to cooperate with our Creator in furthering his design to manifest the inner heart of [the] matter. We prefer to take an escape-route through the dark tunnel of our partial meanings of paltry philosophies or subjective romantic interpretations or literal sense, rather than risk being consumed by Jesus' love. In a more wondrous way than in the burning bush of Moses, he reveals God's presence anew and calls us to bow down in adoration — that is, submit our minds and hearts and surrender ourselves totally to the service of love.

Paradoxically, this Word, who seals the deep core of all experience with reality — the reality of sacrifice, the tenderness of love — claims also our speech-forms in the diversity of their modalities expressing our moods, experiences and levels of understanding. The living Word mysteriously cannot do without our human words of response. We must pronounce our acceptance of Being; we must become at-one with the Word's Being-alive in all things: "This is my body... This is my blood!" This is the great poetry transforming existence into abundant life: the Mystery of Faith!

We have allowed ourselves to become so attached to words themselves, faith's traditional language of *Transubstantiation* and *Real Presence*, that we rarely recognize the reality of Christ's presence to which they point. We even have used such expressions as sharp weapons to crucify Christ in our neighbor or as tools of our intolerance to drive a wedge between ourselves and others whose culture, temperament and religious sense impel them to see the living presence of God in deeds rather than in dogmas. This has been poignantly expressed by Ann Ridler in her poem *Cranmer and the Bread of Heaven*:

> Dear master, was it really for this you died?
> To make that separation clear,
> That heaven is elsewhere, nowise here?

That the divine, bitter yeast is not inside
  Our common bread; this body loved so
In its young crocus light, and the full orb of mankind,
  And the paean of sound, all that our senses know
Is not the matter of God?

The function of dogmas is not only *like* metaphor; it is our noblest kind of metaphor! For, the Word became flesh, that is, a man. And, apart from often employing human analogies, similitudes, "parables of sunlight" (in Dylan Thomas' bright phrase), the same man enacted the most mind-and-body startling metaphor in saying of bread and wine: "This is my body... This is my blood." This leap from Word to deed — that finest deed of sharing which is communion — not only challenges every use of metaphor, but gives metaphor a ring of reality. There is a double challenge here: to stop thinking that words can "say it all" and to start believing in the reality to which the language of faith points through symbols and metaphors, sacraments and liturgy. This, after all, recalls the original significance of "metaphor" which comes from the Greek words meaning: "To bear/carry/point beyond." The challenge of the Word's revelation is to abandon literal-mindedness and to embrace the lovely condition of children, for whom the symbols and figures of speech springing up from the caverns of imagination are no less certitudes and part of the landscape of human experience than are snow-capped mountains, summer rain, or computer games!

Christ — Our Neighbor

Not only has Christ become our companion (cf. French, *co-pain*) in sharing his bread with us and needing us to share our bread with him in the needy, but he also shows himself to be our "neighbor," as Clement of Alexandria points out in commenting on the parable of the Good Samaritan:

> This is He who poured over our wounded souls the wine, the blood of David's vine; this is He who has brought and is lavishing on us the oil, the oil of pity from the Father's heart;

this is He who has shown us the unbreakable bands of health
and salvation, love, faith and hope...[20]

This brief comment echoes the rich eucharistic imagery of the
Didache:

With regard to the giving of thanks (i.e., the Eucharist), in this
way give thanks: first with regard to the cup, "We give thanks
to Thee, our Father, for the holy vine of David Thy Son, which
Thou hast made known to us through Jesus Thy Son."[21]

In giving thanks — our celebration of "Eucharist" — we announce the recapitulation of all creation restored through, with, and
in Christ's presence, a presence-in-mystery or sacrament of the
saving action of love. In essence, this annunciation is no different from
what the Disciple of love proclaimed: "The Word became flesh and
dwelt among us... full of grace and truth" (Jn 1:14). It is utterly dynamic, the most dynamic reality available to human experience: the
call, invitation, challenge, and energy of God's own Word changing
our hearts and the human situation.

This dynamic presence comprises Christ's communication of
the Father's love in the Holy Spirit to which we respond in the liturgy,
in devotion, and in living in brotherly love (cf. 1 Jn 4:11-21). The reality
of this presence is not subjective but is called "ontological" in the
deepest sense by Pope Paul VI in *Mysterium Fidei* since it is indeed
the Being of God: being and action which Christ reveals in his Gift of
Love. This reality, while ever "open" or available to us to be received,
demands our response, commands our utmost respect, invites our
love and deepest adoration of worship "in spirit and in truth" (cf. Jn
4:23).

This transforming dynamism involves the creative communication of being-in-love! The secret of this proclamation, which the
beloved John learned while leaning on Jesus' heart at the Last Supper,
the Church, like the Blessed Virgin Mary, loves to ponder in its heart
(cf. Lk 2:19, 51). While the contemplative dimension of the Church
must always be recognized as having priority over action and "doing,"
as the revelation of God's being-in-love holds primacy over our
response (cf. 1 Jn 4:9-10), it is inspired and impelled by the love of
Christ to discern and serve him in the least of his brothers and sisters.

XXXIII

In other words, Christ in this sacrament of neighborliness makes us signs of a new world — our world becoming God's neighborhood, the environment of grace and truth. Here is "the many-splendoured thing" of Christ's beauty — that is, the way he is content to go incognito — or, in Hopkins' memorable lines:

> Christ — for Christ plays in ten thousand places,
> Lovely in limbs, and lovely in eyes not his
> To the Father through the features of men's faces.

By affirming his presence in the bread and wine, Christ not only expresses the spiritual potential of our material world — a potential, that is, to become a "relational being," sharing existence and its component elements through sacrifice — but he also communicates his own reality to the stuff of our experience and to the whole of creation. The real beauty of the mystery of the Eucharist is the presence of Emmanuel, God-with-us, in us and in our midst.

Our discovery of the way God deals with us in the sacraments makes us aware of the humility of love, which prevents our neglecting him in the hungry while greedily gathering in the *manna of heaven*. The mystery of the Eucharist makes us always keep on asking not only, like the Hebrews in the wilderness, "What is it?" but also in the prayer of discipleship and faith: "Give us this day our daily bread."

The presence of Christ in the eucharistic mystery can best, indeed, *only* be discerned in the prayer of faith, just as his body is discerned in an attitude of faith that works by love (cf. 1 Cor 11:27-34; Gal 5:6). Although we can distinguish the clear signs of the ways wherein his love is at work, the reality of Christ's presence in the world ultimately must not and cannot be divided lest we lose sight of his beauty, *"ever ancient, ever new."*[22]

Eucharistic Worship Reveals Human Worth

Furthermore, being the signature of God's Word of love etched, as it were, into the materials of human experience, the sacrament of the Eucharist throws new light on the real significance of our relationship to and responsibility for all creation. In reflecting at length on the calling of every Christian to relate what is celebrated in eucharistic worship to living, Pope John Paul II concludes his Encyclical Letter on solicitude for human welfare with a splendid affirmation of the Church's faith in Jesus Christ as the unique Savior or Liberator of humanity, who continues to reveal the Kingdom of God in our midst in the sacrament of the Eucharist:

> The Kingdom of God becomes *present* above all in the celebration of the *Sacrament of the Eucharist*, which is the Lord's Sacrifice. In that celebration the fruits of the earth and the work of human hands — the bread and wine — are transformed mysteriously, but really and substantially, through the power of the Holy Spirit and the words of the minister, into the *body and blood* of the Lord Jesus, the Son of God and Son of Mary, through whom the *Kingdom of the Father* has been made present in our midst.

> The goods of this world and the work of our hands — the bread and wine — serve for the coming of the *definitive Kingdom*, since the Lord, through his Spirit, takes them up into himself in order to offer himself to the Father and to offer us with himself in the renewal of his one Sacrifice, which anticipates God's Kingdom and proclaims its final coming.

> Thus the Lord *unites us with himself* through the Eucharist — Sacrament and Sacrifice — and he *unites us with himself and with one another* by a bond stronger than any natural union; and thus united, he *sends us* into the whole world to bear witness, through faith and works, to God's love, preparing the coming of his Kingdom and anticipating it, though in the obscurity of the present time.

> All of us who take part in the Eucharist are called to discover through this Sacrament, the profound *meaning* of our actions in the world in favor of development and peace; and to receive from it the strength to commit ourselves ever more generously following the example of Christ, who in this Sacrament lays down his life for his friends (cf. Jn 15:13). Our personal commitment, like Christ's and in union with his, will not be in vain but certainly fruitful.[23]

This kind of statement goes deeper than that which proclaims a fashionable "social Gospel." It is the fruit of the most profound contemplation of the presence of Christ in the Eucharist — the mystical reality at the heart of the Church, without which the Church would not have any meaning and, indeed, cannot exist. The moral incentives of the Scriptures, the encouragement of the example of Christ's life, the inspiring challenges to the beauty of holiness and integrity of life, can do so much to foster a generous personal response. Something more, however, is required to love, cultivate, and transform our situation in this world in order to realize the significance of our prayer: "Thy will be done on earth as it is in heaven."

This *something more* is *presence*: the Real Presence of God-made-man among us. To acknowledge the cry of the poor for justice, to be sensitive to the needs of the homeless, to seek out the lonely, to be in solidarity and at-one with just anyone — just to be practically a *Christ*-ian, we, who are really poor lovers — though perhaps full of good intentions, fine ideas, and grandiose plans for reforming the world — we need the mystery of Christ's Real Presence. We need to discover in his presence and draw from him the necessary energy which transforms and empowers our hearts to become capable of loving with the same love with which he loves us — that love which redeems the world and reveals the joy of the eternal life of communion.

Pope Paul VI's dramatic words to the *campesinos* at the Thirty-ninth International Eucharistic Congress in Bogotà spring from a heart that knew the experience of Christ's Real Presence in the Mystical Body:

> We have come to Bogotà to honor Jesus in his eucharistic mystery and We are full of joy that We have been given the opportunity to do this in your midst by celebrating the presence of the Lord among you...; you are a sacrament, that is a sacred image of the Lord among us, like a reflected representation, but not hidden, of his human and divine features...; you, beloved children, are Christ for Us and We bow down before you and wish to embrace Christ in you as if he were alive and suffering...; We shall continue to defend your cause, We shall continue to denounce the sinful disparity between

rich and poor, the authoritarian and administrative abuses damaging you and your life together.[24]

But no less than ourselves do the poor, the destitute and refugees, the lonely — not only in the Third or Fourth Worlds, but also in the "world" to which we have not dared to venture, that world around the corner in the horrors of our urban high-rise flats — yes, all these anonymous and unrecognized faces of Christ's *little ones* also crave to behold the beauty of the mystery of "presence become a reality."

There is no more moving an example of the way contemplation of Christ's love in the Eucharist leads to discernment of his presence and service of him in "the distressing disguises of the poor" than that shown by Mother Teresa of Calcutta. Because of her closeness to Jesus in adoration of the Blessed Sacrament this woman who believes in Love has been able to translate the tenderness of loving into practice, as she simply recalls in the many stories of her "encounters" such as the following:

> I remember when we went to Australia, outside Melbourne — they call it "a reserve." People live there and the Sisters and I would go to the poor families and we helped them with their families. So I went to a little house and a man was there. I asked this man whether he would allow me to clean his house, but he said: "I'm all right." And I said to him that he would be more all right if he allowed me to do it. And so I started cleaning and washing his clothes. Then I saw a big lamp in that room; it was covered with dust and dirt. And I said to him: "Do you light this beautiful lamp?" And then he said: "For whom? For years nobody has visited me." And then I said to him: "Will you light the lamp if my Sisters come to you?" "Yes," he said. And so I cleaned the lamp and then the Sisters started going every evening to visit him. After two years I had completely forgotten about him. He sent me a message saying: "Tell my friend the light she lit in my life is still burning."[25]

Our world today — a world which is riven by injustice, exploitation, and racism, which in turn are the results of ruthless materialism, self-indulgence, and sheer pride — suffers the most miserable anguish of alienation and fear. It is to such a world that the presence of Christ in the seemingly voiceless anonymity of the Eucharist mysteriously impels us to proclaim the Good News of the Kingdom of God. In such a world of abject spiritual impoverishment we are called to witness to the joy of sharing the beauty of Christ's humble presence as "our daily *bread*."

The Word — Basis of Belief

While acknowledging that Christ's presence in the Blessed Sacrament cannot be separated from the whole paschal mystery of the Eucharist, it is nevertheless legitimate to ask: What did previous generations of Christians believe regarding it? How did they express their faith? In what way did their language and vocabulary reflect what they believed?

The short answer to our inquiry is found in the New Testament. For here we find the normative basis for the whole fabric of Christian belief and practice through the subsequent centuries. The very nucleus or heart of the good news in the New Testament consists in the early Christians' awareness in faith of their specific heritage from Israel; *God's covenanted presence to his people*. Since this covenant is essentially a lived reality, the people of God are first and foremost not a people of the *Book* or the *Law*, but of the *Dialogue of Love* which God initiated and brought to fulfillment in the *Life-giving Word of God*. The creative imagination of divine love found a way of inserting his presence into human experience as "the bread of life" (cf. especially Jn 6). While the Old Testament prepared the way to hear and receive the divine Word-made-flesh and the New Testament witnesses to his expression and fulfillment, the primary reality is not the ensemble of the sacred books of Scripture, but the person of the Son of God with whom and through whom Christians encounter the living God of *communion*.

The witness of the Gospels and Epistles in the New Testament, therefore, expresses more than a sense of continuity with the rich heritage of the primitive Church's Hebrew background and tradition.

For the distinctive feature of the New Testament is its witness to the *fulfillment* of God's fidelity to his promise to be forever with his people. The disciples of Jesus Christ and those who came to believe in him through their preaching staked their lives on the belief that the Risen Christ is the Lord of history, the concrete manifestation of Israel's hoped-for Emmanuel (God-with-us). They, moreover, proclaimed and celebrated his *presence* in their midst full of grace and truth (cf. Jn 1:14) especially when they gathered to pray in his name and to do what he did at the Last Supper in accordance with his command to imitate his example. Thus, St. Paul, to take one of the earliest witnesses who played no small part in shaping the tradition of eucharistic faith, expressed the nucleus of Christian practice:

> I received from the Lord what I also delivered to you, that the Lord Jesus, on the night when he was betrayed, took bread and, when he had given thanks, he broke it and said, "This is my body which is for you. Do this in remembrance of me." In the same way also the cup, after supper, saying: "This cup is the new covenant in my blood. Do this, as often as you drink it, in remembrance of me." For as often as you eat this bread and drink the cup, you proclaim the Lord's death until he comes (1 Cor 11:23-26).[26]

The expression "the breaking of bread" would seem to be the most ancient description of the distinctively Christian ritual celebration of the Risen Lord Jesus' presence in the midst of the assembly (or "Church") of the new Israel. It came to have a quasi-technical meaning to describe the focal point and central religious action in the Christian community's life, as evidenced in the classic Lucan resumé in the Acts of the Apostles:

> They devoted themselves to the apostles' teaching and fellowship, to *the breaking of bread* and the prayers... And day by day, attending the temple together and breaking bread in their homes, they partook of food with glad and generous hearts, praising God and having favor with all the people. And the Lord added to their number day by day those who were being saved.[27]

This summary text of the primitive Christian community's ideals is particularly important because it highlights the four essential principles regarding its life around the eucharistic celebration — namely, the apostles' teaching and communion, the breaking of bread and the prayers. It may also be considered as determinative of the practical arrangements, organization, and structures developed by later generations. While these very features themselves later came to be incorporated as essential elements of the eucharistic celebration — as "liturgy of the Word" (apostles' teaching and prayers) and "liturgy of the Eucharist" (breaking of the bread and communion) — these features required a division of labor, so to speak, in sharing out the ministries and functions among different members of the community. Furthermore, especially after the death of the apostles or their departure from a particular region, there had to be some person who would act as superintendent or "overseer" (bishop) or a group of senior members ("presbyters" or elders) in taking decisions and acting with competent authority recognized by all.[28]

Not only did this community simply carry on what the Lord was so magnificent in doing, as for instance when he multiplied and distributed the loaves or especially when he revealed the significance of his presence in love at the table of the Last Supper. But it also discovered its coherent inner identity and source of cohesion as a "communion" (*koinonia*) through its obedience in faith to what the Lord himself had taught it to observe as a memorial of his new and eternal covenant. Both its identity and its source of "communion" were one and the same reality which St. Paul was quick to identify as none other than the "body of Christ."[29]

From its very beginning the experience of becoming a community impressed on the Church an implicit and intuitive sense of that awareness which was emphasized at the Second Vatican Council, namely, that the Eucharist builds up ("makes") the Church, just as the Church "makes" the Eucharist.[30] This awareness is directly and intrinsically traced to the early Christians' faith in sharing in the mystery of Holy Thursday and the Lord's Resurrection — specifically through sharing his gift of the Eucharist which they called "the breaking of the bread." We can thus truly say that just as there would have been no Church if there were no Eucharist and no Eucharist if there were no community of the Risen Lord, so also there would be neither community (or Church) nor Eucharist if faith in the Real Presence of the Risen Lord Jesus were absent. The vitality of this experience of faith was not mere subjective enthusiasm. The enthusiasm — and there was plenty of this in the deepest and best sense of the word among the Christians of the early Church — was focused, stimulated, and fed precisely by what they received with deep gratitude.

In the last half century much painstaking scholarship on the New Testament witness to the Eucharist has confirmed the Church's constant faith regarding the simple meaning of the words: "This is my body... This is my blood," as referring directly to Christ's intention to communicate the whole of himself in the forms of bread and wine. The words of the life-giving Word-made-flesh accomplished what he said they meant not only at the Last Supper, but insofar as his believers faithfully kept, lovingly imitated, and re-presented his words and deeds, he guaranteed to be present in communicating himself to them and ministering to their need for salvation — a need to experience the presence of God.

Drawing on the biblical scholarship of recent decades, Karl Rahner thus refers to the original Aramaic meaning and sense of Jesus' words of Institution, which must be understood as a use of Hebrew parallelism of "bread/body-wine/blood" rather than a Greek dualistic mentality, epitomized in the body-soul dichotomy. In other words, these words refer not to two things or concepts, but to one, integral and whole reality, the person of Christ. For this reason, Rahner goes on to explain that what the Synoptic accounts present as "body-blood" really means the same as what Jesus indicated in replying to the dispute over his promise by the unequivocal sentence: "He who eats *me*, will live because of *me*."[31]

In summary, the Institution Narrative — contained in the Synoptic Gospels and the important passage from St. Paul's First Letter to the Corinthians, cited above — has, from the first, been the nucleus of the Church's central celebration of its faith regarding the signs of bread and wine really containing not only Christ's redemptive sacrifice, but also his presence.

The early Christians' response in faith to the Lord's presence in "the breaking of the bread" prepared the way for them to recognize also the presence of the Risen Christ in a diversity of other forms as well — those other forms in which his dynamic presence was discerned in sacramental actions. The root of this faith-response from the very beginning must be none other than the personal reality of the Risen Lord Jesus, present to his Church, which itself being the sacrament of salvation, as the Council highlighted, is a community that joyously believes and acts in the power of the love of the Father, to whom it constantly renders praise and gives thanks in recalling the action of his Spirit in Jesus. This personal reality of Christ's presence is the deepest glory of the Christian people, for his presence called forth — and ever continues to evoke — that faith which concentrates and builds on the rich, living tradition of Israel's awareness of God's nearness, the immanence of transcendent Love.

The "Voices" of History

In the present anthology of witnesses to faith in the Real Presence of Christ in the Holy Eucharist there are representatives from every century. The intention in compiling a book of this kind to cater for as wide an audience as possible has in no way been to provide either a source of references sought by serious students or even a representative sample of texts regarding this central truth of the Catholic faith and experience.[32] The "examples" have been chosen simply — somewhat at random — to illustrate the constancy of faith in this Catholic truth. Without in any respect being prejudicial to one stream of the Christian Tradition — namely, that of the Roman Catholic Church — the selection of authors has not included any samples of writers from other streams of Christian faith.

The production of a comprehensive edition would entail a vastly enlarged, and indeed greatly enriched book, if it were to include writers from the other Christian Churches. One thinks immediately, for instance, of George Herbert or the Wesleys, whose eucharistic hymns are unsurpassed for the depth of insight, beauty of doctrinal content, and intimate quality of devotion. Or again, among more recent authors, one recalls with gratitude the theological contribution to faith in the Real Presence offered by Pusey, Mascall, Macquarrie, Thurian, Frère Roger of Taizé, to name but a few. One might even consider including one or other of Thomas Hardy's two accounts of the Medieval Legend of *The Lost Pyx*,[33] John Betjmann's various acts of poetic devotion, and at least a section of Friedrich Hölderlin's *Brod und Wein (Bread and Wine)*.[34]

C.S. Lewis professes the virtual universality of Christian faith in the Real Presence, a faith and devotion which is almost the criterion of authentic Christianity itself:

Yes, you are always everywhere, But I,
Hunting in such immeasurable forests,
Could never bring the noble Hart to bay....

Therefore I turn my back on the unapproachable
Stars and horizons and all musical sounds,
Poetry itself, and the winding stair of thought,

Leaving the forests where you are pursued in vain
— Often a mere white gleam — I turn instead
To the appointed place where you pursue,

Not in Nature, not even in Man, but in one
Particular Man, with a date, so tall, weighing
So much, talking Aramaic, having learned a trade;

Not in all food, not in all bread and wine
(Not, I mean, as my littleness requires)
But this wine, this bread... no beauty we could desire.[35]

The pursuit of witnesses to faith in the Real Presence of Christ in the Eucharist, somewhat analogously to the *Quest for the Holy Grail*, cannot leave one cold or unaffected as regards one's quality of purpose in living. These witnesses are like "voices" echoing the invitation and challenge of the Life-giving Word of God, Jesus Christ himself, who at that moment of providing sustenance for the multitude not only promised to satisfy their spiritual hunger, but also put to them the crucial question: "Do you, too, wish to go away?" (Jn 6:67).

This existential and personal question cannot be brushed aside casually. It calls for a response. To neglect it is tantamount to denial not only of Christ, but also of the richest dimension of being human, namely, the experience of commitment to Christ who, uniquely among those born of woman, reveals to us the way God alone can satisfy the human heart's deep, divinely-etched craving for personal relationship and converse with God (cf. Gal 4:4-7).

The splendid technological achievements of recent years have not been able to bring about that longed-for *civilization of love* which Pope Paul VI indicated as the focus of genuine human development and progress.[36] Sadly though, material prosperity and success have sometimes only led to decadence in Western society. Some have tried to escape from the emptiness of loneliness, hopelessness, and despair by turning to Eastern religions or techniques of meditation; and there have been others, even among members of the Christian Church — as from its very beginning as in the story of Simon the Magician (cf. Ac 8:9 ff.) — who have been ready to exploit even this sense of spiritual poverty in the commercial consumerism of our times.

But, on the other hand, there is also no dearth of many signs of hope today regarding a genuine search for God — especially evident in the honesty and generosity of young people. What is particularly encouraging and inspiring in all this, however, is the heartfelt need for the Real Presence of God, to which *witnesses* rather than teachers are especially required.[37] Only such as these — like the early Christians in a community of living faith — can bring about the "New Evangelization" which Pope John Paul II calls for in his Encyclical *Redemptoris Missio*.[38]

The intention of this book is to show that throughout the twenty centuries of Christian faith there have not been such witnesses lacking. The witness given by these must be complemented by recalling the way their faith in the Real Presence was depicted in art — such as that of the catacombs — reflecting the climate and cultures of their lives. This anthology makes no claim to demonstrate that these testimonies of faith are of equal value or that they indicate the same or similar style of expression of this faith in eucharistic devotions or acts of worship.

The gradual development in the expression of these devotions and cult, centered on the Blessed Sacrament in Western Catholicism, must be seen and interpreted according to that solid principle of living Christianity which Cardinal Newman so finely illustrated in *The Development of Christian Doctrine*. It is ever a question of the realization of doctrine following or, at least, keeping apace with the life of prayer: *Lex orandi, lex credendi*, as the Fathers of the Church tersely put it.[39]

Thus, at times of the necessary human endeavor of questioning, through which we ourselves may grow and develop spiritually, it is well that our trust and confidence is strengthened by the stability offered to us so thoughtfully by Christ in the sacramental truth of his Presence. This Sacrament is truly called sometimes "the *permanent* sacrament" because it guarantees us reality in a world of rapid change, unreliable economic or social conditions and, sadly, all-too-often unstable relationships even in families. René Voillaume advised:

> Our devotion to the Eucharist must be profound, honest, totally embraced as essential. When one has acquired the disposition of receiving this gift of God with the soul of a child, one is upset by the reasoning of certain people, especially priests and religious, who dispute the devotion towards the Eucharist and sometimes question its legitimacy on liturgical or historical grounds... Why not, in the simple logic of faith, love the Eucharist with all the love with which we love Jesus himself?[40]

It is Christ's fidelity in Love — his *Mystery of Faith* — that provides a glimmer of the light of reality which heady rationalism tends to water down or deny outright. But only such *Reality* can justify and sustain our fragile hopes and threatened aspirations. For Christ the Light of the Nations enkindles in the human heart, which he created and redeemed by his sacrifice, the reality of faith and hope in his *Presence*, the focus and very substance of the Church's *Communion*.

More than anything else in the world, this attitude of faith in the *Reality of Love's Presence* can change the world precisely because it transforms our hearts to be tenderly responsive and truthfully responsible in *Communion* to the Gift of God which Christ our Lord hands over to us.

Biblical Abbreviations

OLD TESTAMENT

Genesis	Gn	Nehemiah	Ne	Baruch	Ba
Exodus	Ex	Tobit	Tb	Ezekiel	Ezk
Leviticus	Lv	Judith	Jdt	Daniel	Dn
Numbers	Nb	Esther	Est	Hosea	Ho
Deuteronomy	Dt	1 Maccabees	1 M	Joel	Jl
Joshua	Jos	2 Maccabees	2 M	Amos	Am
Judges	Jg	Job	Jb	Obadiah	Ob
Ruth	Rt	Psalms	Ps	Jonah	Jon
1 Samuel	1 S	Proverbs	Pr	Micah	Mi
2 Samuel	2 S	Ecclesiastes	Ec	Nahum	Na
1 Kings	1 K	Song of Songs	Sg	Habakkuk	Hab
2 Kings	2 K	Wisdom	Ws	Zephaniah	Zp
1 Chronicles	1 Ch	Sirach	Si	Haggai	Hg
2 Chronicles	2 Ch	Isaiah	Is	Malachi	Ml
Ezra	Ezr	Jeremiah	Jr	Zechariah	Zc
		Lamentations	Lm		

NEW TESTAMENT

Matthew	Mt	Ephesians	Ep	Hebrews	Heb
Mark	Mk	Philippians	Ph	James	Jm
Luke	Lk	Colossians	Col	1 Peter	1 P
John	Jn	1 Thessalonians	1 Th	2 Peter	2 P
Acts	Ac	2 Thessalonians	2 Th	1 John	1 Jn
Romans	Rm	1 Timothy	1 Tm	2 John	2 Jn
1 Corinthians	1 Cor	2 Timothy	2 Tm	3 John	3 Jn
2 Corinthians	2 Cor	Titus	Tt	Jude	Jude
Galatians	Gal	Philemon	Phm	Revelation	Rv

Short Reading List

Bermejo, Luis M. *Body Broken and Blood Shed: The Eucharist of the Risen Christ*, Gujarat Sahitya Prakash, Anand, India, 1986.

Bouyer, L. *Eucharist*, Notre Dame, 1968.

_____ *Le Mystère Pascal*, Editions du Cerf, Paris.

Buxton, R.F. *Eucharist and Institution Narrative*, A Study of Roman and Anglican Traditions (Alcuin Club Coll., No. 58), Mahew-McCrimmon Ltd., 1976.

Corpus Christi: An Encyclopedia of the Eucharist (Michael O'Carroll, ed.), Michael Glazier, Inc., Wilmington, DE, 1988.

Coughlan, P. *The New Mass: A Pastoral Guide*, Geoffrey Chapman, London, 1970.

Crichton, J.D. *Christian Celebration: The Mass*, Geoffrey Chapman, London, 1971.

Daly, Robert J. *The Origins of the Christian Doctrine of Sacrifice*, DLT, London, 1978.

Deiss, Lucien *It's the Lord's Supper*, Collins, 1980.

De Lubac, Henri *Corpus Mysticum*, 2nd ed., Aubier, Paris, 1949.

_____ *Méditation sur l'Eglise*, 2nd ed., Aubier, Paris, 1963.

Didier, Jean-Charles *Histoire de la Présence Réelle*, Collection "Esprit et Vie" 3, CLD, 1978.

Galot, Jean *Eucharistie Vivante*, Desclée de Brouwer, Paris, 1963.

Giraudo, C. *La Struttura Litteria della Preghiera Eucharistica*, Biblical Institute Press, Rome, 1981.

Guzie, Tad *Jesus and the Eucharist*, Paulist Press, New York, 1974.

Johanny, R. *L'Eucharistie Centre de l'Histoire du Salut chez Saint Ambroise de Milan*, (Theologie Historique 9), Beauchesne, Paris, 1968.

_____ *L'Eucharistie Chemin de Résurrection*, Desclée de Brouwer, Paris, 1974.

Jungmann, J.A. *The Eucharistic Prayer* (Revised), Anthony Clark, 1978.

Kilmartin, Edward J. *The Eucharist in the Primitive Church*, Prentice-Hall, Inc., Englewood Cliffs, NJ, 1965.

Lash, N. *His Presence in the World*, Sheed and Ward, London, 1968.

_____ *Theology on the Way to Emmaus*, SCM, London, 1986.

Léon-Dufour, Xavier, *Sharing the Eucharistic Bread: The Witness of the New Testament*, (translated by Matthew J. O'Connell), Paulist Press, Mahwah, New Jersey, 1987.

Ligier, L. "From the Last Supper to the Eucharist" in *The New Liturgy*, Lancelot Sheppard, London, 1970.

Mahoney, R. *The Eucharistic Prayers in Worship, Preaching and Study*, Dominican Publication, Dublin, 1985.

Martelet, G. *The Risen Christ and the Eucharistic World*, Collins, 1976.

Martimort, A.G. (Ed.) *The Church at Prayer*, Geoffrey Chapman, London.

Masure, Eugene *The Christian Sacrifice: The Sacrifice of Christ our Head*, (translated by Illtyd Trethowan), Burns Oates and Washbourne, London, 1944.

Mazza, Enrico *The Eucharistic Prayers of the Roman Rite*, Pueblo Publishing Co., NY, 1986.

Mitchell, Nathan *Cult and Controversy: The Worship of the Eucharist Outside Mass*, Pueblo Publishing Co., NY, 1982.

Musurillo, Herbert A., *The Fathers of the Primitive Church*, Mentor-Omega Books, The New American Library, Inc., NY, 1966.

Nichols, Aidan *The Holy Eucharist From the New Testament to Pope John Paul II*, Oscott 6, Veritas, 1991.

O'Connor, James T. *The Hidden Manna: A Theology of the Eucharist*, Ignatius Press, San Francisco, CA, 1988.

Oxford Dictionary of the Christian Church (Edited by F.L. Cross & E.A. Livingstone), Oxford University Press, 2nd Edition, 1974.

Pennington, M.B. *The Eucharist Yesterday and Today*, St. Paul Publications, London, 1985.

Piolanti, Antonio *Eucaristia Il Mistero dell'Altare nel pensiero e nella vita della Chiesa*, Desclée & Co., Rome, 1957.

Schmemann, Alexander *The Eucharist: Sacrament of the Kingdom*, St. Vladimir's Seminary Press, Crestwood, New York, 1988.

_____ *For the Life of the World*, St. Vladimir's Seminary Press, Crestwood, New York, 1988.

Senn, F.C. (Ed.) *New Eucharistic Prayers*, Paulist Press, New York, 1987.

Sheerin, Daniel J. *The Eucharist* (Message of the Fathers of the Church, 7), Michael Glazier, Wilmington, DE, 1986.

Solano, Juan *Textos Eucaristicos Primitivos*, I & II, Biblioteca de Autores Cristianos 118, Madrid, 1954 (2nd ed. 1973).

Tatre, Raymond (Ed.) *The Eucharist Today*, P.J. Kenedy and Sons, New York, 1967.

Thurian, Max *L'Eucharistie Mémorial du Seigneur Sacrifice d'action de grâce et d'intercession*, Delachaux et Niestlé S.A., Neuchâtel, 1963.

Tillard, J.M.R. *The Eucharist: Pasch of God's People*, Alba House, Staten Island, N.Y., 1967.

Vagaggini, C. *Il senso teologico della Liturgia*, Edizioni Paoline, Rome, 1965.

_____ *The Canon of the Mass and Liturgical Reform*, Alba House, Staten Island, N.Y., 1967.

Van Bruggen, A. *Réflexion sur l'Adoration Eucharistique*, Études Picpuciennes, Padri dei Sacri Cuori, Roma, 1968.

Vonier, A. *A Key to the Doctrine of the Eucharist,* London, 1925.

Wainwright, G. "Recent Eucharistic Revision" in *The Study of the Liturgy,* Ed. Cheslyn Jones et alii, SPCK, 1978, p 280 ff.

Young, Frances *Sacrifice and the Death of Christ,* SCM, London, 1983.

The Heart of the Church's Proclamation of the Mystery of Faith

"The Eucharist is the heart of the Church.
Where the eucharistic life flourishes,
there the life of the Church blossoms."

— John Paul II,
Siena, 14 September 1980

At every Mass the living Word of God comes to dwell among us, communicating the fulness of grace and truth (cf. Jn 1:14; 10:10). The two main "parts" of the celebration of the Eucharist — the liturgy of the Word and the liturgy of the Eucharist — constitute one act of worship.[1] Communication/communion is of the essence.

The Mass is the most perfect sacrifice because it re-presents Jesus Christ's total communication of God's love. At its very heart he, the life-giving Word, consecrates creation into a newness of being in virtue of both the institution narrative of the Gospel and also the Church's prayer of invocation (*epiclesis*) for the breath of God's Holy Spirit of love. The context of this creative interaction of God's Word and Spirit, however, is the Great Prayer of Praise, Blessing, Thanksgiving or *Eucharist*, from which the whole celebration gets its name. This Great Prayer is itself word-in-action creative of communication/communion between God and humanity and, consequently, between human persons themselves. Prayer creates bonds because it is God's gift of inspiration for the beauty of dialogue; it reveals our truth of relational being; it manifests the grace and goodness of wholeness in loving communion. The Eucharist in its wholeness transforms our experience of "I-Thou" in enabling us to discover our *being-in-Christ* as "we" — the communion of saints.

1

Some of the early Fathers of the Church—for example, Cyprian and Tertullian — spoke of two prayers coming from Christ: the "Our Father" and his "Prayer of Blessing and Thanksgiving," which he said or sang at the Last Supper (cf. Mt 26:30; Mk 14:26). Only the former came down to us *verbatim*, the latter having been transmitted *in spirit* in the Church's Eucharistic Prayer. At the end of the sixth century St. Gregory the Great confused the Fathers' expression "Lord's Prayer" (*oratio dominica*), not distinguishing their use of it in two senses. However, despite being muddled about the meaning and history of the expression, Gregory is correct about one vitally important point, namely, that all Christian prayer — and hence, the Church's prayer, *par excellence* during the Eucharist—comes from Christ, the Teacher and Model of our authentic manner of relating to the Father. In this, Gregory's witness is utterly coherent and consistent with the Tradition of the Fathers: Christian celebration in the Eucharistic Prayer proclaims in the most profound way the best of God's *spiritual gifts* to us through Christ's gift of himself as our *Pray-er*! Though the earliest form of the "Eucharistic Prayer" of Christ at the Last Supper has not been identified as it has been lost or left unrecorded, the important point is that the Christian community or Church took the initiative in celebrating the Eucharist in creating its Prayers while remaining faithful to the Spirit at the heart of Jesus' revelation of our communication with the Father. This is in utter accordance with and fulfillment of Jesus' promise to send his Spirit who would lead us into all truth — the deepest truth of the mystery of our relationship to God as his children, empowered and confident to approach him as "Father" (cf. Jn 15:26; 16:13; Rm 8:14ff.; Gal 4:5-7).

Our identity and deepest worth are discovered in worship. The spiritual grace and character of our Christian vocation consists in that we are God's children which we become on receiving Jesus' Spirit at baptism. In virtue of this we are orientated to celebrate the fulness of worship in the Eucharistic Prayer.[2]

It seems not only fitting but also crucial, thus, to begin this anthology of witnesses to the Real Presence of Christ in the Eucharistic Mystery by recalling his Word mysteriously communicating hope, beauty, and life in the proclamation of the Mystery of Faith at the heart of the Church's celebration of its experience of God's life of love. In the two examples given below of the Eucharistic Prayer, we find the expression of the nucleus of all the other witnesses' faith in God's Real Presence in the world.

From the Anaphora of Hippolytus (c. 215)[3]:

Hippolytus of Rome (c. 170 - c. 235), a presbyter resident in Rome until his martyrdom, wrote the Apostolic Tradition, from which the following text comes (ch. 4) as a model to help improvisation of the Eucharistic Prayer.

We give you thanks, O God,	
through your beloved Boy [*pais*],[4] Jesus Christ,	(Cf. Col 1:13)
whom at the end of time you have sent to us	
as Savior and Redeemer and	
Angel of your will.	(Judeo-Christian, cf. Is 9:5 LXX)
He is your inseparable Word	(Jn 1:1-2)
through whom you made the universe.	(Jn 1:3)
When it seemed good to you,	
you sent him from heaven into the womb of a virgin.	
He was conceived and became incarnate,	
and was made manifest as your Son,	
born of the Holy Spirit	(Cf. Apocryphal Bk of Jubilees 1:23-26)
and of the virgin.	(Lk 1:35)
In fulfillment of your will,[5]	
winning for you a holy people,	(1 P 2:9)
he opened his arms on the cross	(Is 65:2; Rm 10:21)
to deliver from suffering those who believed in you.	
While he was being given up to death,	
a death he freely accepted,	(Jn 10:18)
in order to *put an end to death*	(1 Cor 15:26; Rv 2)
and to break the devil's chains, to trample on hell	
and to illuminate the just, to establish the end	
and *to reveal the resurrection,*	(Cf. 2 Tm 1:10)
taking bread, giving thanks to you, he said;	
Take, eat, this is my body,	
which will be broken for you.	(1 Cor 11:24)
Similarly with the cup, saying:	
This is my blood,	(1 Cor 11:25; cf. Heb 13:20)
which is being shed for you.	(Lk 22:20; Mt 26:28)

When you do this,
you are carrying out my memorial. (1 Cor 11:25)
In memory of his death and resurrection
we offer you bread and cup, (Jn 6:35; Ps 115:13)
thanking you for counting us worthy
to stand in your presence and serve you. (Dt 18:5)
And we pray that you may send your Holy Spirit
on the oblation of Holy Church,
that, bringing us into unity, you may grant (Cf. Ep 4:3)
that all who partake of these sacred things
may be filled with the Holy Spirit
and have their faith established in the truth,
so that we may praise and glorify you (Cf. Heb 13:15)
through your Boy [*pais*], Jesus Christ.
Through him (1 Cor 8:6; Col 1:16)
glory to you and honor (Rm 16:27; 1 Tm 1:17)
to the Father and the Son with the Holy Spirit, (Cf. Ep 4:3)
in your Holy Church, now and forever. Amen.

From the First Eucharistic Prayer ("Roman Canon")[6]

Between Hippolytus' anaphora and the following text, which became standard in the West (Canon actionis) under Gregory the Great, a number of modifications and changes took place: the Roman Church abandoned Greek and adopted Latin as its language at worship; a "middle-ground" was found between Eastern and varied Western formulas.

Literal translation:	*ICEL translation:*	
We pray you, O God, deign to	Bless and approve our offering;	
make this offering wholly blessed,	make it acceptable to you,	(1 P 2:2-5)
approved, confirmed, reasonable	an offering in spirit and in	
and acceptable (spiritual),[7]	truth.	(Rm 12:1; 1 Jn 4:24)
so that it may become for us	Let it become for us	
the body and blood of your most	the body and blood of	
beloved Son, our Lord Jesus Christ,	Jesus Christ, your only Son, our Lord.	
Who, on the day before he suffered,	The day before he suffered	
took bread into his holy and	he took bread in his sacred	

4

venerable hands,	hands
and with his eyes lifted up	and looking up
to heaven	to heaven, (Mk 6:41; Jn 17:1)
to you God his almighty Father	to you, his almighty Father,
giving thanks to you,	he gave you thanks
he blessed [it],	and praise.
broke [it],	He broke the bread,
and gave [it] to his disciples,	gave it to his disciples,
saying:	and said:

"TAKE	"TAKE THIS, ALL OF YOU,
AND EAT OF IT ALL OF YOU:	AND EAT IT: (Mt 26:27)
FOR THIS IS MY BODY,	THIS IS MY BODY
WHICH WILL BE GIVEN UP	WHICH WILL BE GIVEN UP
FOR YOU."	FOR YOU." (1 Cor 11:24)

In like manner, after supper,	When supper was ended,
taking also this noble cup	he took the cup.
into his holy and venerable hands,	
again giving thanks to you	Again he gave you thanks
he blessed [it],	and praise,
and gave [it] to his disciples,	
saying:	and said:

"TAKE	"TAKE THIS, ALL OF YOU,
AND DRINK OF IT ALL OF YOU;	AND DRINK FROM IT: (Mt 26:27)
FOR THIS IS THE CUP	THIS IS THE CUP
OF MY BLOOD	OF MY BLOOD, (Cf. 1 Cor 11:25)
OF THE NEW AND	THE BLOOD OF THE NEW AND
ETERNAL COVENANT,	EVERLASTING COVENANT. (Heb 13:20)
WHICH SHALL BE POURED OUT FOR YOU	IT WILL BE SHED FOR YOU
AND FOR MANY [ALL]	AND FOR ALL (Lk 22:20; Mt 26:28)
FOR THE FORGIVENESS OF SINS	SO THAT SINS MAY BE FORGIVEN (Mt 26:28)
DO THIS IN MY REMEMBRANCE."	DO THIS IN MEMORY OF ME." (1 Cor 11:25)
THE MYSTERY OF FAITH.	LET US PROCLAIM THE
	MYSTERY OF FAITH.

"The Rock Was Christ"

Monuments in Stone

Great excitement has always accompanied archaeological finds — especially when these are demonstrated beyond reasonable doubt by independent scientific investigation to corroborate the authenticity of Christian claims of faith. The two examples of this kind of witness given here, it would seem, may be fittingly grouped together in a phrase borrowed from a passage in the Apostle Paul's First Letter to the Corinthians where he refers to the unique source of spiritual nourishment: "I want you to know, brethren, that our fathers were all under the cloud, and all passed through the sea, and all were baptized into Moses in the cloud and in the sea, and all ate the same spiritual food and all drank the same spiritual drink. For they drank from the spiritual Rock which followed them, and the Rock was Christ" (1 Cor 10:1-4).

Epitaph of Abercius (late 2nd century)

The first of the inscriptions in stone is that composed by a certain Abercius, bishop of Hieropolis in Phrygia, for his own tomb. Fragments of it were discovered in 1883 by Sir William Ramsey and it was graciously given by the Sultan of Turkey, Abdul Hamit II, to Pope Leo XIII. It is kept in the Lateran Museum in Rome. Scholars have been able to reconstruct the text of the inscription from what was known of it through a late life of Abercius which is attributed to Metaphrastes.

In the rather cryptic and poetic language, there can be

discerned almost certainly allusions to Christ ("the Chaste Shepherd"), the Church and/or Virgin Mary ("Queen" and "immaculate Virgin"), and the Eucharist ("the Fish"). The genre and tone bespeak a deep, mystical, faith and reverence befitting the Presence of Christ in the sacred Gifts shared in the Christian mysteries.

Citizen of a famous city, I erected this [tomb] in my lifetime,
so that my body might one day repose in it. My name is
    Abercius,
and I am a disciple of the Chaste Shepherd
who pastures the flocks of his sheep on the mountains
and in the plains, and whose great eyes are far-seeing
everywhere. He it is who taught me the scriptures of faith...
He it is who sent me to Rome to contemplate
its majesty, to behold a Queen adorned
in golden apparel and shod with sandals of gold.
I beheld there a people marked with a shining
seal. I also saw the plain of Syria
and all the cities, and Nisibis, beyond
the Euphrates; everywhere I discovered
my companions. With Paul for my guide,
I was led everywhere in faith; everywhere
(faith) served me as food a Fish from the Spring —
large and pure, [it had been] caught by an immaculate
    Virgin.
She constantly offers it to her dearest friends
to eat; she likewise possesses the best of wine
which she serves for their drink with the bread.

I, Abercius, dictated this [text]
engraved in my presence; I am seventy-two years old.
Let the brother who understands these lines
pray for Abercius. Let no one place
any other tomb above this one. If he does so,
he shall pay the Roman treasury [a fine of] two thousand
    coins
and [owe] my beloved Hieropolis a thousand.[1]

Epitaph of Pectorius (2nd Century ?)

This enigmatic inscription on seven marble fragments was found in 1838 in an ancient Christian cemetery near Autun, France. The style of the Greek characters occasioned some scholars to date the epitaph as late as the fifth or sixth centuries. It has been argued, however, by Cardinal J.B. Pitra and G.B. de Rossi that it is probably a copy of a second century original, the imagery and doctrine of its content being reminiscent of Irenaeus' teaching. This epitaph — like the famous epitaph of Abercius — is in essence thoroughly eucharistic, especially because of the identifying symbolism of the Fish.[2]

O divine race of the celestial Fish,
keep your heart pure in the midst of men, for you have
     received
an immortal spring of wondrous waters. Thus
my friend, refresh your soul in the eternal waters
of abundant Wisdom. Receive the honied food
that the Savior gives to his saints. Satisfy
your hunger when you receive the Fish in your hands.
Lord and Savior, I beg you to feed us
with the Fish. I beseech you, Light of the deceased,
that my mother may sleep in peace. Aschandius, O father
most dear to my heart, together with my [sweet mother]
and my brothers, remember [me]
Pectorius [resting in the peace of the Fish].[3]

Early Witnesses

St. Ignatius of Antioch (c. 35 - c. 107)

Probably of Syrian origin, he is thought to have been the successor of St. Peter at Antioch, i.e., the second bishop in that city. During his journey to Rome for martyrdom, under a guard of ten soldiers, he was received with much honor at Smyrna by St. Polycarp and members of some of the Christian communities of Asia Minor. There he wrote letters of encouragement to the Churches of Ephesus, Magnesia, and Tralles and also to the Church of Rome to beg not to be prevented from attaining the privilege of the palm of martyrdom by their well-meaning, though mistaken, kindness. For to be a witness of proclaiming the Good News of Jesus he felt the urgent need also to master his silence in sharing his passion and death. On being taken to the port of Troas he wrote three more letters: to St. Polycarp and to the Churches of Philadelphia and Smyrna.

In all seven letters — but especially in that to the Romans — Ignatius' eagerness to witness to the Gospel by martyrdom is clearly rooted in his passionate devotion to Christ, whose life is manifest in the Eucharist. This Christian sacrament, presided over by the bishop, is the source and bond of unity in faith and love, the hallmark of Christians, whose lives it challenges and empowers to imitate and become what they receive. In "the breaking of bread"[1] Ignatius discerned "the medicine of immortality, our antidote to ensure that we shall not die but live in Jesus Christ for ever" (cf. Ephes. xx).

For we can have no life apart from Jesus Christ; and as he represents the mind of the Father, so our bishops, even those who are stationed in the remotest parts of the world, represent the mind of Jesus Christ... Pray, then, come and join this choir, every one of you; let there be a holy symphony of minds in concert; take the tone all together from God, and sing aloud to the Father with one voice through Jesus Christ, so that he may hear you and know by your good works that you are indeed members of his Son's Body. A completely united front will help to keep you in constant communion with God... Let no one be under any illusion; a man who excludes himself from the sanctuary is depriving himself of the bread of God, for if prayer of one or two individuals has such efficacy, how much more powerful is that of the bishop together with his whole church.[2]

All the ends of the earth, all the kingdoms of the world would be of no profit to me; so far as I am concerned, to die in Jesus Christ is better than to be monarch of earth's widest bounds. He who died for us is all that I seek; he who rose again for us is my whole desire. The pangs of birth are upon me; have patience with me, my brothers, and do not shut me out from life, do not wish me to be stillborn. Here is one who only longs to be God's; do not make a present of him to the world again, or delude him with the things of earth. Suffer me to attain to light, light pure and undefiled; for only when I am come thither shall I be truly a man. Leave me to imitate the passion of my God. If any of you has God within himself, let that man understand my longings, and feel for me, because he will know the forces by which I am constrained.

It is the hope of this world's prince to get hold of me and undermine my resolve, set as it is upon God. Pray let none of you lend him any assistance, but take my part instead, for it is the part of God. Do not have Jesus Christ on your lips and the world in your heart; do not cherish thoughts of grudging me my fate. Even if I were to come and implore you in person, do not yield to my pleading; keep your compliance for this written entreaty instead. Here and now, as I write in the fullness of life, I am yearning for death with all the passion of a lover. Earthly longings have been crucified[3]; in me there is left no spark of desire for mundane things, but only a murmur of living water that whispers within me, "Come to the Father." There is no pleasure for me in any meats that perish, or in the delights of this life; I am fain for the bread of God, even the flesh of Jesus Christ, who is the seed of David; and for my drink I crave that blood which is love imperishable.[4]

Every man who belongs to God and Jesus Christ stands by his bishop. As for the rest, if they repent and come back into the unity of the Church, they too shall belong to God, and so bring their lives into conformity with Jesus Christ. But make no mistake, my brothers; the adherents of a schismatic can never inherit the kingdom of God. Those who wander in outlandish by-ways of doctrine must forfeit all part in the Lord's passion.

Make certain, therefore, that you all observe one common Eucharist[5]; for there is but one body of our Lord Jesus Christ, and but one cup of union with his blood, and one single altar of sacrifice — even as also there is but one bishop, with his clergy and my own fellow-servitors, the deacons. This will ensure that all your doings are in full accord with the will of God.[6]

The Didache
(The Teaching of the Twelve Apostles, c. 2nd Century?)

> The author, date and place of composition of this very early manual or series of "Church Orders" regarding Christian morals and practices at worship are unknown. Its content and style suggest that it describes the life of an isolated Christian community somewhere in Syria. It contains two examples of the primitive kind of prayer extemporized during the eucharistic celebration. In them there is explicit evidence of a sense of faith and reverence for the Real Presence of Christ in this sacrament.

Give thanks in this manner. First, over the cup: "We give thanks to you, our Father, for the holy vine of your child David, which you have made known to us through Jesus your child: to you be glory for ever."

Then over the broken bread: "We give thanks to you, our Father, for the life and knowledge which you have made known to us through Jesus your child: to you be glory for ever. As this broken bread was scattered upon the mountains and was gathered together and made one, so let your Church be gathered together from the ends of the earth into your kingdom: for the glory and the power are yours through Jesus Christ for ever and ever."

Let none eat or drink of your Eucharist except those who have been baptized in the name of the Lord. For on this point the Lord said: "Do not give dogs what is holy."

And when you have been filled, give thanks in this way. "We give thanks to you, holy Father, for your holy name, which you have made to dwell in our hearts, and for the knowledge and faith and immortality which you have made known to us through Jesus your child: to you be glory for ever. You, almighty Master, created all things for your name's sake; you gave food and drink to men for their enjoyment, so that they might give thanks to you; and on us you have bestowed spiritual food and drink, and eternal life through your child. Above all we give thanks to you because you are mighty; to you be glory for ever. Remember, Lord, your Church: deliver it from all evil, make it perfect in your love; make it holy and gather it together from the four winds into your kingdom which you have prepared for it; for the power and the glory are yours for ever."

"Let grace come and this world pass away. Hosanna to the God of David! If any man is holy, let him come; he who is not, let him repent. Our Lord, come [Maranatha]. Amen."

On the Lord's day assemble together and break bread, and give thanks, first confessing your sins, that your sacrifice may be pure. If any man has a quarrel with a friend, let him not join your assembly until they are reconciled, that your sacrifice may not be defiled. For this is the sacrifice spoken of by the Lord: "In every place and time offer me a pure sacrifice, for I am a great king, says the Lord, and my name is great among the nations."[7]

St. Justin Martyr (c. 100 - c. 165)

Born of pagan parents in Samaria, he spent a long time searching for the truth in various philosophies. All this stood him in good stead when eventually he became a convert to Christianity (c. 130), for he employed what he had learned to defend and proclaim the truth of the Gospels and Christian way of life. After first teaching at Ephesus, he moved to Rome where he set up a Christian school. Among his students was the famous Tatian, whose main contribution was the Diatessaron, a history of the life of Christ drawn from the Four Gospels used in the Syrian Church till the fifth century.

Though Justin was not a particularly brilliant philosopher or noted for literary skill, he nevertheless shines as the first Christian thinker to demonstrate the relation between reason and faith. Borrowing from the Stoics, he taught that the traces of truth in all systems of thought ("seminal ideas") lead to the fullest expression of wisdom in the Christian faith whose teacher is the Word of God.

In the first of his two Apologies, from which the following text is taken, Justin offers most interesting information about early Christian belief and practice regarding the Eucharist.

No one may share in the Eucharist except those who believe in the truth of our teachings and have been washed in the bath which confers forgiveness of sins and rebirth, and who live according to Christ's commands.

For we do not receive this food as ordinary bread and as ordinary drink; but just as Jesus Christ our Savior became flesh through the word of God, and assumed flesh and blood for our salvation, so too we are taught that the food over which the prayer of thanksgiving ["eucharistized food"], the word received from Christ, has been said, the food which nourishes our flesh and blood by assimilation, is the flesh and blood of this Jesus who became flesh.

The apostles in their memoirs, which are called Gospels, recorded that Jesus left them these instructions: he took bread, pronounced the prayer of thanksgiving, and said: "Do this in memorial of me. This is my body." In the same way he took the cup, pronounced the prayer of thanksgiving, and said: "This is my blood," and shared it among them and no one else. From that time on we have always continued to remind one another of this. Those of us who are well provided for help out any who are in need, and we meet together continually. Over all our offerings we give thanks to the Creator of all through his Son Jesus Christ and the Holy Spirit.

On Sundays there is an assembly of all who live in towns or in

15

the country, and the memoirs of the apostles or the writings of the prophets are read for as long as time allows.

Then the reading is brought to an end, and the president delivers an address in which he admonishes and encourages us to imitate in our own lives the beautiful lessons we have heard read.

Then we all stand up together and pray. When we have finished the prayer, as I have said, bread and wine and water are brought up; the president offers prayers and thanksgiving as best he can, and the people say "Amen" as an expression of their agreement. Then follows the distribution of the food over which the prayer of thanksgiving has been recited; all present receive some of it, and the deacons carry some to those who are absent.

Those who are well provided for, if they wish to do so, contribute what each thinks fit; this is collected and left with the president, so that he can help the orphans and the widows and the sick, and all who are in need for any other reason, such as prisoners and visitors from abroad; in short he provides for all who are in want.

So on Sundays we all come together. This is the first day, the one on which God transformed darkness and matter and made the world; the day on which Jesus Christ our Savior rose from the dead.[8]

St. Melito of Sardis (mid 2nd Century; d. c. 190)

Though in early times his reputation and prolific writings were held in high esteem, all about him passed into obscurity except a few fragments and a homily on the Paschal Sacrament, which was discovered only in 1940. The reason for the eclipse of one of the great lights of Asia (as was the way he was described by Polycrates in Eusebius' Hist. Eccl.) is unknown. Perhaps, however, his position in the controversy regarding the dating of Easter may have played a part in occasioning his disfavor.

The homily on the Paschal Sacrament is the oldest known example of catechesis or instruction on the relation of the central Christian sacramental rites to the Old Testament, whose fulfillment they are. Faith in the Real Presence is implied in this fulfillment of what was foreshadowed and prefigured. Especially in the peroration — with its rhetorical repetitions: "This is he..." may one not catch an echo of the invitation to Holy Communion: "This is the Lamb of God..."?

The Law is old, the Logos new; the figure is transient, grace is eternal. The sheep is corruptible, the Lord is incorruptible, who was immolated as a lamb, but resurrected as God.

For as a sheep he was led to the slaughter but a sheep he was not; and as a mute lamb, but a lamb he was not. For the figure is past and the truth has been revealed: in place of a lamb it is God who has come, and in place of a sheep, man. And in man, Christ, who contains all.

For born Son-like, and led forth lamb-like, and slaughtered sheep-like, and buried man-like, he has risen God-like, being by nature God and man.

He is all things: inasmuch as he judges, Law; inasmuch as he teaches, Word; inasmuch as he saves, Grace; inasmuch as he begets, Father; inasmuch as he is begotten, Son; inasmuch as he suffers, Sheep; inasmuch as he is buried, Man; inasmuch as he has risen, God.

This Jesus Christ to whom be glory for ever and ever. Amen.

Words and deeds, dearly beloved, are meaningless if they are separated from their symbol and prefigure. Everything said and everything done participates in this prefiguring — words in their parable, and deeds in their prefiguration....

It is the same in a work of art. No work is undertaken without a model. Is not the future work already outlined in its design? That is why a model is first constructed of wax, or clay, or wood, from which the future work can be seen emerging, loftier in height, more durable, gracious in line and rich in appointment, thanks to a miniature and perishable model... When you execute the work, it becomes the sole object of your desire, because in it alone you see model, materials, and reality. As it is in the case of corruptible images so it is in incorruptible; as it is in the earthly so it is in the heavenly...

The earthly Jerusalem was once of value, but now it is valueless because of the heavenly Jerusalem. The narrow inheritance was once of value, but now it is valueless because of the breath of grace.

For it is not in one place or in a narrow piece of land that the glory of God resides, but his grace has been spread to the ends of the earth, and there the Almighty has pitched his tent, through Jesus Christ to whom is glory for ever and ever. Amen.

If you look at this prefiguration you will see its truth through its fulfillment. If you wish to see the mystery of the Lord look to Abel likewise slaughtered, to Isaac likewise bound, to Joseph likewise sold, to Moses likewise exposed, to David likewise persecuted, to the prophets likewise maltreated because of Christ. Look also at the sheep sacrificed in the land of Egypt which smote Egypt and saved Israel by its blood.

By the voice of the prophets the mystery of the Lord has also been proclaimed... Isaiah [says]: "Like a lamb he was led to the slaughter and like a sheep dumb before his shearers this man did not open his mouth. Who shall tell his descent?" (Is 53:7). And many other things were proclaimed by many other prophets concerning the mystery of the Passover which is Christ; to him be glory for ever and ever. Amen.

This is he who is the Passover of our salvation...

Come, then, to me [he says] all you families of mankind sullied with sin, and receive the remission of sins. For I am your forgiveness, I am the Pasch of salvation, I am the lamb immolated for you, I am your redemption, I am you life, I am your resurrection, I am your light, I am your salvation, I am your king. I lead you to the heights of heaven. I will show you the Father eternal. I will raise you by my right hand...

He is the *alpha and the omega*, he is the beginning and the end, the inexplicable beginning, the incomprehensible end. This is the Christ. This is the King. This is Jesus. This is the commander. This is the Lord. This is he who rose from the dead. This is he who sits at the Father's right hand. This is he who carries the Father and is carried by the Father. To him be glory and power for ever and ever. Amen.[9]

St. Irenaeus of Lyons (c. 130 - c. 200)

He is thought to hail from the East (Smyrna) since he heard St. Polycarp as a boy. After studies in Rome, he became a presbyter of the church of Lyons. After fulfilling his commission of taking letters to Pope Eleutherius regarding toleration for the Montanist sect of Asia Minor, he was made bishop on his return to Lyons (c. 178) to succeed the martyred Pothinus.

Irenaeus' achievement in his great work *Adversus Haereses* — against all kinds of false teachings pervading the Church through Gnosticism — rightly earns him the title of being the first great Catholic theologian. He develops the Pauline notion of "recapitulation" (cf. Ep 1:10) in showing not only how God's revelations to previous ages are summed up in the Incarnation, but also that, through his filial obedience of love, Christ reconciles and restores all humanity and creation into communion with God. His Christ-centered approach brings out the wholesomeness of creation, especially in the Eucharist, in which the new creation comes about. The presence of Christ is real, though spiritual, for Christ guarantees the continuity of revelation while uniting and integrating our material world into the communion of God's design, which consists in bringing all things under the Lordship of Christ, the Head. For in him is manifest the glory of God: man fully alive.

We must [...] make an offering to God and show ourselves in everything grateful to him who made us, in the purity of our thoughts, the sincerity of our faith, the firmness of our hope and our burning charity, as we offer him the first fruits of the creatures that are his. This is the pure offering that the Church alone makes to her creator, presenting her gift to him gratefully from his creation.

We offer to him what belongs to him, as we appropriately recall our fellowship and union and confess the resurrection of flesh and spirit. For as the earthly bread, once it has received the invocation of God upon it,[10] it is no longer ordinary bread, but the Eucharist, and is made up of two elements, heavenly and earthly, so too our bodies, once they have received the Eucharist, are no longer corruptible, but contain within themselves the hope of resurrection.[11]

If the flesh is not saved, then, the Lord did not redeem us with his blood, the chalice of the Eucharist is not a share in his blood, and the bread which we break is not a share in his body. For blood cannot exist apart from veins and flesh and the rest of the human substance which the Word of God truly became in order to redeem us with his blood, as his own apostle states: "In him we have redemption, the forgiveness of sins" (Ep 1:7).

Since we are his members, and are nourished by his creation, and since he also gives us his creation, by making his sun rise and rain fall according to his own good pleasure, he declared that the chalice of his creation is his own blood, from which he augments our own blood, and he affirmed that the bread of his creation is his own body, from which he gives growth to our bodies.

So when the mixed chalice and the baked loaf receive the word of God, and when the eucharistic elements become the body and blood of Christ, which bring growth and sustenance to our bodily frame, how can it be maintained that our flesh is incapable of receiving God's gift of eternal life? For our flesh feeds on the Lord's body and blood, and is his member.

So St. Paul writes in his letter to the Ephesians: "We are members of his body, of his flesh and his bones" (Ep 5:30). He is not speaking about some spiritual and invisible man, "for a spirit has not flesh and bones as you see that I have" (Lk 24:39); on the contrary, he is speaking of the anatomy of a real man, consisting of flesh, nerves and bones, which is nourished by his chalice, the chalice of his blood, and gains growth from the bread which is his body.

When a vine-stock is set in the ground, it bears fruit in due season; when a grain of wheat falls into the earth, it dies, only to be restored to life and multiplied by the Spirit of God, who holds all creatures in being. Then by the providence of God the grape and the vine become available for man's use, and when they receive God's word, they become the Eucharist, the body and blood of Christ. In the same way, if our bodies are nourished by the Eucharist, after being buried in the earth and decaying there they shall rise again in due season, when the word of God confers resurrection upon them for the glory of God the Father (cf. Ph 2:11). For God confers immortality on what is mortal, and bestows incorruptibility on what is corruptible, because his power is made perfect in weakness.[12 & 13]

Alexandrian Catechists

Clement of Alexandria (c. 150 - c. 215)

Probably of Athenian origin, Clement came to Alexandria after studying philosophy and Christianity in various places. He succeeded his master, Pantaenus, as head of the Catechetical School at Alexandria in 190. Some years later (in 202) persecution made him flee. His teaching is reflected in his many writings, in which he gives a new orthodox meaning to "gnosis" — revealed religious knowledge or illumination as communicated in the Christian teaching through the Holy Scriptures and the Sacraments. Chiefly through the instrumentality of Baptism and the Eucharist Christ, the Teacher or "Logos," enables humankind to partake of divine Life and immortality.

We, however, are they who are "taught by God" (1 Th 4:9), and who boast in the name of Christ. Is there any reason, then, that we should not understand the Apostle to be referring to this when he speaks of the "milk of little ones" (cf. 1 Cor 3:21)? Whether we are the shepherds who rule the churches in imitation of the Good Shepherd (cf. Jn 10:11), or the sheep, should we not understand that in speaking of the Lord as the milk of the flock, he is merely safeguarding the unity of his thought by a metaphor? Certainly, the passage, "I gave you milk to drink not solid food for you were not yet ready for it," can be adapted to this sense, too, if we only take "solid food" as substantially the same thing as milk, not something superior to it. Either way, it is the same Word, whether light and mild as milk or become firm and solid as food.

Still, taking it in this sense, we can also consider preaching as milk, poured out far and wide, and faith as food, made solid by instruction as the foundation. Faith is more substantial, in fact, than hearing, and is assimilated into the very soul and is, therefore, likened to solid food. The Lord presents the same foods elsewhere as symbols of another sort, when he says in the Gospel according to John: "Eat my flesh and drink my blood" (Jn 6:55). Here he uses food and drink as a striking figure for faith and for the promise. Through these the Church, made up of many members, as man is, takes her nourishment and grows; she is welded together and formed into a unit (cf. Ep 2:21; 4:16) out of both body, which is faith, and soul, which is hope; just as the Lord, out of flesh and blood. Hope, indeed, which holds faith together as its soul, is the blood of faith. Once hope is extinguished, then the life-principle of faith expires, as when blood is drawn from the veins....

O mystic wonder! The Father of all is one, the Word who belongs to all is one, the Holy Spirit is one and the same for all. And one alone, too, is the virgin Mother. I like to call her the Church. She alone, although a mother, had no milk because she alone never became a wife. She is at once virgin and mother: as virgin, undefiled; as mother, full of love. Calling her children about her, she nourishes them with milk that is holy: the Infant Word. That is why she has no milk, because this Son of hers, beautiful and all hers, the Body of Christ, is milk. The new people she fosters on the Word, for he himself begot them in the throes of his flesh and wrapped them in the swaddling clothes of his precious blood. What a holy begetting! What holy swaddling clothes! The Word is everything to his little ones, both father and mother, educator and nurse. "Eat my flesh," he says, "and drink my blood" (Jn 6:55). He himself is the nourishment that he gives. He delivers up his own flesh and pours out his own blood. There is nothing lacking his children, that they may grow. What a mystical paradox! He bids us put off the former mortality of the flesh and, with it, the former nourishment, and receive instead this other new life of Christ, to find place in ourselves for him as far as we can, and to enshrine the Savior in our hearts that we may be rid of the passions of the flesh.

Yet, possibly you do not relish this turn of thought, but prefer to be more down to earth. Then listen to this interpretation: the flesh is a figure of speech for the Holy Spirit, for it is he, in fact, who created the flesh; the blood means the Word, for he has been poured forth as precious blood to give us life; the union of the two is the Lord, nourishment of little ones: the Lord, both Spirit and Word. Our nourishment, flesh, flesh from heaven made holy. This is our nourishment, the milk flowing from the Father by which alone we little ones are fed. I mean that he, the "well-beloved" (Mt 3:17), the Word, our provider, has saved mankind by shedding his blood for us. Therefore, we fly trustfully to the "care-banishing breast" (*Iliad* 22:83) of God the Father; the breast that is the Word, who is the only one who can truly bestow on us the milk of love.[1]

...[T]he natural and pure drink demanded by ordinary thirst is water. This is what the Lord supplied for the Hebrews, causing it to gush from the split rock (cf. Ex 17:6; Nb 20:11), as their only drink, a drink of sobriety; it was particularly necessary that they who were still wandering should keep far from wine. Later on, a sacred vine put forth a cluster of grapes that was prophetic (cf. Nb 13:24); to those who had been led by the Educator to a place of rest after their wanderings it was a sign, for the great cluster of grapes is the Word crushed on our account (cf. Is 53:5, 10). The Word desired that the "blood of the grape" (cf. Gn 49:11; Ec 50:16) be mixed with water as a symbol that his own blood is an integral element in salvation.

Now, the blood of the Lord is twofold: one is corporeal, redeeming us from corruption (1 P 1:8); the other is spiritual, and it is with that we are anointed. To drink the blood of Jesus is to participate in his incorruption (cf. Jn 6:55). Yet, the Spirit is the strength of the Word in the same way that blood is of the body. Similarly, wine is mixed with water and the Spirit is joined to man; the first, the mixture, provides feasting that faith may be increased; the other, the Spirit, leads us on to incorruption. The union of both, that is, of the potion and the Word, is called the Eucharist, a gift worthy of praise and surpassingly fair; those who partake of it are sanctified in body and soul for it is the will of the Father that man, a composite made by God, be united to the Spirit and to the Word. In fact, the Spirit is closely joined to the soul depending upon him, and the flesh to the Word, because it was for it that "the Word was made flesh" (Jn 1:14).[2]

Origen (c. 185 - c. 254)

This Alexandrian biblical scholar and theologian has enjoyed a mixed reputation: on the one hand he has been recognized as one of the brightest lights of Christian intellectualism; and, on the other, he has been regarded with great caution. His tendency for symbolic speculation and spiritual interpretation of Scripture made him somewhat suspect as regards orthodoxy. There is also the question of the irregularity surrounding his ordination by the bishops of Palestine in defiance of Demetrius, his own ordinary in Alexandria. Because of persecutions, which occasioned his flight from his native city, he became widely known. Translations of some of his writings — most of the original Greek texts of which have been lost (through ecclesiastical censure imposed on him) — were made by Rufinus into Latin. Through these some of his seminal ideas and insights passed over to the West.

"Each one shall bring as a contribution to the Lord, therefore, as he has conceived in his heart" (Ex 35:5). Ask yourselves if you are conceiving, or taking in; and if you are retaining: lest what is said should flow away and perish... You who are wont to take part in the divine mysteries know how carefully and reverently you guard the body of the Lord when you receive it, lest the least crumb of it should fall to the ground, lest any thing should be lost of the hallowed gift. For you regard, and rightly regard, yourselves as culpable if any part should fall to the ground through your carelessness. When you show, and rightly show, such care in guarding his body can you suppose it less blameworthy to neglect the word of God than his body?[3]

That which is "sanctified through the word of God and prayer" (1 Tm 4:5) does not of its own accord sanctify the recipient; for if this were so it would sanctify him who eats the bread of the Lord unworthily and no one through this food would become "ill or weak" or "sleep" (1 Cor 11:30). Thus even in respect of the bread of the Lord the advantage to the receiver depends on his partaking of the bread with a pure mind and a clear conscience. We are not deprived of any good merely by not eating of the bread sanctified by the word of God and prayer; neither do we abound in any good by the mere eating. What causes our deprivation is wickedness and sin; what causes our abundance is righteousness and well-doing (cf. 1 Cor 8:8)... The food which is "sanctified"... "goes into the belly," in respect of its material nature, and is "discharged into the privy" (Mt 9:17). But in respect of the prayer which is added to it, it becomes profitable, "according to the proportion of faith" (Rm 12:6), and is the cause of spiritual discernment in the mind which has an eye to its spiritual profit. It is not the material bread that profits the man who eats the bread of the Lord not unworthily; rather it is the word which is spoken over it.[4]

The morsel which Jesus gave to Judas was of the same kind as that which he gave to the rest of the Apostles when he said, "Take, eat." But to them the result was salvation; to Judas it was condemnation, so that "after he had received the morsel Satan entered him" (Jn 13:27). Let this bread and the cup be understood by the simpler folk according to the more general acceptation of the Eucharist; but by those who have been schooled to a more profound apprehension let it be interpreted in reference to the diviner promise, the promise of the nourishing word of truth. I might illustrate the point by the physical effect of the most nutritive bread, which aggravates a latent fever, although it is conducive to health and well-being. Thus a true word supplied to a sick soul, which does not require such nourishment, often irritates it, and becomes the occasion for its deterioration: in such a case it is dangerous to speak the truth.[5]

Church of Martyrs

Tertullian (c. 160 - c. 225)

This African came from a pagan family in Carthage where he was well-educated in literature and law, and may have practiced as a lawyer. This rich foundation, his literary skill and brilliant style ennobled Latin theology as well as literature in the West. After his conversion to Christianity in c. 190 he seems to have remained a layman (though St. Jerome says he was ordained a priest). Later he became a member of a heretical sect called the Montanists — a sect noted for rigorism in its rather severely depressing attitudes toward the material world, marriage, and so on, despite the fact that many excesses and inconsistencies prevailed among its adherents. Though Tertullian's copious writings thus fall into two periods — those of his orthodox and those of his heterodox days, the short passages cited below regarding faith in Christ's Real Presence in the Eucharist reflect nothing contrary to Catholic faith. Rather, they enhance it.

[Commenting on the parable of the Prodigal Son — Lk 15.] He receives the ring for the first time when, after being questioned [during the rites of initiation], he seals the covenant of faith and thus afterwards feeds on the rich food [lit. "fatness," i.e., "fatted calf"] of the Lord's body, that is, on the Eucharist.[1]

The flesh is the hinge of salvation [*adeo caro salutis est cardo*]... The flesh feeds on the body and blood of Christ that the soul also may feast [lit. "be fattened"] on God.[2]

We receive the sacrament of the Eucharist... when we meet before dawn only from the hand of those who preside. We offer sacrifices for the dead, and for birthdays, on the anniversaries... We take great care to prevent any of our wine or bread being dropped on the ground.[3]

[Care required when the Sacrament is reserved at the home of a Christian woman married to a pagan.] Your husband will not know what it is that you are eating secretly before you begin your meal of [ordinary] food. Even if he knows that it is bread he does not believe that it is what it is said to be.[4]

We understand in a spiritual sense the words: "Give us this day our daily bread." Christ is indeed our bread, because Christ is our life and life is "bread." "I am the bread of life," he said (Jn 6:31); a little before this he said, "Bread is the word of the living God which comes from heaven."[5] His body is also understood [as being] in the bread — as when he said: "This is my body" (Mt 26:26; Mk 14:22; Lk 22:19). Therefore, when we ask for daily bread, our request is[6] to live eternally in Christ and to receive from his body our indivisibility.[7]

Thus, after announcing that he longed passionately to eat the Passover, as it was his own — for it would have been unfitting for God to desire what belonged to someone else — [Christ] took the bread and distributed it to the disciples, after having made it his own body, saying: "This is my body," that is, the figure of my body. But it could not have been the figure except that it were the body of a real thing. An unreal thing — like a dream ["phantasma"] — cannot possess a figure. On the other hand, if he moulded bread into a body for himself, if his body were not real, then what he should have offered up for our sakes would have been bread. This would be the kind of foolish reasoning that Marcion employs: that bread be crucified! But he called bread his body — not the pumpkin which Marcion seems to have for a brain. For Marcion fails to appreciate that bread was prefigured as the body of Christ in Jeremiah, through whom already Christ said: "They were hatching their plots against me, saying: 'Let us give him a taste of wood with his bread'" (Jr 11:19), that is, the cross pertaining to his body [the cross part of his very life]. So, he who clarifies the past showed just what "bread" he intended by calling his body "bread." In the same way, when he established the covenant sealed with his blood in speaking of the cup, he likewise demonstrated his body's reality. For only a living body of flesh has blood....

In order that you may discern also the ancient figure of blood in wine, listen to Isaiah: "Who is this that comes from Edom, in crimsoned garments from Bozrah, he that is glorious in his apparel, marching in the greatness of his strength? Why is thy apparel red, and thy garments like his that treads in the wine press?" (Is 63:1-2) ... Thus, he who once signified his blood by wine now has consecrated his blood into wine.[8]

St. Cyprian (d. 258)

When Cyprian, a pagan rhetorician was converted to Christianity in 248, who would have thought that within the compass of a decade he would have left so significant a mark on the life not only of the Church in Africa but also on that of all subsequent centuries of the Christian Church? For within this short span, which comprised his pastoral ministry as a priest and bishop and, indeed, almost the entire extent of Cyprian's Christian life, his teaching became recognized as a compellingly fascinating witness to and powerful influence on the Universal Church regarding its mission to be a sacrament of unity. His life and teaching offer an inspiring lesson about the spirituality of the Eucharist as the unique sacrifice capable of transforming our personal existence into an offering or gift for others. This teaching is particularly evident in his famous Epistle 63 — the earliest work exclusively devoted to the Eucharist. This letter tackles the division of the African Church brought about by the "Aquarian" controversy, which debated the use of water alone or wine mixed with water for the eucharistic celebration. Cyprian insisted, using the most persuasive argument of all, on fidelity to what Christ did, taught, and commanded. Herein is found the Church's unity. More compelling still was his fidelity in deed to Christ, by offering the supreme witness of pouring out his life-blood in martyrdom in imitation of the supreme sacrifice of Christ which he celebrated in the Eucharist. Thus, in this age of martyrs his life itself demonstrated Tertullian's renowned saying: "As frequently as we are bled by you, the more we increase in number; the blood of Christian martyrs waters the seed of faith" (*Apology*, 50).

No one is more a priest of the Most High God than our Lord Jesus Christ: he sacrificed to God the Father, offering nothing other than what Melchisedech had offered, namely bread and wine, his body and blood... Insofar as Christ bore our sins, our whole burden, we recognize water as signifying the people and wine the blood of Christ. But the mingling of water with wine in the cup signifies the people's union with Christ; the multitude of believers becomes associated and one with him, the focus of their faith. So complete is this association and mingling of water and wine in the Lord's cup that it is impossible to separate these elements from one another. Hence, nothing can separate from Christ the Church, which comprises the vast assembly of the faithful staunchly persevering in their belief in him; nothing can prevent its adherence to indivisible love, in which it abides. For this reason, when consecrating the Lord's cup, we cannot use only water. Neither will just wine alone do for the offering. For, if wine is offered by itself, it signifies only the blood of Christ, without our part in it; whereas water by itself signifies the people without Christ. When both are mingled and are fused in an indiscriminate manner of union with each other, however, then the spiritual and heavenly sacrament comes about. Thus the Lord's cup means neither water alone, or wine alone, but both mixed together, in the same way as flour alone or water alone cannot constitute the body of the Lord, unless both have been united and kneaded into the solid, single substance of bread. In this holy sign or sacrament the unity of our people is manifested. Just as a single loaf of bread is made up from many grains, which have been collected, milled and mixed, so let us understand that in Christ, the heavenly bread, there is but one body, to which we, though many, have been joined and united.[9]

In the [Lord's] prayer we go to ask: "Give us this day our daily bread." These words can have both a spiritual and a literal meaning. Both senses can be understood, through God's goodness, as fostering our salvation. Christ is truly the bread of life (Jn 6:35). This bread is ours, and not for everyone. Just as we say "Our Father," because he is the Father of those who know and believe in him, so we call Christ "our bread," because he is the bread of those who are feasted on his body. We ask for this bread every day in order not to be separated from the body of Christ by some serious sin, which would prevent us from communion in the daily Eucharist, the bread of salvation, and from the heavenly bread. He himself has proclaimed: "I am the living bread who has come down from heaven. Whoever eats this bread will live for ever. The bread that I shall give is my flesh for the life of the world" (Jn 6:51). When he says that anyone who eats his bread lives for ever, he clearly declares that this pertains only to those who eat his body and who have the right to share in the eucharistic communion. On the other hand, it is necessary to fear and to pray lest by keeping away from the body of Christ one may not become separated and remain far from salvation. For we must heed the warning which he himself gave: "If you do not eat the flesh of the Son of man and drink his blood, you shall not have life in you" (Jn 6:53). For this reason we ask to be given every day our bread, that is, Christ. Thus, abiding and living in Christ, we are not cut off from his sanctification and from his body.[10]

A Golden Age of Catechesis

St. Ephraem (c. 306-373)

This Syrian deacon became famous for his ascetical life of holiness and his great learning. His preaching is lyrical with enthusiasm about his experience of Christ in the "sacred mysteries" or divine liturgy. His deep devotion led him to compose many hymns (*"memra"* or "rhythms"), some of the most beautiful being to the Holy Spirit and the Blessed Virgin Mary.

O Lord, drive away the darkness from our minds with the light of your wisdom, so that enlightened in this way we may serve you with renewed purity. The beginning of the sun's passage through the sky marks the beginning of the working day for us mortals: we ask you, Lord, to prepare in our minds a place where the day that knows no end may give its light. Grant that we may have within us this light, the life of the resurrection, and that nothing may take away our delight in you. Mark us with the sign of that day that does not begin with the movement and the course of the sun, by keeping our minds fixed on you.

In your sacraments we welcome you every day and receive you in our bodies. Make us worthy to experience within us the resurrection for which we hope. By the grace of baptism we conceal within our bodies the treasure of your divine life. This treasure increases as we eat at the table of your sacraments. Let us rejoice in your grace. We have within us, Lord, a memorial of you, which we receive at your spiritual table; may we possess the full reality in the life to come.

Let us appreciate the great beauty that is ours through the spiritual beauty that your immortal will arouses in our mortal nature. Your crucifixion, Lord, was the end of your bodily life: help us to crucify our will to give birth to the spiritual life. May your resurrection, Jesus, fill our spirits with greatness: may we see in your sacraments a mirror in which we may be able to recognize the resurrection.

Your divine ordering of the world, O Savior, is the image of the spiritual world: let us live in it as truly spiritual men.

Do not take away from our minds, Lord, the signs of your spiritual presence and do not withdraw from our bodies the warmth and delight of your presence. The mortal nature of our bodies is a source of corruption within us: let the outpouring of the spirit of your love wipe away the effect of mortality from our hearts. Grant, Lord that we may hasten to our true home, and, like Moses on the mountaintop, let us have a glimpse of it.[1]

St. Cyril of Jerusalem (c. 313-387)

> Like many of his contemporaries, Cyril was taken up in resolving disputes of doctrine concerning the nature of Christ — disputes which sadly divided the body-politic of the Empire as well. Despite such taxing endeavors, he carefully prepared catechumens for the sacraments of Christian initiation at Easter. While the eighteen pre-baptismal instructions attributed to him have never been questioned, the authorship of five post-baptismal treatises ("Mystagogical Catecheses" or "Instructions about the Mysteries") has been long debated. They provide, however, a clear idea about faith in the eucharistic presence in 4th century Jerusalem.

The blessed Paul's teaching (cf. 1 Cor 11:23-25) itself gives you ample and full assurance about the divine mysteries into which your admission has made you one body and blood with Christ... Since, then, Christ himself clearly described the bread to us in the words, "This is my body," who will dare henceforward to dispute it? And since he has emphatically said, "This is my blood," who will waver in the slightest and say it is not his blood?

So let us partake with the fullest confidence that it is the body and blood of Christ. For his body has been bestowed on you under the figure of bread, and his blood under the figure of wine, so that by partaking of Christ's body and blood you may become one body and blood with him. This is how we become bearers of Christ ["Christophers"], since his body and blood spreads throughout our limbs; this is how, in the blessed Peter's words, "we become partakers of the divine nature" (2 P 1:4).

Christ once said in conversation with the Jews: "Unless you eat my flesh and drink my blood, you have no life in you" (Jn 6). They were scandalized because they did not interpret his words spiritually; they retreated from his presence, thinking he was exhorting them to cannibalism.

Even in the Old Testament there were "Loaves of the Presence," but since they belonged to the old dispensation they have come to an end. But in the New Testament the bread is of heaven and the chalice brings salvation, and they sanctify the soul and the body; for as the bread relates to the body, so the Word harmonizes with the soul.

Do not, then, regard the bread and wine as nothing but bread and wine, for they are the body and blood of Christ as the master himself has proclaimed. Though your senses suggest otherwise, let faith reassure you.

You have been taught and fully instructed that what seems to be bread is not bread, though it appears to be such to the sense of taste, but the body of Christ; that what seems to be wine is not wine, though the taste would have it so, but the blood of Christ; that David was speaking of this long ago when he said, "Bread strengthens the heart of man that he may make his face glad with oil" (Ps 103:15). So strengthen your heart by partaking of that spiritual bread, and gladden the face of your soul.

May you unveil it with conscience undefiled, and reflect the glory of the Lord, and pass from glory to glory in Christ Jesus our Lord. To him be honor, power and glory for ever and ever. Amen.[2]

St. Basil the Great (c. 330-379)

St. Basil the Great was the brother of Saint Gregory of Nyssa
and Saint Macrina and the friend of St. Gregory Nazianzus.
He was educated at Caesarea in Cappadocia and the great
centers of pagan and Christian culture, Constantinople and
Athens. Forsaking worldly renown, however, he embraced
the monastic and eremetical life, which the Emperor Julian,
his former fellow-student, could not persuade him to abandon
in favor of life at the court. He succeeded his bishop Eusebius
to the see of Caesarea in 370, defending the orthodox faith
against Arianism. He possessed a capacity for organization —
apart from his gifts of learning and eloquence — so that his
stamp was left on Eastern monasticism which at his time
stood in need of coordination and coherence; various works
of charity — hostels for the poor and hospitals — were also
undertaken under his administration. Largely due to his
teaching on the Holy Spirit, the Council of Constantinople in
381-382 saw the virtual end of the Arian controversy with the
acceptance of the Creed of Nicea. The "Liturgy of St. Basil,"
which is celebrated in the Eastern Church on certain important days (e.g., the eves of Christmas and Easter, Sundays of
Lent, Maundy Thursday, etc.) may be traced to his influence,
though it has undergone considerable modification since his
time.

To communicate every day, to be a sharer in the holy body and
blood of Christ is, indeed, a good and beneficial practice, for He says
plainly: "He who eats my flesh and drinks my blood, has eternal life"
(Jn 6:55). Who doubts but that to share continually in life is nothing
other than to live in manifold ways? We, for our part, communicate
four times each week: on the Lord's day, on the fourth day [Wednes-
day], on the day of preparation [Friday], and on the Sabbath [Satur-
day], also on the other days if there is a commemoration of a saint.

But as to a person's being compelled in times of persecution, in
the absence of a priest or minister, to receive communion from his
own hand — it is a waste of time to prove that this is no offense at all,
since events themselves attest the long-standing, traditional character of this practice.

For all those living the solitary life in the wilderness, where there is no priest, reserve communion at home, and receive it from themselves. In Alexandria, and in Egypt, each one, even of the laity, very commonly keeps communion in his house and receives it from himself when he wishes. For when once the priest has consecrated and imparted the sacrifice, he who has received it as complete, once and for all, ought rightly to believe that he is partaking and receiving it from the hand of him who imparted it, even when he partakes of it everyday. Indeed, even in church the priest distributes a portion, and the one who receives it has it at his disposal, and thus moves it to his mouth with his own hand. And so, it is the same situation whether one receives a single portion or many portions at the same time from the priest.[3]

Question No. 172: With what fear, with what sort of assurance and disposition should we partake of the body and blood of Christ?

Reply: Fear is taught us by the Apostle when he says: "He who eats and drinks unworthily eats and drinks condemnation to himself" (1 Cor 11:29). Assurance is created in us by belief in the words of the Lord: "This is my body which is given for you. Do this in remembrance of me" (Lk 22:19), in the testimony of John who described first the glory of the Word, and then added the manner of the Incarnation by saying: "And the Word became flesh and dwelt among us, and we beheld His glory, glory as of the Only begotten of the Father, full of grace and truth" (Jn 1:14), and in the testimony of the Apostle, as he writes: "Being in the form of God, He did not reckon it robbery to be equal with God, but He emptied Himself taking the form of a servant, being made in the likeness of men, and found in fashion as a man; He humbled Himself, becoming obedient unto death, indeed the death of the Cross" (Ph 2:6-8). When, therefore, the soul believes these words, words so very momentous, it learns the greatness of the glory, and is astonished at the surpassing quality of the humility and obedience, that One so great obeyed the Father unto death for the sake of our life, then I think it is disposed towards love for God the Father who "did not spare His own Son, but delivered Him up for us all" (Rm 8:32), and for His Only begotten Son who became obedient unto death for our redemption and salvation. And thus is the soul able to obey the Apostle who establishes a good conscience as a sort of benchmark for those who are sound in these matters by saying: "For the love of Christ presses us on, for we judge that if One died for all, then all died. And He died for all, that living they should no longer live for themselves, but for Him who died and rose for their sakes" (2 Cor 5:14-15). He who partakes of the bread and the cup should have such a disposition and such readiness.[4]

St. Gregory of Nyssa (c. 330 - c. 395)

> This younger brother of St. Basil came from Cappadocia. After following Basil to monastic life, Gregory was made the bishop of Nyssa in c. 371. He was present at the Council of Constantinople in 381, where he stoutly defended the faith of Nicea. His eloquence as a preacher brought him renown wherever he went. His gifts lay also in the calibre of his thought, the originality and poetic turn of which contributed to developing the doctrines of the Trinity, Incarnation, and Redemption, and preparation of catechists responsible for instructing others on the Sacraments of Christian Initiation: Baptism, Confirmation, and the Eucharist. He applied his knowledge of Platonism and Neoplatonism with skill in scriptural exegesis, some of his finest work being his commentaries on the Canticle of Canticles, the Lord's Prayer and the Beatitudes of the Gospel.

But since human nature is twofold, a composite of soul and body, those who are being saved must grasp Him who leads the way towards life by means of both. Now the soul, being blended with Him by faith, received from it the beginnings of its salvation. For the union with Life involves a sharing of life. But the body comes into association and blending with its Savior in a different way.

Those who have through treachery received poison neutralize its destructive force by means of another drug. But the antidote, like the poison, must enter the vital organs of the person, in order that the effect of the remedy may by passing through them, be distributed through the entire body. So, when we had tasted of that which brought destruction to our nature, of necessity we needed in turn something to restore what was destroyed, in order that such an antidote passing into us might, by its own counteracting influence, repel the harm already brought into the body by the poison.

What is this then? It is nothing else but that body which was shown to be mightier than death and which inaugurated our life. For just as a little leaven, as the Apostle says (1 Cor 5:6), makes the whole lump like itself, so the body which was made immortal by God, by passing entire into our body alters and changes it to itself... But it is not possible for anything to enter the body, unless it is mingled with the vital organs by way of food and drink. Therefore the body must receive the life-giving power in the way that its nature permits...

It is admitted that the subsistence of the body comes from nourishment, and that this nourishment is food and drink, and that in food bread is included, and in drink water sweetened with wine. It is admitted, further, that the Word of God, who... is both God and Word, mingled with our human nature, and He entered our body, He did not devise some other constitution for our nature, but provided for the continuance of His own body by the customary and appropriate means, maintaining its subsistence by food and drink, the food being bread... He who sees bread sees, in a way, the human body, for the former by passing into the latter becomes what it is, so too in His case, the body which was the receptacle of divinity, receiving the nourishment of bread, was, in some sense, identical with it, seeing that the nourishment... was changed into the nature of the body.... With good reason, then, do we believe that now also the bread which is sanctified by the word of God is changed into the body of God the Word....

For that body, too, was potentially bread, and it was sanctified by the indwelling of the Word who dwelt in the flesh (cf. Jn 1:14). The manner, then, whereby the bread which was changed in that body was changed to divine power is the same which now brings about the like result. For in that case the grace of the Word sanctified the body which derived its subsistence from bread and, in a sense, was itself bread; whereas in this case, likewise, the bread, as the Apostle says, is sanctified by the word of God and prayer (1 Tm 4:5). Not by the process of being eaten does it go on to become the body of the Word, but it is changed immediately into the body through the word, even as the Word has said: "This is my body."

But all flesh is nourished also by moisture for without being combined with this, the earthly part of us cannot continue in life. As we maintain the solid part of the body by solid and firm food, in a similar way we make an addition to the moist element from the nature which is akin to it. And this, on entering our bodies, is changed into blood by the faculty of assimilation, especially if through wine it receives the power of being changed into heat. Since, then, that flesh which was the receptacle of divinity received this element also in order to maintain itself, and the God who manifested Himself mingled Himself with our perishable nature in order that by communion with his divinity humanity might at the same time be divinized, for this reason He plants Himself by the economy of His grace, in all believers by means of the flesh which derives its subsistence from both wine and bread, mingling Himself with the bodies of believers, in order that, by union with that which is immortal, man also might partake of incorruption. And this He bestows by power of the eucharistic prayer (*eulogia*), transforming the nature of the visible elements into that immortal thing.[5]

St. John Chrysostom (c. 347 - 407)

After serving the church of Antioch, where his eloquent homilies on the Scriptures earned him the surname "the golden mouthed" (Chrysostom), he was called to be Patriarch of Constantinople in 398. His powerful preaching here against the abuses of a corrupt court and church soon won him enemies in both circles so that after being condemned at the "Synod of the Oak" (403), this reformer was exiled. He regained his see for a brief period, but was again sent into exile, in which he died as a result of the hardships imposed on him, particularly because the enfeebled aging bishop had to travel on foot in most inclement weather.

His dedication to the worship of God continues to be the glory of the Greek Church, which celebrates the Divine Liturgy of St. John Chrysostom, the rich heritage he left it. His sense of the holiness of God in the "awe-inspiring mysteries" shaped his preaching regarding showing reverence for the "body of Christ" in the Eucharist and in the faithful, particularly the poor. This great pastoral exegete drew from the word of God and divine worship inspiration for practical living no less than for the beauty of spiritual contemplation.

Do you wish to know the power of Christ's blood? Let us go back to the ancient accounts of what took place in Egypt, where Christ's blood is foreshadowed.

Moses said: "Sacrifice a lamb without blemish and smear the doors with its blood." What does this mean? Can the blood of a sheep without reason save man who is endowed with reason? Yes, Moses replies, not because it is blood but because it is a figure of the Lord's blood. So today if the devil sees, not the blood of the figure smeared on the door posts, but the blood of the reality smeared on the lips of the faithful, which are the doors of the temple of Christ, with all the more reason will he draw back.

Do you wish to learn from another source the power of this blood? See where it began to flow, from what spring it flowed down from the cross, from the Master's side. The Gospel relates that when Christ had died and was still hanging on the cross, the soldier approached him and pierced his side with the spear, and at once there came out water and blood. The one was a symbol of baptism, the other of the mysteries [the sacrament of the Eucharist]. The soldier, then, pierced his side: he breached the wall of the holy temple, and I found the treasure and acquired the wealth. Similarly with the lamb. The Jews slaughtered it in sacrifice, and I gathered the fruit of that sacrifice — salvation.

"There came out from his side water and blood." Dearly beloved, do not pass the secret of this great mystery by without reflection. For I have another secret mystical interpretation to give. I said that baptism and the mysteries were symbolized in that blood and water. It is from these two that the holy Church has been born "by the washing of regeneration and the renewal of the Holy Spirit," by baptism and by the mysteries. Now the symbols of baptism and the mysteries came from his side. It was from his side, then, that Christ formed the Church, as from the side of Adam he formed Eve...

Have you seen how Christ has united his bride to himself? Have you seen with what kind of food he feeds us all? By the same food we are formed and are fed. As a woman feeds her child with her own blood and milk, so too Christ himself continually feeds those whom he has begotten with his own blood.[6]

Would you honor the body of Christ? Do not despise his nakedness; do not honor him here in church clothed in silk vestments and then pass him by unclothed and frozen outside. Remember that he who said, "This is my body," and made good his words, also said, "You saw me hungry and gave me no food," and "insofar as you did it not to one of these, you did it not to me." In the first sense the body of Christ does not need clothing but worship from a pure heart. In the second sense it does need clothing and all the care we can give it.

We must learn to be discerning Christians and to honor Christ in the way in which he wants to be honored. It is only right that honor given to anyone should take the form most acceptable to the recipient not to the giver. Peter thought he was honoring the Lord when he tried to stop him washing his feet, but this was far from being genuine homage. So give God the honor he asks for, that is give your money generously to the poor. God has no need of golden vessels but of golden hearts.

I am not saying you should not give golden altar vessels and so on, but I am insisting that nothing can take the place of almsgiving. The Lord will not refuse to accept the first kind of gift but he prefers the second, and quite naturally, because in the first case only the donor benefits, in the second case the poor get the benefit. The gift of a chalice may be ostentatious; almsgiving is pure benevolence.

What is the use of loading Christ's table with gold cups while he himself is starving? Feed the hungry and then if you have any money left over, spend it on the altar table. Will you make a cup of gold and withhold a cup of water? What use is it to adorn the altar with cloth of gold hangings and deny Christ a coat for his back! What would that profit you? Tell me: if you saw someone starving and refused to give him any food but instead spent your money on adorning the altar with gold, would he thank you? Would he not rather be outraged? Or if you saw someone in rags and stiff with cold and then did not give him clothing but set up golden columns in his honor, would he not say he was being made a fool of and insulted?[7]

WESTERN FATHERS

St. Hilary of Poitiers (c. 315 - 367)

St. Hilary of Poitiers has been called the "Athanasius of the West" because of his vigorous and untiring defense of orthodoxy regarding the doctrine of the Trinity against the Arian heresy. He was converted from Neoplatonism and soon became bishop of Poitiers c. 353, from where he was exiled to Phrygia by the Emperor Constantius for four years in 356. His works include commentaries on the psalms and the Gospel of Matthew, a treatise on the sacraments (*Tractatus Mysteriorum*), and, most notably, *De Trinitate* in twelve books. The originality and greatness of his writings — especially in the treatise on the sacraments, which was intended as a guide to preachers and catechists in preparing people for Christian Initiation — consist in his attempt to work out a balanced approach between traditional scriptural exegesis (e.g., in Zeno of Verona) and the method of Platonist allegorizing (e.g., in Gregory of Nyssa). The Spring Term at the Law Courts and the universities of Oxford and Durham derives its name from the Middle Ages when his feast (January 13) became the day on which sessions and lectures resumed after the Christmas holidays.

If the Word was truly made flesh, and if we truly receive the Word made flesh in the Lord's food, why should we not hold that he remains within us naturally? For when he was born as a man he assumed the nature of our flesh in such a way that it became inseparable from himself, and he joined the nature of his flesh to the nature of his eternity in the sacrament of his flesh which he allows us to share. Accordingly we are all one, because the Father is in Christ and Christ is in us. He is in us through the flesh, and we are in him; and being united with him, what we are is in God.

His own words testify to the fact that we are in him through the sacrament by which we share in his flesh and blood: "And this world will see me no more, but you will see me; because I live, you will live also. For I am in my Father, and you in me, and I in you." If he wished us to conceive solely of a unity of will, why did he speak of a kind of graduated scale to be achieved? Surely it was to teach us that, while he is in the Father by the nature of his divinity, we on the contrary are in him through his bodily birth, and he again is in us by the mystery of the sacraments. From this we can learn the unity which has been achieved through the Mediator; for we abide in him and he abides in the Father, and while abiding in the Father he abides in us. In this way we attain to unity with the Father. For while Christ is in the Father naturally according to his birth, we too are in Christ naturally, since he abides in us naturally.

We can learn how natural this unity is in us from his own words: "He who eats my flesh and drinks my blood abides in me, and I in him." No one can be in Christ unless Christ is in him; for Christ has taken to himself the flesh only of those who receive his flesh.

He had earlier revealed to us the sacrament of this perfect unity when he said: "As the living Father sent me, and I live because of the Father, so he who eats my flesh will live because of me." He lives because of the Father; and just as he lives because of the Father, we live because of his flesh.

Every comparison is chosen to help our understanding, so that we may grasp what is being discussed by means of an example. These then are the facts about our life: since we are made of flesh we have Christ abiding in us, because of his flesh, so that we can live because of him on the same condition as he lives because of the Father.[8]

St. Ambrose (c. 339 - 397)

St. Ambrose was born at Trier of an aristocratic family. Ambrose's natural abilities and inclination to study secured him a high-ranking position in the Roman civil service. When, as governor in a northern province of Italy near Milan he intervened in the interest of public order to settle the wrangling between Arian and Catholic factions following the death of the Arian Auxentius, he was chosen by popular acclaim to succeed the latter as the bishop of this see, even though he was still a catechumen. He applied himself with great energy and zeal to this demanding service of pastoral charity, such as in fearlessly rebuking the Emperor Theodosius for a massacre in Thessalonica by debarring him from Communion.

He took a deep interest in the psalm-singing of his flock's worship and devoted his lyrical gifts to composing some of the most beautiful Latin hymns, many of which are still sung in our vernacular translations. His knowledge of the Greek Fathers enabled him also to enrich Western theology with valuable insights in the course of his commentaries on Scripture and teachings as a pastor. He left two famous treatises on the Holy Eucharist (*De Mysteriis*, a polished work, and *De Sacramentis*, which was probably a compilation of his Easter catechetical lectures to the newly baptized), sermons thought to be preached between 380-390. The substance of these instructions would have been heard by his most illustrious convert, Augustine of Hippo, at that memorable Easter in 387.

You approached [the altar after being baptized and anointed] in the sight of the angels, who on beholding the transformation of your sin-disfigured human state suddenly made resplendent cried out in amazement: "Who is this coming up from the desert, all gaily clad?" (Sg 8:5). Are you curious about their astonishment? Listen to what the apostle Peter says regarding the way the angels long to look upon those things which have been bestowed on us (cf. 1 P 1:12). Or again, listen [to Paul]: "What no eye has seen, nor ear heard, God has prepared for those who love him" (1 Cor 2:9). Then go on to reflect on what you have received....

You approached with yearning. Since you had beheld so great a gift, you longed to receive from the altar the sacrament. Your inner self says: "I will go to the altar of God, to God who rejoices my youth" (Ps 42:4). In despoiling yourself of the garments of the old man of sin, you clothed yourself in the grace of youth. The heavenly sacraments have given this to you. Listen to what David says: "Your youth will be renewed like the eagle's" (Ps 102:5). In beginning to look down on earthly things, like a soaring eagle you are seeking heaven. Around the altar [behold] the great eagles, for "Wherever the body is, there too the eagles gather" (Mt 24:28). The shape of the altar is like that of a body, and on the altar is Christ's body. You are eagles who, by the cleansing of wrong-doing, have been renewed. When you came to the altar, you noticed the sacraments on it. No doubt you were filled with awe [on seeing] what was there. But this is ordinary and familiar. It may perhaps be said: "God shows the Jews the same great favor in raining down manna from heaven on them. What greater thing has he given his faithful? What greater gift has he lavished on those to whom he has made greater promises?"

Pay close attention to my words now: the Christian mysteries are more ancient than those of the Jews; the Christian sacraments are more sacred than those of the Jews. How? Listen... It was not before Abraham's great-grandson [Judah] that they came to be called Jews in holy Moses' time, when God showered down manna from heaven on the grumbling Jews. But, there existed for you a prefiguring of these [our Christian] sacraments long before [the manna]. It goes back to Abraham's day... The priest Melchisedech approached him, offering bread and wine (cf. Gn 14:14-18). Who offered the bread and wine? Not Abraham. But who had it to offer? It was Melchisedech. He, therefore, is the author of the [Christian] sacraments. Who is this Melchisedech, who is called "the king of righteousness, the king of peace" (Heb 7:21)? Who is this king of righteousness but the Righteous One of God himself? Who is the peace of God, but the very wisdom of God (cf. 1 Cor 1:30)? It is none other than he who can say: "My peace I give you, my peace I leave you" (Jn 14:27). Therefore, take note that these sacraments which you receive are more ancient than those sacraments claimed by the Jews. We, the Christian people, go back — through our predestination — to before the time of the Jews, though they have the name [of being the people of God]... Just as Melchisedech was a priest... Christ too is a priest; of him it is said: "You are a priest forever according to the order of Melchisedech" (Ps 109:4; Heb 7:17). Hence, who is the author of the sacraments other than the Lord Jesus? These sacraments came down from heaven, because all counsel is from above.

What a great and, indeed, divine miracle that God showered down the manna from heaven on his people, who ate it without having to work (Ws 16:20)! Perhaps you will say: "Mine is only an ordinary kind of bread." Yes, indeed, it is mere bread before the sacramental words. But once [the word of] consecration has been added, what was bread becomes Christ's flesh. Now, let us examine how bread can become the body of Christ.

In whose words, in whose speech is the consecration pronounced? They are the Lord Jesus' words. Everything that is said before it is the priest's words: the praise and prayer offered to God, petitions are made on behalf of the people, rulers, and others. But when the moment comes for confecting the venerable sacrament, then the priest employs not his own words, but the words of Christ. So, Christ's word confects this sacrament. What is the word of Christ? It is surely none other than the same as that by which all things were made. At the Lord's command, heaven... earth... the seas were made. At his command, every creature came to be. So, you can see how effective Christ's word is. For, if the word of the Lord Jesus is so powerful as to bring into existence things which were not, then *a fortiori* those things which already exist can be changed into something else!... I therefore answer you: before the consecration [the bread] was not Christ's body. He spoke and it was made; he commanded and it was created. Though you existed, you were an old creation. After your consecration, your life as a new creature began.[9]

St. Gaudentius of Brescia (4th - 5th Century)

> This friend of St. Ambrose became bishop of Brescia before 397. He was sent in the delegation by Pope Innocent I (in 406) to plead with the Emperor to restore St. John Chrysostom to his see of Constantinople. Many of his homilies survive. The following section from his catechesis to the newly baptized at the Easter Vigil offers an example of the way people were taught both about the significance of the gifts of bread and wine and also to believe in Christ's presence in the Eucharist.

One man died to save everyone. Thus, in every house, namely every church [*par singulas Ecclesiarum domos*], where the mystery of bread and wine is celebrated, he who has been sacrificed restores us, he who is believed enlivens us, he who has been made holy sanctifies those who consecrate.

This is the flesh of the Lamb; this is his blood. For the Bread who came down from heaven says: "The bread which I will give you is my flesh for the life of the world" (Jn 6:51-52). Rightly, also, does the appearance of wine manifest his blood, for he himself says in the

47

Gospel: "I am the true vine" (Jn 15:1). This sufficiently demonstrates that the wine which is offered as a sign of his passion is his blood....

The Creator and Lord of all nature, therefore, who provides bread from the earth, is able to make from bread his own body as he promised. Likewise, he who turned water into wine, made from wine his blood....

We hear the words: "It is the Lord's Pasch" — that is, the passover of the Lord. Lest you think of this heavenly event in an earthly way, it is brought about through him by his passing into it when he made it his body and blood [*per eum qui transit in illud, et fecti illum suum corpus et sanguinem*].

You receive the body of that heavenly bread and the blood of that holy vine. For when he gave his disciples the consecrated bread and wine, he declared: "This is my body; this is my blood" (Mt 26:26, 28). We who believe in him, I beseech you, must believe this. Truth does not know deceit.

So when he was speaking to the crowd about eating his body and drinking his blood, they were amazed and began murmuring: "This is a hard saying. For who can listen to it?" However, he dispels by heavenly fire those thoughts which I have just been telling you to avoid when he added: "It is the Spirit that gives life, the flesh is of no avail. The words that I have spoken to you are spirit and life."

Christ instituted a heavenly sacrifice which is truly the legacy of his new testament. What he left on that night when he was handed over to be crucified was given to us as a pledge of his presence [*tamquam pignus suae praesentiae*].

This is the provision [*viaticum nostri itineris*] which feeds and nourishes us during life's journey towards coming to him when we depart from this world. Telling us of this the Lord himself said: "Unless you eat my flesh and drink my blood, you will have no life in you."

For he willed that his gifts should remain among us and that those whom he had redeemed by his precious blood be always made holy through the pattern of his own passion. To realize this he ordered his faithful disciples, whom he had appointed as the first priests of his Church, to carry on ceaselessly these mysteries of eternal life. Every priest in every church through the world, therefore, must celebrate them until Christ's return from heaven. This ensures that priests and all the faithful people have daily before them the example of Christ's passion. By holding it in our hands and even receiving it in our mouths and hearts, we hold onto the indelible remembrance of our redemption. By this sweet medicine we are forever protected from the Devil's poison. For the Holy Spirit encourages us to "Taste and see that the Lord is good" (Ps 33:9)...

[Here he describes the Pauline image of the one bread made from many grains, the one cup of wine from many grapes.]

All you, who escape from the enslavement of Egypt and Pharaoh — that is, the Devil — discern with the fervent longing of a religious heart this paschal sacrifice of salvation. Receive it with us so that he whom we believe to be present in his sacraments, our Lord Jesus Christ himself, may make our inmost hearts holy. The power of his priceless sacrifice remains for ever.[10]

St. Augustine of Hippo (354 - 430)

One of the best-known books of Christian literature is the *Confessions* of St. Augustine — a masterpiece that is considered the forerunner of modern autobiography and even of the existential novel. It situates the personal story of conversion — his psychological, intellectual, moral, and spiritual odyssey — within the vast perspective of the whole of creation's yearning for eternal communion with God: a yearning which itself originates in God, being etched into the heart of every man by the Creator himself: "You have created us for yourself, O Lord, and our hearts are restless until they rest in you" (*Conf.* I, 1).

Augustine's extensive writings — mainly during the forty years of his pastoral activity as bishop of the north African provincial town of Hippo Regius — played no small part in shaping not only all subsequent development of Christian doctrine, practice, and theology (Western and Eastern, Catholic and Protestant), but also the thought-patterns and cultural values of Western civilization.

Central to his awareness is that conviction in faith which brought about his conversion to Christianity—namely, belief in the truth expressed by John that "the Word was made flesh and dwelt among us" (Jn 1:14), a verse of Scripture he never tired of citing. Belief in this truth is the key to his rich teaching on the Eucharist as the focal point of the whole life of and worship of the Church — worship which gives and celebrates the worth of living.

O eternal truth and true charity and beloved eternity! This is you my God for whom I sigh at night and by day. From the very first instant that I knew you, you raised me up to make me recognize that there was something to behold, which as yet I was unable to see. The brilliance of light emanating from your splendor bedazzled my weak eyes. All I could do was tremble with love and awe. I realized that I was very far away from you — as if in some region utterly remote from you while I heard your voice calling out to me from the very heights: "I am the food of grown men; grow up and you shall eat me. Do not imagine that you will change me into your substance as happens to your bodily food, but you will be transformed into me."[11]

On the altar you are looking at the same thing as you saw there last night. You have not yet heard, however, what this is, what it signifies, or about the greatness of the reality of which it is a sacrament. Your eyes are looking at bread and a cup. This is the evidence before your physical sight. But your faith must be instructed concerning it — this bread being Christ's body and the cup containing his blood. Though perhaps these few words may be enough to initiate faith, faith must be further instructed in accordance with the Prophet's words: "Believe that you may understand" (Is 7:9). Thus, you can ask me: "Since you have brought us to believe, help us now to understand...."

The reason, brethren, these things are called sacraments is that what one sees in them is not the same as that which one understands them to be. Its physical appearance is seen; its spiritual significance understood. So, if you want to comprehend the body of Christ, listen to what the Apostle tells the faithful: "You are the body of Christ, his members" (1 Cor 12:27). Since you make up the body of Christ and are his members, your mystery rests on the table of the Lord; you receive your own mystery. You answer "Amen" to the reality of what you are; your reply gives your consent to it. For on hearing the words,

"The Body of Christ," you reply, "Amen." Be in fact a member of Christ's body for your affirmation, "Amen," to ring true.

But why use bread? I do not claim to offer my own explanation, but rather I refer to the Apostle's words concerning this sacrament. Let us listen to them: "Though we are many, we make one loaf of bread, one body" (1 Cor 10:17). Understand and be glad. Unity! Truth! Piety! Charity! "One loaf of bread." What is this one [substance of] bread? "Many... one body." Recall how bread is not made up from just one grain, but from many. When you were exorcized, you were, it seems, as if you were being ground to flour. When baptized, you were moistened into dough. On receiving the fire of the Holy Spirit, you were baked. Be what you see; receive what you are.

This is how the Apostle speaks about the bread. By implication he has adequately indicated what we must understand regarding the cup as well. As in the case of the bread being prepared... "They were of one mind and one heart turned towards God" (Ac 4:32), so likewise in the case of the wine. Recall, brethren, how wine is produced. From many grapes hanging in a cluster, their crushed liquid fuses into a unity. Christ the Lord also described us in this imagery. He desired us to be his. At his table he sanctified the mystery of our peace and unity. Whoever receives the mystery of unity without maintaining firmly the bond of peace, does not receive the mystery into himself, but a condemnation against himself.

Being converted towards the Lord God, the Father Almighty, let us with a pure heart truly offer him as much gratitude as we can. With our whole soul let us request him to favor us with his unique kindness in hearing our prayers, driving far from us by his power the enemy who thwarts our actions and good intentions; may he increase our faith, guide our minds to a spiritual way of thinking, and lead us to delight in his holiness, through Jesus Christ his Son. Amen.[12]

What should we worship? "His footstool!..." Take notice, brethren, of what we are ordered to worship. Scripture elsewhere tells us: "Heaven is my throne, and the earth my footstool" (Is 66:1). Are we being told to worship the earth insofar as this passage tells us that the earth is the Lord's footstool? But, how may we adore the earth when Scripture states clearly "You shall only adore the Lord, your God" (Dt 6:13)? ... I am in a quandary. I hesitate to bow down in adoration to the

51

earth for fear of being condemned by him who made heaven and earth (Ps 133:3). On the other hand, however, I am afraid not to carry out what the Psalm tells me to do: "worship the Lord's footstool." In seeking to know what is meant by his footstool, I find Scripture telling me: "the earth is my footstool." In my dilemma I turn to Christ, since he is the one I am looking for all the while. I discover how I may worship the earth without offense to God. Since the flesh is of the earth, when he took our flesh from Mary's, he indeed took earth from earth. Having walked among us in that flesh, he gave us the same flesh as food for our salvation. However, no one feeds on that flesh without first adoring it.

Here we know that it is right to worship God's footstool. Moreover, we learn both that it is not only not sinful for us to worship it, but also that we would sin by not worshipping it. But, the flesh cannot give life, can it? It was the Lord himself who said this in treating of what comes from the earth: "It is the spirit that gives life, the flesh is of no avail" (Jn 6:63)....

The Lord spoke these words when making the promise about his flesh: "Unless a man eat my flesh.. he has no life in him" (cf. Jn 6:53). At this, certain disciples — about seventy — were scandalized, and objected: "This is a hard saying, who can abide it?" (Jn 6:60)... They misunderstood what he was saying, interpreting his words in a physical [carnal] way... They were really the ones who were hard, not the saying of Jesus. For, if they were not obdurate, but docile, they would have thought to themselves: "There is a good reason for him to say this; there must be some sacramental meaning hidden here in his words..." When these others had left him... Jesus instructed [those remaining with him], saying: "It is the spirit that gives life, the flesh is of no avail. The words that I have spoken to you are spirit and life" (Jn 6:63). Try to understand my meaning in a spiritual way. You are not going to eat this body which you see with your eyes, nor drink the blood which will be shed when they crucify me. What I have provided is a sacrament. If understood in a spiritual way, it will give you life. While visibly celebrated, its meaning must be understood spiritually.[13]

St. Leo the Great (d. 461)

> The period during which Leo was Pope (440-461) was marked by the Christological controversy. The famous letter (called "the Tome of Leo"), which he sent to Flavian, the Patriarch of Constantinople, in 449 was accepted as an authentic expression of the Church's faith regarding Christ by the Council of Chalcedon in 451. He managed to secure the authority of the papacy as the sign of unity at a time of great turmoil. His pastoral preaching proclaimed Christ's incarnation as revelatory of human dignity, which is celebrated and strengthened by the sacraments of the Church.

There is no doubt, dearly beloved, about the fact that the Son of God so intimately united himself to human nature that he is one and the same Christ in that man who is the firstborn of the whole of creation and in all his saints. Just as a head cannot be separated from the rest of the body, neither can the members be divided from the head....

Just as the Good Shepherd graciously gave his life for his sheep, so too countless sheep, who have been strengthened by the food of love [*dilectionis pinguedine*], do not baulk to lay down their lives for his name's sake....

We fittingly celebrate, therefore, the Lord's Passover with the unleavened bread of sincerity and truth. Once the leaven of our past malice has been purged out, the new creature can satisfy its thirst and feed upon the Lord himself.

For, to participate in the body and blood of Christ is nothing other than to become what we receive. This means that we bear constant witness in our spirit and our flesh to him, in whom we have died, been buried, and risen to life.[14]

The Lord's resurrection filled us with joy on Easter Day; so too his ascension into heaven is the cause of our gladness now as we commemorate and solemnize the day on which our lowly nature was raised up in Christ above all the host of heaven....

This is the strength which is given to great minds, this is the light of truly faithful souls, that unhesitatingly they can believe what they cannot see with the eyes of the body, and direct their longings beyond the range of their sight. How could this devotion be born in our hearts, how could anyone be justified by faith, if our salvation were to be found in those things alone which are open to our gaze? The visible presence of our Redeemer passed over into sacraments [*quod itaque Redemptoris nostri conspicuum fuit, in sacramenta transivit*]; and so that faith might be more noble and firmer, it is grounded now not on sight but on doctrine. The hearts of those who believe follow this doctrine by a light that comes from above. This faith which is increased by the Lord's ascension and strengthened by the gift of the Holy Spirit, could not be dismayed by chains, by prison... For this faith people all over the world have striven to witness to it even to shedding their blood — not only men, but also women, young lads and even lovely lasses.[15]

Byzantine Mystagogy

Dionysius the Areopagite (End of the 5th Century?)

The obscurity enshrouding the identity of this Eastern theologian may be taken as symbolic of the profundity of his thought and mystical insights. Possibly a monk or even bishop, this writer assumed the pseudonym of St. Paul's illustrious Athenian convert perhaps in order to give his teaching authority, as was not unknown in past times. He is first mentioned in 533 at the Council of Constantinople in support of Monophysite teaching. St. Maximus elucidates his doctrines in a splendid commentary in the 7th century. Not until the 9th century, however, was the West introduced to his various treatises through Erigena's Latin translation, which Medieval scholastics devoured; St. Thomas Aquinas referred to or quoted from them quite often, though admitting they were difficult to comprehend at times. It is reported that: "The Mystical Divinity ran across England like deer." The Rhineland mystics appealed to these writings, Ruysbroeck finding in them staple diet.

The importance of Dionysius' mystical theology consists particularly in this, that it manifests a mature quest for reality, which lies beyond all articulation in dogmas and any human expression — or even comprehension. The best that our words or rituals can offer is that they afford us symbols or sacraments of the ultimate Ineffability of God. We are called to share the Transcendence of God, however, precisely because we are "deified" through participating in the Mystery of Christ, which we celebrate in the "sacred mysteries" of Christian Initiation: Baptism, Confirmation, Eucharist. Dionysius likens ministerial priests to the angels since they come as near God as is possible in this world; they lift up their eyes to contemplate the "blessed refulgence of Jesus" (cf. *Eccles. Hier.*, i, 1).

This is indeed the sacrament of sacraments... For a start, let us reverently behold what is above all characteristic of this, though also of the other hierarchic sacraments, namely, that which is especially referred to as "Communion" and "gathering" [*synaxis*]. Every sacredly initiating operation draws our fragmented lives together into a one-like divinization.[1] It forges a divine unity out of the divisions within us. It grants us communion and union with the One. But I submit that the perfection of the other hierarchical symbols is only achieved by way of the divine and perfecting gifts of Communion. For scarcely any of the hierarchic sacraments can be performed without the divine Eucharist as the high point of each rite,[2] divinely bringing about a spiritual gathering to the One for him who receives the sacrament, granting him as a gift from God its mysterious perfecting capacities, perfecting in fact his communion with God. Each of the hierarchic sacraments is incomplete to the extent that it does not perfect our communion and "gathering" to the One, and by being thus incomplete it cannot work our full perfection.[3]

The goodness of the Deity has endless love for humanity and never ceased from benignly pouring out on us its providential gifts. It took upon itself in a most authentic way all the characteristics of our nature, except sin. It became one with us in our lowliness, losing nothing of its own real condition, suffering no change or loss. It allowed us, as those of equal birth, to enter into communion with it and to acquire a share of its own true beauty... This imitation of God, how else are we to achieve it if not by endlessly reminding ourselves of God's sacred works and doing so by way of the sacred hymns and the sacred acts established by the hierarchy? We do this, as the Scriptures say, in remembrance of him. This is why the hierarch, the man of God, stands before the divine altar. He praises the divine works which I have mentioned, those sacred works wrought gloriously by Jesus, exercising here his most divine providence for the salvation of the human race. This he does, as Scripture tells us, for the good pleasure of the most holy Father and the Holy Spirit. And the hierarch sings the praises of all this venerable work and beholds with the eyes of the mind this spectacle for conceptual contemplation. He proceeds to the task of the symbolic sacred act. He does this in accordance with the rules laid down by God himself, which is the reason why, at the same time, having sung the sacred praises of the divine works he apologizes, as befits a hierarch for being the one to undertake a sacred task so far beyond him. Reverently he cries out: "It is you who said, 'Do this in remembrance of me.'"

He prays, then, to be made more worthy to do this holy task in imitation of God. He prays that, like Christ himself, he might perform the divine things. He prays too that he might impart wisely and that all those taking part may do so without irreverence. Then he performs the most divine acts and lifts into view the things praised through the sacredly clothed symbols. The bread which had been covered and undivided is now uncovered and divided into many parts. Similarly, he shares the one cup with all, symbolically multiplying and distributing the One in symbolic fashion. With these things he completes the most holy sacred act. For because of his goodness and his love for humanity the simple, hidden oneness of Jesus, the most divine Word, has taken the route of incarnation for us and, without undergoing any change, has become a reality that is composite and visible. He has beneficently accomplished for us a unifying communion with himself. He has united our humility with his own supreme divinity. But we in our turn have to cling to him like the members of one body and we do so by the conformity that comes with a divine life of sinlessness... If our longing is for communion with him, then we must give our full attention to his divine life in the flesh.[4]

St. Maximus the Confessor (c. 580 - 662)

The life of this monk (and later abbot), who came from the Byzantine aristocracy and held an important position in the Imperial Court as secretary, was taken up in combatting the heresy of Monothelitism (denial of a human will in Christ). Despite being exiled, he continued his prolific writing on doctrine, asceticism, Scripture, and liturgy. His vision presents the Incarnation at the center of history as its purpose for the sake of the restoration of the divine image in human nature (divinization). Thus, he describes the mystagogical significance of the Divine Liturgy:

The closing of the doors which takes place after the sacred reading of the holy Gospel and the dismissal of the catechumens signifies the passing from material things which will come about after that terrible separation and even more terrible judgment and the entrance of those who are worthy into the spiritual world, that is, into the nuptial chamber of Christ, as well as the complete extinction in our senses of deceptive activity.

The entrance into the holy and august mysteries... is the beginning, a prelude of the new teaching which will take place in the heavens concerning the plan of God for us and the revelation of the mystery of our salvation which is in the most secret recesses of the divine. For as the Word of God says to his disciples, "I shall not drink of the fruit of the vine until that day when I drink it anew with you in the kingdom of my Father."

The spiritual kiss which is extended to all prefigures and portrays the concord, unanimity, and identity of views which we shall all have among ourselves in faith and love at the time of the revelation of the ineffable blessings to come. In this situation those who are worthy will receive intimate familiarity with the Word of God. For the mouth is a symbol of the Word, precisely through whom all those who share in reason as reasonable beings are united to the first and unique Word who is the cause of every word and meaning....

The profession "One is Holy" and what follows, which is voiced by all the people at the end of the mystical service, represents the gathering and union beyond reason and understanding which will take place between those who have been mystically and wisely initiated by God and the mysterious oneness of the divine simplicity in the incorruptible age of the spiritual world. There they behold the light of the invisible and ineffable glory and become themselves together with the angels on high open to the blessed purity. After that, as the climax of everything, comes the distribution of the sacrament, which transforms into itself and renders similar to the causal good by grace and participation those who worthily share in it. To them is there lacking nothing of this good that is possible and attainable for men, so that they also can be and be called gods by adoption through grace because all of God entirely fills them and leaves no part of them empty of his presence.[5]

St. John Damascene (c. 675 - c. 749)

There is not a great deal known about the life of this Greek theologian and Doctor of the Church. He retired from public office at the court of the Caliph because his duties conflicted with his Christian faith and entered a monastery near Jerusalem. He made a most forceful contribution in defense of images in the iconoclast controversy. His writings bear the influence of the Cappadocian Fathers, as is evident in the following passage concerning the real change effected in the Eucharist.

[The Eucharist contains] the body which was received from the Blessed Virgin and indeed united to the divine nature. This does not mean that the same body which ascended into heaven has come down again, but that the bread and wine themselves are changed into God's body and blood. If you were to ask how such a change is brought about, all you need know is that it is the work of the Holy Spirit, through whom also the Lord took flesh from the Holy *Theotokos* and made the flesh subsist in himself as his own [body]. For we know nothing more than this — that God's word is true and carries out what it purposes, being full of power [omnipotent]. The manner in which this happens, however, is quite beyond our capacity to comprehend. The following may be stated without hesitation: just as what happens, according to the laws of nature, when bread is eaten and wine and water drunk they are changed into the body and blood of a person who consumes them, so, in a supernatural way, the bread which has been offered [*prothesis*] and the wine and water by the prayer of invocation [*epiklesis*] and the coming down of the Holy Spirit are changed into the body and blood of Christ. They no longer remain as two substances but become one and the same [reality]....

The bread and wine are more than merely [symbolic] types of Christ's body and blood, but the Lord's own divine [deified] body itself. For what he said was: "This is my body," not, "This is a type of my body"; and also, "my blood," not, "a type of my blood." Moreover, on an earlier occasion, he told the Jews: "Unless you eat the flesh of the Son of Man, you cannot have life in you. For my flesh is real food and my blood is real drink"; and further, "He who eats me lives of me" (Jn 6:54-58).

Hence, when we come forward, let us do so most reverently with a clear conscience and unwavering faith. It will then be truly as our faith teaches us, without doubt. Our reverence must express the purity of both our body and soul, for it is twofold. Let us come forward to receive the body of the Crucified with ardent longing, our hands held in the form of the cross. Touching our eyes, lips, and brows [with the sacrament], let us receive into ourselves the Divine Coal, so that the fire of our desire, set ablaze by the intensity of heat from the Coal, may utterly consume our sins and enlighten our hearts.[6] In this way may we become completely alight and divinized by contact with the fire of God. Isaiah beheld a coal (cf. Is 6:6): a coal is not mere wood, but wood penetrated by fire. Similarly, the communion bread is not merely bread, but bread united to divinity.[7]

Gregorian Counsel
to Enjoy the Lord's Supper

St. Gregory Agrigentinus (late 6th Century)

St. Gregory takes his surname from the city in the south of Sicily, Agrigentum, near which he was born and of which, after a pilgrimage to the Holy Land, he was made bishop. He suffered as a result of an attack on his character. Pope Gregory wrote many letters to him. He was deposed, or died, in 594. The extract given here is taken from a commentary on Ecclesiastes attributed to him.

"Come, eat your bread with enjoyment, and drink your wine with a merry heart; for God has already approved of what you do. Let your garments all be white; let not oil be lacking on your head." If we wished to explain the meaning of this saying in the obvious and literal sense, we could say, appropriately enough, that it seems to be a righteous counsel whereby the Preacher urges us to adopt a simple style of living and adhere to the teachings of a sincere faith in God so that we may eat our bread with enjoyment and drink wine with a merry heart. He warns us not to fall into evil talk or to have anything to do with crooked ways of speech. Instead, our thoughts should be of the things that are right and, insofar as it is proper, we should, with compassion and generosity, help beggars and the needy. In short, we should give ourselves to the duties and deeds that give pleasure to God himself.

However, the spiritual meaning carries our thoughts up to higher things and teaches us to consider the heavenly and mystical bread that came down from heaven and brought life to the world; and to drink the spiritual wine with a merry heart, that wine which flowed from the side of the true vine at the time of his sufferings that saved us. Of these, the Gospel of our salvation says, "And when Jesus had taken bread and blessed it, he said to his holy disciples and apostles, 'Take and eat; this is my body that is broken for you so that sins may be forgiven'; and in the same way with the cup, saying, 'Drink from this all of you, this is the blood of the new covenant that is shed for you and for many so that sins may be forgiven.'" They who eat this bread and drink this mystical wine are indeed gladdened and exult and can cry out, "You have given joy to our hearts."

Moreover, it seems to me that Christ our Savior, the subsistent Wisdom of God, gave another meaning to this same bread and same wine in the book of Proverbs as well when he said, "Come, eat of my bread and drink of the wine I have mixed for you," referring to our mystical sharing in the Word. It is the glory of those who do so share that at all times their clothing, that is the works of light, shine as brightly as the light, in accordance with what the Lord said in the Gospels, "Let your light so shine before men that they may see your good works and give glory to your Father who is in heaven." Their heads too, will be seen to overflow perpetually with oil, that is, with the Spirit of truth who protects and defends from all the harm of sin.[1]

St. Gregory the Great (c. 540-604)

In mid-life this well-to-do and successful Roman turned his back on worldliness, by resigning his important position of prefect of the City of Rome and selling his considerable properties, the proceeds from which he devoted to the poor and to founding several monasteries, including one in Rome itself. He entered this monastery in 574, but shortly afterwards was prevailed upon by Pope Pelagius II to serve the Church's interests at the Imperial Court of Constantinople. In 585 he returned to Rome and reentered his former monastery of St. Andrew, of which he was made abbot. During this time the famous meeting in the Forum of the fair-haired Saxon slaves from Britain recounted by Bede ("Non Angli, sed angeli": "Not Angles but angels") took place. After Pelagius' death, Gregory was pressed to succeed him as Pope in 590. It seems that he endured a terrible interior struggle in taking on this most onerous service, not only because of his sense of unworthiness but also because of the general state of demoralization, which his experience taught him, prevailed in Italy: famine, disease, tension between Church and Imperial power, invasion of the Lombards, and so on. But this son of a senator of Rome turned monk was the man to meet this critical time. He left his stamp so decisively on the See of Peter that he is still, fourteen centuries later, called the "Father of the Medieval Papacy."

Gregory's great humility made him adopt the title "servus servorum Dei" ("the servant of the servants of God"). This quality of humility served him well in being of service to the Christian Church precisely at a time when it needed one who was not so much a man of great speculative gifts, but practical, diligent, hard-working and experienced in dealing with problems of the secular and ecclesiastical worlds. He adapted the teachings of St. Augustine of Hippo for the needs of his contemporaries and popularized the mystical ideas of Dionysius the pseudo-Areopagite. He took a keen interest in the liturgy, on which his influence is recognized by his name being associated with plainsong (Gregorian Chant) and the Gregorian Sacramentary which, though compiled later, contains prayers composed by him. Being a deeply religious and practical man of God — he was ever a monk at heart — his stance shows the value, beauty, and joy of worship as the soundest basis of living.

There is this difference, Dearly Beloved Brethren, between the delights of the body and those of the soul, that the delights of the body, when we do not possess them, awaken in us a great desire for them; but when we possess them and enjoy them to the full they straightaway awaken in us a feeling of aversion. But spiritual delights work in the opposite way... For spiritual delights, when they fill the soul, increase in us the desire of them; and the more we savor them, the more do we come to know what we should eagerly love... The psalmist exhorts us, saying: "O taste and see that the Lord is sweet" (Ps 33:9)! As though he were saying: You know not His sweetness if you have not tasted it. But try this Food on the palate of your heart, so that when you see how sweet it is then you will love it. Man lost this delight when he sinned in Paradise (Gn 3:6); he went forth from there when he closed his mouth against the sweetness of the eternal Food....

"A certain man made a great supper and invited many." Who is this man? He has made a great Supper, for He has prepared for us the fulness of inward delight. He has invited many, but few come; for oftentimes those who are subject to Him in faith, are hostile to the eternal Supper He has prepared because of their evil way of life....

When I exhort you to despise the world, I come to invite you to God's supper. Let no one in this place despise me for myself. And if I appear to you far from worthy to invite you, nevertheless great are the joys which I promise you....

Those who listen are thinking of *what* it is they hear, and *from* whom they hear; not *through* whom they hear. So let you also; and if perhaps you have reason to despise us, yet always keep reverence in your heart for the Lord Who is inviting you. Accept with readiness, and become the guests of the Supreme Father of the family. Search into your own hearts and drive out from them this deadly aversion. But if you are still earthly minded, you will perhaps be seeking for earthly food. Behold how even earthly food has been changed for you into spiritual nourishment. To take away this distaste from your soul, the matchless Lamb has been slain for you in the Supper of the Lord.[2]

Celtic and Anglo-Saxon Faith

St. Columbanus (543-615)

In his missionary travels to Europe, this Celtic monk stirred up much opposition when setting up monastic communities with a severe Celtic rule of life. Expelled from Burgundy and later from Bregenze on Lake Constance, his monks went to Bobbio in North Italy, which developed into an important center of learning.

My dearest brethren, give ear to our words, as men about to learn something essential; slake the thirst of your mind from the streams of the divine fountain of which we now wish to speak, but do not quench it; drink, but be not sated; for now the living fountain, the fountain of life, calls us to himself, and says, "Let him who is thirsty come unto me and drink." What you are to drink, take note... The Lord himself, our God Jesus Christ, is the fountain of life, and so he calls us to himself, the fountain, that we may drink of him. He who loves drinks of him, he drinks who is satisfied by the word of God, who sufficiently adores, who longs sufficiently, he drinks who burns with the love of wisdom.

Observe whence that fountain flows; it flows from that place whence also the bread came down; since he is the same who is bread and fountain, the only Son, our God Christ the Lord, for whom we should ever hunger. Though we eat him in loving, though we feast on him in desiring, let us still desire him as though hungering for him. Likewise as the fountain, let us ever drink of him with overflowing love, let us ever drink of him with the fulness of longing, and let us be gladdened by some savor of his loveliness.

The Lord is lovely and pleasant; though we eat and drink of him, yet let us ever hunger and thirst, since our food and drink can never be consumed and drained entire; for though he is eaten he is not consumed, though he is drunk he is not lessened, since our bread is eternal, and our fountain is perennial, our fountain is sweet... If you thirst, drink the fountain of life; if you hunger, eat the bread of life. Blessed are they who hunger for this bread and thirst for this fountain; ever eating and drinking they still long to eat and drink. For that is lovely to excess which is ever eaten and drunk, and ever hungered and thirsted after, ever tasted and ever desired; wherefore the prophet-king says, "Taste and see how lovely, how pleasant is the Lord."

The author of life is the fountain of life, the creator of light, the fount of glory; and thus, spurning the things that are seen, making a passage through the world, let us seek the fount of glory on the heights of heaven, the fountain of life, the fountain of living water, like intelligent and most wise fish, that there we may drink the living water which springs up to eternal life... Inspire our hearts, I beg you, O our Jesus, with that breath of your Spirit, and wound our souls with your love... Jesus Christ, that physician of righteousness and health, deign to wound the inward parts of our soul, who with the Father and the Holy Ghost is one unto ages of ages. Amen.[1]

St. Bede the Venerable (673-735)

Born at Wearmouth in Northumbria, Bede was entrusted by his parents at the age of seven to the Abbot Benedict Biscop for his education and upbringing at the new monastery of St. Peter. Shortly afterwards, in 682 when a foundation of St. Paul's was made at Jarrow, he was transferred there where he remained as a monk all his life. He was ordained deacon at the exceptionally young age of nineteen and eleven years later a priest by Bishop John of Hexham (St. John of Beverley). The account of his last hours is movingly recorded in a letter of St. Cuthbert, one of Bede's pupils, to a fellow monk.

His loving devotion to the common prayer of the monastic brethren, the Divine Office of singing the Psalms, is preserved in a letter written by Alcuin, who recounts that Bede would not absent himself from the brethren's devotions even when ill because he believed the angels, who were present at the canonical Hours, would ask: "Where is Bede?" He industriously applied himself to study the Sacred Scriptures and Fathers of the Church, which is evident in his writings and sermons. The work for which Bede is best remembered, however, is his *History of the English Church,* completed in 731. From this work we can learn much about the conditions of the times and life of the Church, such as St. Gregory the Great's answers to various questions concerning the celebration of the Eucharist among the Anglo-Saxons. In this document, such as the following extracts illustrate, we can discern the reverent way in which the Sacrament was reserved and treated, implying faith in the Real Presence.

[St. Gregory's reply] A man should not approach his wife until her child is weaned. But a bad custom has arisen in the behavior of married people that women disdain to suckle their own children, and hand them over to other women to nurse... Even apart from childbirth, women are forbidden to [approach their husbands] during their monthly courses, and the Old Law prescribed death for any man who approached a woman during this time. But a woman should not be forbidden to enter church during these times; for the workings of nature cannot be considered culpable, and it is not just that she should be refused admittance, since her condition is beyond her control. We know that the woman who suffered an issue of blood, humbly approaching behind our Lord, touched the hem of his robe and was at once healed of her sickness. If, therefore, this woman was right to touch our Lord's robe, why may not one who suffers nature's courses be permitted to enter the church of God? ... A woman, therefore, should not be forbidden to receive the mystery of Communion at these times. If any out of a deep sense of reverence do not presume to do so, this is commendable; but if they do so, they do nothing blameworthy. Sincere people often acknowledge their faults even when there is no actual fault, because a blameless action may often spring from a fault... Therefore, when women after due consideration do not presume to approach the Sacrament of the Body and Blood of the Lord during their courses, they are to be commended. But if they are moved by devout love of this holy mystery to receive it as pious custom suggests, they are not to be discouraged. [end of quote from St. Gregory][2]

Caedmon was a deeply religious man who humbly submitted to regular discipline and hotly rebuked all who tried to follow another course. And so he crowned his life with a happy end. For, when the time of his death drew near, he felt the onset of physical weakness for fourteen days, but not seriously enough to prevent his walking or talking the whole time. Close by, there was a house to which all who were sick or likely to die were taken. Towards nightfall on the day when he was to depart this life, Caedmon asked his attendant to prepare a resting-place for him in this house. The attendant was surprised at this request from a man who did not appear likely to die yet; nevertheless, he did as he was asked. So Caedmon went to the house, and conversed and jested cheerfully with those who were already there; and when it was past midnight, he asked: "Is the Eucharist in the house?" "Why do you want the Eucharist?" they inquired. "You are not likely to die yet, when you are talking so cheerfully to us and seem to be in perfect health." "Nevertheless," he said, "bring me the Eucharist." And taking It in his hands, Caedmon asked whether they were all charitably disposed towards him, and whether they had any complaint or ill-feeling against him. They replied that they were all most kindly disposed towards him, and free from all bitterness. Then in turn they asked him to clear his heart of bitterness towards them. At once he answered: "Dear sons, my heart is at peace with all the servants of God." Then, when he had fortified himself with the heavenly Viaticum, he prepared to enter the other life, and asked how long it would be before the brothers were roused to sing God's praises in the Night Office. "Not long," they replied. "Good, then let us wait until then," he answered; and signing himself with the holy Cross, he laid his head on the pillow and passed away quietly in his sleep.[3]

The Oldest Eucharistic Hymn (Compiled 680-691)

Perhaps originally composed earlier than the Antiphonary of
Bangor, this hymn, *Sancti venite*, has found its way to the
Ambrosiana Library in Milan, where it was taken from the
monastery of Bobbio by Frederigo Borromeo in 1609. It
leaves no doubt as to the faith of people at the end of the
seventh century regarding Christ's Real Presence in the
Bread and Wine of the Eucharist.

Come, faithful Christians, take your heavenly food;
All drink this chalice, Christ's redeeming blood.
Saved by his body and by his blood,
All by them nourished, let us praise our God.

Body and Blood under sacramental veil,
Rescue all Christians from the gates of hell.
Bringer of salvation, Christ the Son of God,
Saved all mankind by his cross and blood.

And now inviting to his sacred feast,
Christ is himself the victim and the priest.
Victims were offered in the Temple's shrine,
All were but shadows of the Victim divine.

Light of the world and savior of our race,
Filled all our hearts with his heavenly grace.
Come all and take, full of faith and love,
God's own protection, given from above.

Christ is our guide, our guard and saving Lord,
Giver of life to believers in his word.
Souls who are hungry eat the heavenly bread;
Thirsty they drink the blood which he has shed.

Alpha and Omega, the universe's Head,
Soon comes again, to judge the living and the dead.[4]

Controversy, But Firm in Faith

St. Paschasius Radbertus (c. 790-865)

This Abbot of the Benedictine monastery of Corbie wrote the first treatise formally devoted to the sacrament of the Eucharist, *De corpore et sanguine Domini* (c. 831). The work immediately caused a sensation, that is, it stirred up a lively controversy because of its realism in identifying Christ's sacramental body and the one he received from the Blessed Virgin Mary. In the following paragraphs there is a serious attempt to clarify the underlying principle of sacramentality, a principle which was only properly understood and lucidly expounded later by St. Thomas Aquinas. This endeavor is noteworthy, however, insofar as it raises a new question, unconsidered by the Fathers, viz. "How is Christ present?"

No one who believes the divine words doubts what the body and blood truly (*in veritate*) becomes by the consecration of the mystery; since Truth says: "For my flesh is food indeed, and my blood is drink indeed" (Jn 6:55). And to clarify the disciples' misunderstanding about what he said of his flesh and his blood, he openly added: "He who eats my flesh and drinks my blood abides in me, and I in him" (ibid., 56). Therefore because it is indeed food and truly flesh; and because it is indeed drink and truly blood, he elsewhere says how this is true: "The bread which I shall give for the life of the world is my flesh" (ibid., 51). Unless it is truly flesh would he have said also, "bread which comes down from heaven"? However, because it is not fitting to chew Christ, he wished that this bread and wine become his true flesh and blood in the mystery by the consecration of the Holy Spirit: he creates it indeed in a mystical way by his daily immolation for the life of the world. Just as his real flesh is created through the Spirit without the Virgin having human intercourse, so through the same Spirit the body and blood of Christ is mystically consecrated from the substance of bread and wine... He indeed speaks of nothing other than his real flesh and blood, though in a mystical way.

Since this sacrament is mystical, we cannot deny that it is an image (*figuram*). But if it is an image, we must ask how it can be real. For every image is an image of something else, and always refers to it as to something real (*res vera*), of which it is an image. No one who reads the Scriptures denies that the images of the Old Testament were shadows; this mystery is either truth or an image, and thus a shadow. The question that certainly must be asked is whether this whole thing may be called real without any shadow of falsehood or whether this kind of thing ought to be regarded as a mystery.

It seems to be an image when it is broken, when something different is understood about the visible species than what our natural senses of seeing and tasting suggest, when blood is mixed with water in the chalice. But all the same time, this sacrament of faith is rightly called Christ's true body and blood. It is truly this when the body and blood of Christ are brought by the power of the Spirit in the word from the substance of bread and wine. It is an image, however, insofar as some external gesture of the priest serves to recall the sacred Passion at the altar while at the same time the lamb is daily sacrificed. But if we consider the matter correctly, it is rightly called simultaneously both image and truth. What is experienced externally bears the image or character of what is truly there. But what is properly understood and believed internally about this mystery is indeed truth. For not every image is merely shadow or falsehood. Thus, Paul speaks in Hebrews about God's only Son[1]: "He reflects the glory of God and bears the very stamp of his nature, upholding the universe by his word of power and making purification for sins" (Heb 1:3). In these words he declares that Christ's two natures are both real.[2]

Ratramnus (+ 868)

This disciple of St. Paschasius Radbertus also wrote a treatise entitled *De corpore et sanguine Domini*. In this work, at the request of the Emperor Charles the Bald, he reacted against the crude "realism" of his teacher, particularly where the latter resorted to strange legends of bleeding hosts, etc. The basis of his approach he claimed was St. Augustine's teaching. However, the texts he rallies in his support are mainly from St. Ambrose. Ratramnus enjoyed a mixed fortune: his writings were referred to by St. John Fisher in his treatise on the Eucharist, as also by the more symbolist-minded Reformers and, perhaps for this very reason of being open to ambiguous interpretation, they were even placed on the Index. There is no question that *both* these monks of Corbie believed wholeheartedly in Christ's presence in the Sacrament of the Eucharist. The controversy was about *how* this can be explained.

We are taught by the authority of a most learned man[3] that there is a great difference between the body in which Christ suffered and the blood which flowed from his side while on the cross and this body which the faithful celebrate daily in the mystery of Christ's passion and this blood which the faithful drink in order that it may be the mystery of that blood by which the world was redeemed. For this bread and this drink do not appear to be the body and blood of Christ, but are taken in a spiritual way to refer to the nature of his life. That body, however, in which Christ once suffered bears no resemblance to any other thing than what it seemed to be: for it was what it indeed seemed, what was tangible, what was crucified, what was buried. Likewise, the blood that flowed from his side did not appear to be one thing outwardly while it signified another inner meaning. But now the blood of Christ which believers drink and the body which they eat, are one thing in appearance while holding another meaning; as bodily food it nourishes the body while as the substance of eternal life it satisfies the mind....

For if that mystery is not celebrated figuratively, it is no longer correctly called a mystery, since it cannot be called a mystery if there is nothing hidden, nothing covered with some sort of veil. But that bread which becomes the body of Christ through the ministry of the priest is revealed externally to the sense as one thing, and yet internally it demands that the minds of the faithful discern it as something different. Externally, it retains the form of bread which beforehand it was; the color of bread is seen; the aroma of bread is caught. Internally, however, something else far more precious, far more excellent, is intimated, since here is shown what is heavenly, what is divine, that is, the body of Christ, which is seen not by the bodily senses, but, perceived by the minds of the faithful, received and eaten....

St. Augustine clearly teaches us that just as the body of Christ is signified in the bread placed on the altar, so also it signifies the people who receive it... What is placed on the altar of the Lord contains both his mystery and also that of believers in accordance with what the Apostle testifies: "One bread, one body though we are many in Christ...."

It should not be thought that because we say these things that the Lord's body and blood is not consumed by the faithful in the mystery of the sacrament. For faith receives not what the eye sees but what is believed. This is spiritual food and spiritual drink that spiritually nourishes the soul and provides life an everlasting fulness. The Savior himself speaks in this manner, commending this mystery: "It is the spirit that gives life; the flesh profits nothing...."[4]

The Carolingian Renaissance: Texts of Personal Devotion

Carolingian Texts (9th Century)

During Charlemagne's reign a renaissance took place, largely due to the endeavors of his two tutors: Alcuin and Theodulf of Orleans. This climate of renewal and, indeed, originality of thought had a direct effect in theological approach and devotion. Thus, it is from this period that there appear the first examples of private prayers being introduced into the liturgy. *The Sacramentary of Amiens* (late 9th Century) contains prayers for the priest's private devotional use during the preparation for and celebration of Mass. The two prayers cited below are familiar to us since, with slight modifications, they have been retained in our current Missal of Paul VI (1970).

Lord Jesus Christ, Son of the living God, by the will of the Father and the work of the Holy Spirit, your death brought life to the world. By your holy body and blood free me from all my sins, and from every evil. Keep me faithful to your teaching, and never let me be parted from you.[1]

What we have received with our mouth, Lord, may we also bear in our mind: so that this temporal gift may become an everlasting remedy.[2]

The *Prayerbook* of Charles the Bald (+ 877) offers another example of this kind of personal devotion within the liturgy. The following prayer was incorporated in missals throughout the Middle Ages and even in those for the dioceses of Lyons (1904) and Braga (1924):

Lord, holy Father, almighty and eternal God, may I so receive the body and blood of your Son, our Lord Jesus Christ, that I may find forgiveness of my sins and be filled with your Holy Spirit. For you are God, and in you is God, and beside you there is no other; your kingdom lasts forever and ever.[3]

An old Sarum manuscript instances that the practice of priests saying private prayers during the liturgy just before communicating was likewise followed in England. These prayers are almost unique in that they are addressed to Christ in the Blessed Sacrament:

God, Father, Font and Origin of all goodness, your mercy caused your only-begotten Son to descend for us to the depths of the world. You willed that he take the flesh which I now hold here in my hands (*here the priest bows and speaks to the host*): I adore you; I glorify you; with all the intensity of my heart I praise you. And I pray that you will not leave your servants, but that you will forgive our sins....

(*Before he receives, let him humbly say to the body*): Hail forever, most holy flesh of Christ, before all else and above all else the highest sweetness...!

(*Then, with great devotion, let him say to the blood*): Hail forever, heavenly drink, before all else and above all else the highest sweetness![4]

Faith Seeking Understanding

Lanfranc (1010-1089)

Not before his thirty-third year did the wanderings of this itinerant scholar from Pavia in North Italy come to an end when in 1042 Lanfranc entered the newly founded monastery at Bec, of which he soon became Prior. He was destined for yet higher responsibilities — as Abbot of Caen (1063) and then as Archbishop of Canterbury (1070). Apart from various scholarly commentaries on the Scriptures, his theological reputation became better known for his criticism of Berengar of Tours, *De Corpore et Sanguine Domini* (c. 1070), the first widely known work of this kind. He also possessed a talent for administration, which is evident in his tactful negotiations between Church and State in the delicate business of, among other things, gradually replacing Saxon abbots and bishops by Normans during those days of the Conquest. He rebuilt Canterbury Cathedral, established a library, and wrote a set of interesting regulations for the monks, the *Monastic Constitutions*. The passages given here are from this important document. The last below pertains to the novel practice of introducing the Blessed Sacrament into the ritual of the Palm Sunday procession; this detailed account, nine-hundred years old, is the earliest extant one of a eucharistic procession or congress.

When the cantor begins the antiphon *"Occurrunt turbae"* two priests, vested in albs, shall come forward to carry the shrine which they brought there a little before daybreak. In this shrine the Body of Christ shall have been lain. Those who carry the banners and cross and the other items already mentioned shall go to this shrine. All shall

77

stand on either side, to the right and left, of those carrying the shrine and venerate it in an orderly fashion.

The boys will approach and with their masters and some cantors, who will assist [in the singing], will take their place facing the sacred reserve (*ad ipsos reliquos*).

The older ones will face one another as they do in choir.

The assembly (*statio*) will be in orderly ranks so that there will be a slight space between the boys and the older brethren. At the end of the antiphon "*Occurrunt turbae*" the boys and those with them will begin the antiphon "*Hosanna filio David*," at the beginning and end of which they will genuflect because "*Hosanna*" occurs each time. The choir shall repeat this antiphon and likewise genuflect.

Then the boys will sing the antiphon "*Cum angelis*," only at the end of which shall they genuflect. These antiphons shall be repeated by the congregation....

After this, when the abbot or a cantor begins the antiphon "*Ave Rex noster*" the bearers of the shrine shall lead off through the midst of the assembly... As they pass, all shall genuflect, though not all together but as the shrine is borne past each one....

When they come to the gates of the city they shall come to a halt, forming two ranks with such space between as there is room; the shrine shall be placed on a table covered with a cloth at the city gates while the bearers will stand on either side facing it. The place shall be fittingly adorned, the gateway prepared with fine hangings, curtains, carpets....[1]

St. Anselm (1033-1109)

Originating from Aosta, Anselm was the son of a Lombard landowner. Endowed with a passionate and headstrong nature his youth was spent in a rather unruly way, as he more than hints at in many of his prayers, such as the prayer before receiving Holy Communion (below). In 1059 he entered the monastic school at Bec in Normandy and submitted to the direction of Lanfranc of Pavia, who with Abbot Maurilius of Rouen counselled him to take the vows of religion in the monastery in 1060. Shortly afterwards his outstanding intel-

lectual qualities and sound judgment were recognized so that
he succeeded Lanfranc as prior (1063). He was to follow his
mentor once again, this time to the See of Canterbury as
Archbishop in 1093, the Chair having been vacant for about
four years after Lanfranc's death in 1089. His inclination to
decline accepting this high office may well have had something to do with what he knew of the conflicts between
Church and State, or more precisely, between Rome and
politics in England. Soon enough he was not spared from
becoming enmeshed in these troubles. On appealing to Rome
he found himself exiled from his See and adopted country.

Despite the turbulence of these times of controversy,
Anselm somehow managed to produce theological works of
the highest quality, such as *De Incarnatione Verbi* in 1095 and
Cur Deus Homo, his greatest treatise, while in Italy in 1098. He
bridges the approach in theological inquiry between the
Fathers and scholastics, employing the dual authority of the
word of God and human thought. Thus theology becomes
"fides quaerens intellectum" (faith seeking understanding).
More, Anselm the man of faith sought to *experience* God.

Lord Jesus Christ, by the Father's plan and by the working of the
Holy Ghost, of your own free will you died and mercifully redeemed
the world from sin and everlasting death. I adore and venerate you as
much as ever I can, though my love is so cold, my devotion so poor.
Thank you for the good gift of this your holy Body and Blood, which
I desire to receive, as a cleansing from sin, and for a defense against
it. Lord, I acknowledge that I am far from worthy to approach and
touch this sacrament; but I trust in that mercy which caused you to lay
down your life for sinners that they might be justified, and because
you gave yourself willingly as a holy sacrifice to the Father. A sinner,
I presume to receive these gifts so that I may be justified by them. I
beg and pray you, therefore, merciful lover of men, let not that which
you have given for the cleansing of sins be unto me the increase of sin,
but rather for forgiveness and protection.

Make me, O Lord, so to perceive with lips and heart and know
by faith and by love, that by virtue of this sacrament I may deserve to
be planted in the likeness of your death and resurrection, by mortify-
ing the old man, and by renewal of the life of righteousness.

May I be worthy to be incorporated into your body "which is the Church," so that I may be your member and you may be my head, and that I may remain in you and you in me.

Then at the Resurrection you will refashion the body of my humiliation according to the body of your glory, as you promised by your apostle, and I shall rejoice in you for ever to your glory, who with the Father and the Holy Spirit lives and reigns for ever. Amen.[2]

Monastic Mystical Theology

William of St. Thierry (1085-1148)

This abbot of the Benedictine monastery at St. Thierry near Rheims long desired to join his friend St. Bernard in a more contemplative way of life. Though the latter discouraged him, he eventually resigned his responsibility and joined some Cistercian monks in setting up a community at Igny in the Ardennes. His deep spirituality is evident in his writings on prayer and reflections on the Scriptures, and his tract on the Eucharist, which he sent to St. Bernard. He is best known for his "Golden Letter" to the Brethren of Mont Dieu of the Solitary Life. He distinguishes finely between the external sign of receiving the Sacrament, and the inner reality it contains and communicates to believers. This teaching concerns the heart of *spiritual communion,* which is not merely a matter of subjective "feelings" since its reference point is the Lord's intention to give himself in love through the reality of the Sacrament.

Those who have experienced the sweetness of kissing know how their breath is mutually exchanged with their beloved's.[1] How delicious it is to be drowned, as it were, in the perfume of the other's breathing. Receive my sighs, O Lord, and do not be repulsed by the foulness of the odor I exhale. Pour into me all your breath, which spreads everywhere such a delicate perfume that my staleness may disappear. Remain, O delightful Lord, in me for an even longer time. This takes place when we do what you commanded us to do in remembrance of you. In fulfilling your command for the salvation of your little ones, we cannot think of anything sweeter nor more powerful than when we eat and drink at the incorruptible banquet of your body and blood, like your pure animals: in the delight of thought, in the intimate depths of memory, we mull over what we have received in our mouths; and in order that the effect of our salvation may abide for ever, we meditate with renewed affection over and over again and recall most lovingly nothing other than the memory of what you did for us, how you suffered.

So, say to the yearning soul: "Open wide your mouth and I will fill it" (Ps 81:11). In tasting and beholding your loveliness in this great and incomprehensible sacrament, the soul becomes what it eats, bone of your bone and flesh of your flesh (cf. Gn 2:23). Just as you prayed to the Father on the eve of your passion, may the Holy Spirit bring about in us now by grace what you are eternally in the Father by nature. That is, just as you are one, so also may we be one (cf. Jn 17:21).[2]

Everyone, who has the mind of Christ, knows how it befits Christian piety and how worthwhile it is for the servant of God and minister of Christ's redemption, to apply himself for at least an hour each day in pondering over the benefits of the [Lord's] redeeming passion, whose tenderness is enjoyed inwardly when kept faithfully in mind. This is nothing other than a spiritual eating and drinking of the Body and Blood of Christ in memory of him who asked all who believe in him: "Do this in remembrance of me..." Only a few, to whom this ministry is entrusted to be carried out duly at its proper time and place, only they may celebrate the mystery of this holy and awesome memorial. However, what this sacrament and mystery signifies may always in any place where God reigns be realized, handled, and received according to the Lord's intention — that is, in loving devotion — by everyone. For it is said: "You are a chosen race, a royal priesthood, a holy nation, a people set apart in order that you may declare the wonders of him who has called you out of darkness into his wonderful light" (1 P 2:19). While, indeed, all receive the sacrament, it gives life to those who are rightly disposed, but brings death and condemnation to the wicked. But the reality it signifies is received only by those who have the right intentions and attitude. What most deeply matters — whether one communicates sacramentally or not — is to receive the inner reality of the sacrament. This is eternal life. So, if you desire most truly you may receive this in your cell at every hour of the day or night. For as often as you are moved in devotion by remembrance of him who suffered for you, and recall in faith his deed, you eat his Body and drink his Blood. So long as you abide in him by love, and he in you by carrying out his work of holiness and justice, you thus remain part of his body, of which you are a member.[3]

St. Bernard of Clairvaux (1090-1153)

It was because he was one of those truly rare "all or none" personalities intent singlemindedly on one thing alone, the love of God, that Bernard came to exercise so important and wide a religious influence on his age. The nobleman-turned-monk, whose attractive and forceful personality drew thirty other young fellow Burgundians (including his four brothers and an uncle) to follow him to enter the monastery of Citeaux, continues today to offer a stark challenge to discover the joy of serving God in an authentically "alternative lifestyle" to that of materialism and consumerism. Three years after entering Citeaux, his abbot (the Englishman, St. Stephen Harding) sent the twenty-five-year-old monk, Bernard, to establish a new monastery at Clairvaux. Thus began the Cistercian Order, a simplified and rigorous observance of the Rule of St. Benedict, which under Bernard's direction made Clairvaux a spiritual source of Christian renewal for all Europe.

His gifts as a powerful preacher were recognized widely when he promoted the Second Crusade. But the "Doctor Mellifluous" ("Honied Teacher," as he was later called) is better celebrated for his sublime mystical commentary on the holy Word of God, which he assimilated more through the experience of contemplative prayer than erudite scholarship. Not unlike the great teachers of the Patristic Age, the sermons and scriptural commentaries of the last of the Fathers breathe a wholly refreshing atmosphere of grace. Through his fine poetic prose, which at times may be somewhat too flowery for us, he sings, as it were, of God's own passion to communicate the word of life. Though the Real Presence in the Eucharist does not occupy the focus of his attention, the following samples of his homilies offer ample evidence of his

deep faith in the reality of Christ the giver of life in this manner
of abiding in his Church.

There are some things to eat that yield their savor on the spot,
whereas with others you must work to get at it. It is the same with
spiritual foods; the open, obvious ones require no explanation, but the
closed ones do. A mother does not give a whole nut to her little child;
she cracks it open and gives him the kernel. And in the same way,
brethren most beloved, I ought to open the closed sacraments to you;
but, as I am not equal to the task, let us beseech Wisdom, our mother,
to crack these nuts for you and me alike....

The word sacrament denotes a sacred sign or sacred mystery.
Many things are nothing but what they are in themselves; but others
represent some other thing, and they are called signs... The Lord, as
He approached His passion, invested His own with His grace and saw
to it that every unseen grace should be attached to a sign that could
be seen. All the sacraments were instituted on this principle; the
Sacrament of the Eucharist, the Feet-washing, and even Baptism... I
have told you often enough that we — all of us — fell in the fall of the
first man. We fell, however, both in the mud and on a heap of stones;
so that we were not only rendered dirty, but were also wounded and
severely shaken up. We can be washed quite quickly; but our wounds
require a lengthy process of healing. So we are washed in Baptism, for
the writ of our condemnation is then blotted out; and we are given
grace so that no concupiscence can harm us, so long as we refuse
consent to it. And when our condemnation is taken away, the sentence of death which resulted from it also is removed, like the pus that
comes from a long-standing ulcer.

But who can subdue these passionate upsurgings? Who can
endure the itching of this ulcer? Here also you have grace to help you,
you may be quite sure; to keep you safe, you are invested with the
Sacrament of the Lord's precious Body and Blood, for that sacrament
effects two things in us: it lessens our inclination to lesser sins, and it
prevents our consenting at all to those that are more serious. If any of
you feels the urge to anger or jealously or self-indulgence or is guilty
of any of those things less often and less sharply than he used to do,
let him thank the Body and Blood of the Lord; for the power of the

84

sacrament is at work in him, and he may rejoice that a very bad ulcer is on the way to being healed.[4]

Consider... that it is in Bethlehem of Judah that He is born; and think how you also may make of yourself a Bethlehem of Judah, so that He will not disdain to be born in you. Bethlehem means "the house of bread"; Judah means "confession." Therefore you, if you fill your soul with the food of God's words; if faithfully, though unworthily, and with all the devotion of which you are capable, you receive that Bread which came down from heaven and gives life to the world, that is, the Body of the Lord Jesus, so that the glorified flesh of the Resurrection may renew and strengthen the old wineskin which is your body, which thus renewed will be able to hold the wine in it; if finally, you live by faith and if you never have to admit with tears that you have forgotten to eat your bread; then you will have become a Bethlehem, worthy indeed to receive the Lord into you. Only take care also that Judah, confession, be not lacking. Let Judah, then, be your sanctification; adorning yourself with confession and justice, these being the robes most pleasing to Christ on those who serve Him. The Apostle commends these two things to you very briefly: "With the heart," he says, "we believe unto justice; but, with the mouth, confession is made unto salvation." Justice in your heart is as important as bread in your house. Justice is as bread, for "Blessed are they that hunger and thirst after justice, for they shall have their fill."[5]

St. Aelred of Rievaulx (1109-1167)

He was the son of a Saxon priest of Hexham and as a boy served at the court of King David of Scotland. On entering the Cistercian monastery at Rievaulx in Yorkshire in 1133 he seems to have disappointed his father and friends, for they could not understand why he should dash his prospects of a career and marrying well at court. (Celibacy had only recently become the discipline for the secular clergy in the Western Church.)

Aelred became Abbot of Revesby in 1143, then of Rievaulx in 1147. His abilities were recognized by St. Bernard, who invited him to write the *Speculum Caritatis (The Mirror of Charity),* his first important work. Like another great contemporary, William of St. Thierry, whose approach he shared in many respects, Aelred offers a superbly sensitive analysis of human emotionality and affections. His treatise on friendship *(De Spiritali Amicitia)* offers not only a Christian interpretation of Cicero's famous work, but by becoming the most complete medieval treatise on this subject also became a classic in its own right.

If we wish to love ourselves in the way God wants us to love ourselves, we must not be corrupted by the pleasures of the flesh. And in order that we be not overcome by these pleasures, the remedy is to turn all our love of the flesh to the flesh of Our Blessed Lord. Finally, in order to reach the state of perfect love for our fellow men, we must take even our enemies to our hearts. But we cannot remain in this perfect state unless we think always of the patience of Our Blessed Lord and Savior in His sufferings.

When we have been purified by the twofold love of which we have just treated, we can find our way into God's own sanctuary and be embraced by Him there. Our longing breaks through the limitations of our flesh, and there we see Jesus Christ as God. We are drawn into His glorious light, and lost in His unbelievable joy. Everything that belongs to our human nature, everything fleshly and perceptible and transitory is stilled. All we can do is to gaze on the One who is forever changeless, and as we gaze on Him, we are perfectly at rest; so great is the delight we find in His embrace that this is indeed the Sabbath of all Sabbaths *(The Mirror of Charity,* III, 5-6).

For the moment we have only a foretaste of this Sabbath of Sabbaths, whereas we already know and enjoy the Sabbath of days and the Sabbath of years. But who shall speak of these various Sabbaths in any way transcending what anyone may read in the Scriptures? Who is there, sufficiently enlightened by the Spirit of God, to speak of these things from his own experience? Come then, good Jesus, come to Thy poor servant who begs for crumbs. He looks for nothing from the rich man's table, but, like a dog, he waits at his master's board for whatever may fall from it. And his master, in this case, is none other than Moses, who feasted royally at Thy table.[6]

Thou hast said, kind Lord, that it is not a good thing for the bread of Thy sons to be thrown to dogs, but nonetheless the dogs were in fact allowed to eat up the scraps that were thrown to them, and so I know that bread will be broken even for me. And when the bread is too hard for me, do Thou break it into crumbs (Ibid., III, 1).

We are meant to love, and to feel the warmth of love, but in all things reason must have the last word. Joseph showed his love for his brethren by the tears he wept. If he had allowed reason to hold back those tears, his brothers would not have had the chance to ask pardon for their conduct towards him. Our Lord, likewise, wept over Jerusalem, but this did not prevent Him from punishing the city which had earned destruction through the evil ways of its people. If only those who rule the Church could do the same. Do we not find bishops and even abbots whose houses give us an impression of Sodom and Gomorrah when we go in? There they have about them a host of young relatives, whose vices they make no attempt to correct, in no wise drawing them away from worldly vanity and pleasure, but even indulging their depraved tastes and paying for them with the price of Christ's blood. They, as Joel said, have put their sons in a brothel, encouraging them in effeminate ways, and having them grow their hair long and dress in clothes that reveal the body shamelessly. Amongst these Thy Sacrifice, O Christ, is offered, and Thy Cross they raise up, and all the while they see Thy wounds, yet scorn Thy scourging and crucify Thee afresh in the poor whom they oppress, as they go about hawking and hunting on hard-driven horses. Thou must see it, dear Lord, yet Thou art silent. Wilt Thou ever be silent? No, surely Thou must speak some day! (Ibid., III, 24).[7]

On feast days, when we are bound to hear the Word of God preached, we must not spend the time instead in daily business. In the solemn seasons of penance, we do not deck ourselves out in all our finery. In fact, we must always remember where we are, and what season we are in. Anyone who conducted business in church or had sexual intercourse there would be judged guilty of sacrilege. Paul accused the Corinthians of not taking their food and drink at the right time when he wrote: "When you come therefore into one place, it is not now to eat the Lord's supper, for everyone takes his own supper to eat." Instead of observing the proper time, they ate common food before taking the Eucharist, which was against the tradition they had received from Paul. And so one would be hungry and another one drunk. "Had they not houses to eat and to drink in?" he asked, and "Did they then despise the church of God?" (Ibid., III, 29).[8]

St. Hildegard of Bingen (1098-1179)

The Benedictine Abbess of Rupertsberg (near Bingen), who was called the "Sibyl of the Rhine" for her learning and wisdom, came of noble stock. Her confessor instructed her to record her visions, which received only the guarded approval of Pope Eugenius III. Hildegard's influence was extensive; it included correspondence with none less than the Emperor Frederick Barbarossa and many kings and archbishops, etc. Her renown spread and she was invited to address groups not only of religious, but also the clergy and laity in Mainz, Wurzberg, Bamberg, and Trier (at Pentecost 1160). During her last years she was embroiled in a controversy with the Mainz Chapter over the burial of an excommunicated person near her abbey. The controversy concluded with her vindication in March 1179, six months before she died on September 17. She was not canonized until the 15th century. In 1979, the German bishops petitioned the Holy See to recognize her as a Doctor of the Church.

Apart from her herbal prescriptions, which have attracted the attention of practitioners of homeopathy in recent times, her best-known work is the *Scivias*, a compilation of mystical visions, from which the following passages are taken. The title of the work is derived from "Scito vias Domini" (Know the Ways of the Lord). While quite unique as a visionary account of the orders of creation, redemption, and sanctification, this work has been compared to similar compendiums of Christian doctrine of the period, such as Hugh of St. Victor's *Summa on the Sacraments of the Christian Faith*, which preceded the *Scivias* by about a decade.

The Blessed Virgin heard true words of consolation from the angel in secret, and believed; she uplifted the sighs of her soul and said, "Behold the handmaid of the Lord; be it done unto me according to your word" (Lk 1:38). Thus she conceived the Only-Begotten of

God. This indicates that the priest who is performing this office must invoke with his words Almighty God, faithfully believing in Him, offering Him in devotion of heart a pure oblation and speaking the words of salvation in the service of humanity; then the Supernal Majesty will receive this oblation and transmute it with miraculous power into the body and blood of the Holy Redeemer. How? As My Son miraculously received humanity in the Virgin, so now this oblation miraculously becomes His body and blood on the altar. Therefore this sacrament is wholly perfect, being invisible and visible, as My Only-Begotten is wholly perfect, Who is invisible as to His Divinity and visible on earth as to His Humanity.

For as a chick emerges from an egg, or a butterfly springs from a cocoon, and the living creature flies away while the thing it came from remains, so also in this oblation the truth that My Son's body and blood are there must be held by faith, though the oblation appears to human sight as bread and wine....

This bread is the flesh of My Son, which is obscured by no shadow of sin and clouded by no stain of iniquity, so that they who receive it are bathed with heavenly light in soul and body and cleansed by faith from their inner uncleanness. And therefore let there be no doubt about this most sacred flesh; for He Who formed the first man neither from flesh nor from bone is certainly able to produce the sacrament in this way. Therefore, O virginal Origin, You arise, grow, spread out and produce a great branch with many shoots from which to build the heavenly Jerusalem, beginning not in a man's semen but in a mystical breath. You are bound by no stain of sin at Your beginning, but developed in miraculous virtue, for You arose in an unplowed field, a flower so excellent that it will never wither from an accident of mortality, but in full freshness will last forever. Wherefore this sacrament of Your body and blood must be worshipped in the Church in a true service, until the last person to be saved by the mystery appears at the end of the world. For it comes from the secret mind of God to bring salvation to believers.[9]

Baldwin of Ford (+ 1190)

> Originating from Exeter, he entered the Cistercian abbey of
> Ford, Devon, where he was elected abbot within a year. After
> a few years he was made bishop of Worcester and four years
> later Archbishop of Canterbury (1184). His austere manner of
> life and ideals did not appeal to the monks of Christ Church.
> He was the first Archbishop of Canterbury to obtain the
> submission of Wales to the primatial see of Britain. Very
> disheartened at the Christian army's cruelty and lack of
> human restraint, he died after taking part in the Crusade in
> 1190.

By his word, Jesus manifests what he has done; he proclaims in
word the effect of his deed. First he made it, then said: "This is my
body." When he created the world, on the other hand, he first spoke
and then acted. For instance, in creating light: "God said: 'Let there
be light'; and there was light." Once light was created we do not read
of anything further being spoken: "This is light." It was unnecessary
because the power of him who spoke had instantly been confirmed in
the obedience of his work: the word remained hidden until the
appearance of his work of creation brought it clearly to light. One
word was enough to express the intention to create: immediately, at
a nod from the Creator, creatures hastened into existence. Created
things pronounced what was contained in the Creator's word, whose
power was such that a single word is the operative principle of all
things. Thus, "his invisible nature, namely, his eternal power and
deity, has been clearly perceived in the things that have been made"
(Rm 1:20). In creatures God's power can therefore be discerned and,
in a certain way, his command for their very existence can be
contemplated. There is a vast difference, however, when we consider
such a wonderful change effected in creation. A work so profound that
human reason could not detect it needed to be revealed by his word.
This is why he blessed creation saying: "This is my body." Through
these words, the Word of the all-powerful God manifested a unique
work of his power which holds us all in awe. He acted and he spoke,
so that on his word we might believe.

Although Christ is metaphorically called the vine, lamb, or rock,
and whatever may appropriately describe him, no one, however,

regards as mere figurative speech his words: "Take and eat, this is my body." What clearly he gave to be taken and eaten is called the body of Christ not in a merely symbolic or metaphorical way of speaking. But, it is truly — in the strict sense of the word — the body of Christ given for us by Christ himself, who says in Luke's account: "This is my body which is given for you" (Lk 22:19)... This is exactly what the Church believes and understands what Christ intended. This is what the Spirit of truth, which leads to all truth (cf. Jn 14:17, 26; 16:13), has taught the Church. It is what it has received, and faithfully receiving it, passes on to us....

We believe with devout faith that bread is changed (*mutatio panis facta*), although the evangelist does not explicitly say so... This is the Church's confession — as appears without shadow of doubt in the tradition of the Orthodox Fathers, who teach that in virtue of "the divine blessing, bread becomes Christ's body," is made into his body, is transubstantiated or changed or converted into Christ's body;[10] they also use many other ways of speaking of this mystery of faith. Although this proclamation of faith knows a great diversity of expressions, the piety of faith, however, witnesses an undivided unity of confession.[11]

The Renewal of the Church

The Ancrene Riwle or Wisse (c. 1220)

The *Ancrene Riwle* or *Wisse* was originally written in English in the West Midlands (Herefordshire?) as a "guide for anchoresses." Its author seems to have been a talented and well-educated cleric, who was capable of adapting the spiritual teaching of many of the Fathers and scholastics (including Augustine, Gregory, Anselm, Bernard, and Aelred) to the life undertaken by a group of women recluses. The work has come down in various versions, the best text being kept in Corpus Christi College, Cambridge (MS. 402), which Tolkien edited. The Riwle was well known even in Tudor times and illustrates the English spiritual tradition.

The following quotation from this Riwle provides one of the earliest explicit instances of devotional prayer directly addressed to the Sacrament of Christ's presence in the pyx, which was reserved in the tabernacle. The devotions recommended here were to be carried out on rising in the morning. The invocations suggested, it seems, were familiar to people at about that time. These invocations — among which are also our motets at Benediction, e.g., the "*O Salutaris Hostia,*" "*Ave Verum*" — were introduced into the Mass at the moment of the elevation of the Sacred Host and Chalice and before Holy Communion to stimulate devotion to the presence of Christ. They encouraged an attitude of spiritual communion not in order to substitute for sacramental Communion, but to make up for the common practice of not communicating sacramentally. The practice of visiting the Blessed Sacrament in churches or chapels was fervently encouraged among these pious women as also among the communities of the Beguines and Cistercians of Flanders.

93

When you are quite ready, sprinkle yourself with holy water, which you shall always keep by you, and turn your thoughts to the Body and precious Blood of God on the high altar and fall on your knees towards Him with these greetings: Hail, author of our creation. Hail, price of our redemption. Hail, viaticum of our journey. Hail, reward of our hope. Hail, consolation of our time of waiting. Be thou our joy, who art to be our reward, be always with us, take away the dark night, wash away all our sin, give us Thy holy relief. Glory be to Thee, O Lord, who wast born of a virgin... You shall say these prayers also when the priest holds up the Host during the Mass, and before the Confiteor if you are going to communicate.[1]

St. Francis of Assisi (1182-1226)

Francis is one of the most well-loved saints of the Christian tradition. He and St. Clare have had a remarkable influence on spirituality. The story of his conversion hardly needs retelling! His fervent faith and loving devotion to the humanity and person of Jesus Christ were focused on the Holy Sacrament, wherein the extremity of Christ's love is manifest in becoming poor for our sakes. The influence of the endeavors of the Fourth Lateran Council (1215) to improve the quality of doctrine and devotion regarding the Blessed Eucharist is clearly evident in Francis' writings.

Through his angel, Saint Gabriel, the most high Father in heaven announced this Word of the Father — so worthy, so holy and glorious — in the womb of the holy and glorious Virgin Mary, from which He received the flesh of humanity and our frailty. Though *He was rich* beyond all other things (2 Cor 8:9), in this world He, together with the most blessed Virgin His mother, willed to choose poverty. And, as the Passion drew near, He celebrated the Passover with His disciples and, taking bread, gave thanks, and blessed and broke it, saying: *Take and eat; this is My Body* (Mt 26:26)....

The will of the Father was such that His blessed and glorious Son, Whom He gave to us and [Who] was born for us, should, through His own blood, offer Himself as a sacrifice and oblation on the altar of the cross: not for Himself through Whom all things were made (cf. Jn 1:3), but for our sins, leaving us an example that we should follow in His footprints (cf. 1 P 2:21). And [the Father] wills that all of us should be saved through Him and that we receive Him with our pure heart and chaste body. But there are few who wish to receive Him and be saved by Him, although His *yoke is sweet* and His *burden light* (cf. Mt 11:30)... Oh, how happy and blessed are those who love God and do as the Lord Himself says in the Gospel... Let us love God, therefore, and adore Him with a pure heart and a pure mind because He Who seeks this above all else has said: *The true worshippers will adore the Father in spirit and in truth* (Jn 4:23). For all those *who worship Him* are to worship Him *in the spirit* of truth (cf. Jn 4:24).

And let us praise Him and pray to Him *day and night* (Ps 31:4), saying: *Our Father Who art in heaven* (Mt 6:9), since *we should pray always and never lose heart* (Lk 18:1).

We must also confess all our sins to a priest, and receive from him the Body and Blood of our Lord Jesus Christ. He who does not eat His Flesh and does not drink His Blood (cf. Jn 6:55, 57) *cannot enter the Kingdom of God* (Jn 3:5). Yet let him eat and drink worthily, since he who receives *unworthily eats and drinks judgment to himself, not recognizing* — that is, not discerning — *the Body of the Lord* (1 Cor 11:29)....

We must also visit churches frequently and venerate and show respect for the clergy, not so much for them personally if they are sinners, but by reason of their office and their administration of the most holy Body and Blood of Christ which they sacrifice upon the altar and receive and administer to others.[2]

Afterward the Lord gave me and still gives me such faith in priests who live according to the manner of the holy Roman Church because of their order. [...] And I do not wish to consider sin in them because I discern the Son of God in them and they are my masters. And I act in this way since I see nothing corporally of the Most High Son of God in this world except His Most holy Body and Blood which they receive and which they alone administer to others.[3]

Schooled in Faith

St. Albert the Great (1206-1280)

Born at Lauingen on the Danube, near Ulm in Germany, Albert studied first at Padua where he entered the Order of Preachers (Dominican Mendicant Friars) in 1223. On returning to Germany he taught at different Dominican houses of study. In 1241 he was sent to Paris, where he was honored by being given a chair of theology. While here, he taught St. Thomas Aquinas who followed him to Cologne in 1248. He composed a *Summa Theologica* and various other works of commentary on Holy Scripture and Aristotle. His vast erudition — including knowledge of Graeco-Arabic sources — greatly influenced the scholastic approach to philosophy and theology. He rightly earned the title "Magnus," for he was greatly gifted with the ability, in the words of the prayer for his feastday (November 15), "for reconciling human wisdom with divine faith." Roger Bacon, perhaps somewhat out of "sour grapes," complained that he was revered as if he were an ancient authority.

"Do this in remembrance of me." There are two points to be noted here. First, we are commanded to use this sacrament. Jesus intended this by saying, "Do this." In the second place, we do it in memory of his going to death for us.

So he said, "Do this." He could not have laid down a commandment more profitable or delightful, one more healthful or attractive, one more like to life eternal. We shall study these, point by point. The sacrament profits us by forgiving our sins, and is of utmost use to us by the outpouring of grace in our life. "The Father of spirits...

disciplines us for our good, that we may share his holiness." Christ's holiness lies in his sacrificial action, that is, he offered himself in the sacrament: to his Father to redeem us; to us for our use. "For their sake I consecrate myself," he said. "Christ, who through the eternal Spirit offered himself without blemish to God, will purify our conscience from dead works to serve the living God."

Then there is nothing more delightful we could do. What could ever be more delightful than that in which God offers us infinite delight? "Without their toil you supplied them with bread from heaven ready to eat, providing every pleasure and suited to every taste. For your sustenance manifested your loving kindness towards your children; and the bread, ministering to the desire of the one who took it, was changed to whatever each one desired."

Again, nothing more healthful could have been commanded. This sacrament is the fruit of the tree of life: when any man receives it with the devotion of heartfelt faith, then he shall never taste death for ever. "It is a tree of life to those who take hold of it: those who hold it fast are called blessed." "He who eats me shall live by me."

Nothing more attractive could have been commanded. This sacrament is operative to produce both love and union with Christ. The greatest showing of love is to give oneself as food. [The phrase], "If the men of my tent had not said, 'Who will give us of his flesh that we may be filled?'"... is as if Christ had said: "I have loved them so greatly, and they me, that I desire to be eaten by them: they have desired to receive me within them, to be embodied in me as my members. In no deeper way, or one more consonant to nature, can they be in me and I in them."[1]

St. Thomas Aquinas (1225-1274)

The Sermon on Maundy Thursday 1264 was probably preached at Orvieto in the presence of Pope Urban IV. This sermon is preserved in the 14th century manuscript of the library of Troyes. In the autumn of 1264 the same Pope instituted the Feast of Corpus Christi for which St. Thomas composed the liturgical offices and various hymns. The familiar *"Adoro te"* is given after extracts from the Sermon.

The joyful memory of the feast we keep today reminds us that it is our duty and our privilege ever to find our gladness in praising the most sacred Body of Christ. Is there any more fitting employment to Christians than to magnify the abyss of divine charity?...

Yours is the wonderful work, O Christ, whose power is without bounds in your faithful kindness. You yourself recall the memory of former wonders. You have in this sacred food and supersubstantial bread wonderfully found a means and the way for those who became ill by eating of the forbidden tree and lost thereby the unfading and imperishable crown of everlasting glory to be healed through eating the spotless, pure Lamb.

Most truly wonderful and utterly praiseworthy is God's goodness towards us. In his generous and untiring love he meets us and greets his children in the sacrament which is the goal and final realization of all acts of sacrifice: he abides among them ceaselessly until the end of the world. He provides us for our refreshment the bread of angels; he pours out for our drink (though we are only his adopted children, and not of his blood) strong wine, his Son's Blood.

Humility — which Christ so praised — we know pleases God. In this sacrament he truly preaches by the example of an incomparable humility which does not turn aside from any dwelling but consents to come as a guest to all and sundry, even unworthy hearts....

In the breaking of bread, You are not broken nor divided. You are eaten, but like the burning bush You are not consumed. No, You remain whole and entire as that ancient meal and oil which wonderfully lasted without diminishing or becoming spoilt.

O marvelous sacrament in which God is hidden, and our Jesus, like a new Moses, conceals his face under the creatures made by him! May every generation praise him! Wonderful is this sacrament in which, in virtue of the words of institution, the species signify and are changed into flesh and blood charged with the divine power; appearances remain in their proper substance; and, without violating the law of nature, the one and whole Christ himself is present in different places because of the consecration as a voice is heard and exists in many places — continuing unchanged and remaining inviolable when partaken nor being diminished at all. He is whole and entire and perfect in each and every fragment of the host, just as a hundred mirrors multiply the same visual appearance reflection.

Christ is fittingly offered by the faithful under the twofold species — though he truly exists under either — to signify that the salvation he imparts to humanity affects both parts of our being, soul and body, and to remind us that his bitter passion was likewise twofold.

O how unspeakable is this sacrament which sets the affections ablaze with the fire of charity and sprinkles our home's lintel, on both doorposts [lips], with the immaculate Lamb's blood! What wholesome provision for our dangerous journey we receive in this food! What strengthening manna enriches the traveller! It invigorates the weak, brings back health to the sick; it increases virtue, makes grace abound, purges away vices, refreshes the soul, renews life in the languid, binds together all the faithful in the union of charity! This Sacrament of Faith also inspires hope and increases charity. It is the central pillar of the Church, the consolation of the dead, and the fulfillment of Christ's Mystical Body....

O table of the infinite God! The many wonders of this Feast amaze the mind... more pleasing than any form of grace, more desirable than every other food. In this banquet Christ entertained those who were his earthly companions who sat with him at table... O living Bread, begotten in heaven, prepared in the Virgin's womb, baked in the furnace of the Cross, offered on the altar disguised as a wafer: strengthen my heart to be generous, keep it faithful on life's journey, gladden my mind, purify my thoughts!

This is the true Bread which while being eaten is not consumed... without losing its life-giving energy. Its power saves and completes the work [of redemption]. It is the source of life and fountain of grace. It forgives sin and weakens the grip of selfish desires. The faithful discover here their nourishment—a food for the soul, whose intelligence is enlightened, whose affections are inflamed, whose defects are purified, whose longings are lifted up... The smallness of the host reminds us to be humble; its roundness to be obedient; its simplicity to appreciate what is essential; its whiteness to be pure; its unleavened quality to be patient and kind. The fact that it was produced by baking reminds us to become charitable; its inscription calls us to become discreet; its appearances to our senses to remain steadfast and enduring; its circularity to round off a life of holiness. O rich unleavened bread! O hiding place of the highest power! Though what we see is small, what is concealed there is wonderful and excellent. O body and soul of the Divinity — divine being inseparable from both!...

This is the work of your power, Lord. You, who alone do great and wonderful deeds, transcend our senses and understanding, exceeding our reason's capacity and imagination. You yourself instituted this sacrament and entrusted it to your disciples.

Let no one, therefore, approach this wondrous Table without reverent devotion and fervent love, without true penitence or without remembering his redemption. For it is the pure Lamb that is eaten in the unleavened bread... Approach the Lord's Supper, the table of wholeness and holiness, child of faith, in such a way that at the end you may enter into the wedding feast of the Lamb... There we shall be filled with the abundance of God's house; then we shall behold the King of Glory and the Lord of Hosts in his beauty, and shall taste the bread of our Father's kingdom; our host shall be our Lord Jesus Christ, whose power and reign are without end. Amen.[2]

Adoro Te

Godhead here in hiding, whom I do adore,
masked by these bare shadows, shape and nothing more,
see, Lord, at thy service low lies here a heart
lost, all lost in wonder at the God thou art.

Seeing, touching, tasting are in thee deceived;
How says trusty hearing? That shall be believed;
What God's Son hath told me, take for truth I do;
Truth himself speaks truly, or there's nothing true.

On the Cross thy Godhead made no sign to men;
Here thy very manhood steals from human ken;
Both are my confession, both are my belief,
And I pray the prayer of the dying thief.

I am not like Thomas, wounds I cannot see,
But can plainly call thee Lord and God as he;
This faith each day deeper be my holding of
Daily make me harder hope and dearer love.

O thou our reminder of Christ crucified,
Living Bread, the life of us for whom he died,
Lend this life to me then; feed and feast my mind,
There be thou the sweetness man was meant to find.

Jesu, whom I look at shrouded here below,
I beseech thee send me what I long for so,
Some day to gaze on thee face to face in light
And be blest for ever with thy glory's sight.[3]

A Mirror for Simple Souls (13th Century)

This little work, around which there is so much that is
obscure — unknown author and undiscovered original manuscript — deserves to be better known. The author, who it is
agreed must have been French, speaks from direct experience of contemplative life and tradition, to which his contribution is a gem of late medieval spirituality. In this treatise the
central theme concerns the quest and movement of those
desiring to pass from the service of God into the very existence of God — a mystical theme stemming from the time of
the Christian Neoplatonists, notably the writings of Pseudo-
Dionysius (5th or 6th Century). This quest for intimate and
ultimate union with God is seen to be that of the "indwelling"
of the presence of the divine and "divinization" of the redeemed creature. Abandonment of all sense experience and,
as the soul advances, abandonment of "spiritual experience"
as well, bring the soul to the supreme ecstasy of Existence —
the soul moving "outside" ("without") itself into the Being of
God, which is reciprocated by God moving into the soul. This
work was influenced strongly by the Augustinian-orientated
School of St. Victor, among whose most prominent teachers
were William, Hugh, Richard, the most famous Prior, and
Thomas of St. Victor (Thomas Gallus). Long before St. John
of the Cross, the image of the "dark night" was developed in
this work, *A Mirror*, in which the doctrine of the Victorines is
reflected.

The style, reflecting the scholastic manner of disputa-
tion, offers a dramatic interplay of dialogue between the

tortuous questing of Reason to know and understand and the serenely assured responses of Love and Faith — as is well illustrated in the following passage concerning "everything and nothing: the Trinity and the Blessed Sacrament." (The comment of the text's 15th Century English translator is also interesting.) This section presents a masterly synthesis of Christian theology in its deepest and simplest sense, namely, divinely revealed faith focused on the inner, eternal life of the communion of the Three Persons' Being and on their dynamic action as One, God. The divine Sacrament presents the same perspective for our participation, communication and communion.

Reason: Please stick to my question, Lord. This book says that this soul has everything and has nothing. What do you mean by this?

Love: This soul has God in her through divine grace, and whoever has God has everything. But what she has of God in her seems to her nothing compared to what she loves of God, which is in God and remains in God — the fulness of the divine life. So, by realizing this, the soul has everything and nothing, knows all and knows nothing. Through faith she knows everything: God is almighty, all wise, all good; he sent his Son into the world and the Son left us the Spirit, while the Son and the Holy Spirit also did the work of the Incarnation. The Father has in this way joined and united human nature to the person of the Son; the Son has joined it to himself, and the Spirit has joined it to the Son. The Father has one nature, a divine nature, whereas the Son has two natures, human and divine, and the Spirit the same divine nature. True contemplation consists in believing, saying and thinking this. God is one might, one wisdom and one will; one God in three persons and three persons in one God. His divine nature sets him above everything, but he has glorified our humanity by uniting it to the person of the Son, who is in heaven glorified and, apart from there, only in the Blessed Sacrament. So when Christians receive the sacrament, they receive the divinity and humanity of Christ. We know through Faith how truly we receive the humanity.

Faith: But let me give you a simile to show you how to understand the humanity of Christ in the sacrament. If you take a host and pound it in a mortar with other things till no trace of it remains, it ceases to exist, since it can neither be seen nor felt. You might then ask: "Where has it gone?" The truth is that it was and now is not — referring to the humanity alone. "So, did it come as it went?" The truth is that the humanity of Christ neither comes nor goes. "How so?" doubters will ask.

Love: So, Reason, there is your answer. This is how the soul set free knows everything and knows nothing. Faith teaches her what she needs to know in order to be saved, but she knows nothing of what God is in himself, of himself, for himself, which is reserved to him alone. So, she knows everything, and she knows nothing.[4]

Meister Eckhart (c. 1260-1327)

This German Dominican was born of a noble family at Hochheim in Thuringia. He completed his studies with the degree of master in theology at Paris, where he taught for a short time after being provincial of the Saxon province of his order. On returning to Germany he lived first at Strassburg and then at Cologne, where he became a most noted preacher. Though thoroughly versed in the method of scholasticism, his originality in appreciating the place of paradox and his preference for apophatic expression ("the way of negative statement of the inexpressible mysteries of faith") led him to be misunderstood as promoting pantheism. He died during the proceedings when, after appealing to the Pope against the decision of his trial for heresy by the court of the Archbishop of Cologne, his writings were being reexamined. In 1329 twenty-eight of his opinions were posthumously condemned as heretical or dangerous to faith by John XXII.

As a result of this ecclesiastical censure many of his writings were lost and his teaching largely neglected in Catholic circles until the present century, though his influence continued among his disciples, among whom were Tauler and de Suso. Some romantic poets and philosophers found in him a kinship of ideas, while being for the most part ignorant of his strongly theological tradition of faith or out of sympathy with his undeterred loyalty to the faith of the Church. His insights, while being among the most daring and difficult in the history of Western thought, have recently become recognized as offering a bridge with Eastern mysticism. The following passage on receiving Holy Communion shows, however, an unquestionable lucidity and encouragement of devotion.

Whoever would gladly receive the Body of our Lord ought not to wait until he discovers certain emotions or sensations in himself, or until his inwardness and devotion are great; but he ought to make sure that he has the proper will and intention. You should not attach such importance to what you feel; rather, consider important what you love and what you intend.

The man who freely wants and is able to go to our Lord should as the first condition have a conscience free from every reproach of sin. The second condition is that his will be turned to God, that he intends nothing and delights in nothing except in God and what is wholly godly, and that everything should displease him that is unlike God. And it is in this way too that a man should test how far away from God or how close to him he may be, and this will tell him how near or far away from God he is. The third condition is that his love for the Blessed Sacrament and for our Lord ought to grow in him more and more, and that his reverent awe for it should not decrease because of his frequent receiving; because often what is life for one man is death for another. Therefore you should observe whether your love for God grows and your reverence does not decrease; and then the oftener that you go to the sacrament, the better by far will you be, and the better and more profitable by far will it be for you. So do not let people talk and preach you away from your God; the oftener, the better, and the dearer to God. For it is our Lord's delight to dwell in man and with him.

Now you may say: "Alas, sir, I know how empty and cold and inert I am, and that is why I dare not go to our Lord!"

But what I say is, all the more reason for you to go to your God; for it is in him that you will be warmed and kindled, and in him you will be made holy, to him alone will you be joined and with him alone made one, for you will find that the sacrament possesses, as does nothing else, the grace by which your bodily strength will be united and collected through the wonderful power of our Lord's bodily presence, so that all man's distracted thoughts and intentions are here collected and united, and what was dispersed and debased is here raised up again and its due order restored as it is offered to God. The senses within are so informed by our indwelling God, and weaned from the outward distractions of temporal things, and all at once become godly; and as your body is strengthened by his Body it becomes renewed. For we shall be changed into him and wholly united, so that what is his becomes ours, and all that is ours becomes his, our heart and his one heart, our body and his one Body. Our senses and our will, our intention, our powers and our members shall be so brought into him that we sense him and become aware of him in every power of our bodies and our souls.

Now you may say: "Alas, sir, I can find nothing better than poverty in myself. How could I dare to go to him?"

Be sure of this, if you want all your poverty to be changed, then go to that abundant treasury of all immeasurable riches, and so you will be rich; for in your heart you should know that he alone is the treasure that can satisfy and fulfill you. So say: "This is why I want to come to you, that your riches may replenish my poverty, that your immeasurable wealth may fill out my emptiness, that your boundless and incomprehensible divinity may make good my so pitiful and decayed humanity."

"Alas, sir, I have committed so many sins that I cannot atone for them!"

Go to him for this, for he has made fitting atonement for all guilt. In him you may well offer up to the heavenly Father an offering worthy enough to atone for all your sins.

"Alas, sir, I should like to utter my praises, but I cannot!"

Go to him, for he only is the thanks the Father will accept and he alone is the immeasurable, truth-revealing, perfect praise of all the divine goodness.

In short, if you want all your sins to be wholly taken from you and be clothed in virtues and graces, if you want to be led back joyfully to the source and to be guided by every virtue and grace, see to it that you are able to receive that sacrament worthily and often; so you will become one with him and be ennobled through his Body. Yes, in the Body of our Lord the soul is joined so close to God that not even the angels, not the cherubim or seraphim, can find or tell the difference between them. For as the angels approach God they approach the soul, as they approach the soul they approach God. There was never union so close; for the soul is far more closely united with God than are the body and soul that form one man. This union is far closer than if one were to pour a drop of water into a cask of wine; there, we still have water and wine, but here we have such a changing into one that there is no creature who can find the distinction.[5]

Medieval Gems

St. Catherine of Siena (1347-1380)

This Dominican tertiary was one of twenty-five children (thirteen of whom survived to adulthood) born to a Sienese dyer, Ser Giacomo Benincasa, and his wife Lapa, daughter of a forgotten poet, Mucio Piagenti. Her ordinary background was hardly auspicious for the most important role which she was to exercise in the politics of her day, a role no less demanding than that of persuading the Pope to return to Rome from France where he had been virtually a pawn in the hands of the French king. Of special interest is the fact that Catherine's spiritual director was an English Augustinian, William Flete, who abandoned his Cambridge studies to go into voluntary exile and live as a hermit at Lecceto on the outskirts of Siena. On her deathbed, Catherine is reported to have entrusted this friar with the continuation of her work. She was declared a Doctor of the Church with St. Teresa of Avila in 1970 by Pope Paul VI. In the extract from *The Dialogue*, she presents God as teaching her.

The person of the incarnate Word was penetrated and kneaded into one dough with the light of my Godhead, the divine nature, and with the heat and fire of the Holy Spirit, and by this means you have come to receive the light. And to whom have I entrusted it? To my ministers in the mystic body of holy Church, so that you might have life when they give you his body as food and his blood as drink.

I have said that this body of his is a sun. Therefore you could not be given the body without being given the blood as well; nor either the body or the blood without the soul of this Word; nor the soul or body without the divinity of me, God eternal. For the one cannot be separated from the other — just as the divine nature can nevermore be separated from the human nature, not by death or by any other thing past or present or future. So it is the whole divine being that you receive in that most gracious sacrament under the whiteness of bread.

And just as the sun cannot be divided, so neither can my wholeness as God and as human in this white host. Even if the host is divided, even if you could break it into thousands and thousands of tiny bits, in each one I would be there, wholly God and wholly human.[1] It is just as when a mirror is broken, and yet the image one sees reflected in it remains unbroken. So when this host is divided, I am not divided but remain completely in each piece, wholly God, wholly human.

Nor is the sacrament itself diminished by being divided, any more than is fire, to take an example. If you had a burning lamp and all the world came to you for light, the light of your lamp would not be diminished by the sharing, yet each person who shared it would have the whole light. True, each one's light would be more or less intense depending on what sort of material each brought to receive the fire. I give you this example so that you may better understand me....

O dearest daughter, open wide your mind's eye and look into the abyss of my charity. There is not a person whose heart would not melt in love to see, among all the other blessings I have given you, the blessing you receive in this sacrament.

And how, dearest daughter, should you and others look upon this mystery and touch it? Not only with your bodily eyes and feeling, for here they would fail you. You know that all your eyes see is this white bit of bread; this is all your hand can touch and all your tongue can taste, so that your dull bodily senses are deceived.[2] But the soul's sensitivity cannot be deceived, unless she so chooses by extinguishing the light of holy faith through infidelity.

What tastes and sees and touches this sacrament? The soul's sensitivity. How does she see it? With her mind's eye, so long as it has the pupil of holy faith. This eye sees in what whiteness the divine nature joined with the human; wholly God, wholly human; the body, soul, and blood of Christ, his soul united with his body and his body and soul united with my divine nature, never straying from me.[3]

Pearl (Late 14th Century)

Considered the most important work of this period in English literature, this splendid elegy is by an anonymous poet, probably from the area between Cheshire and Northern Staffordshire. Its interweaving themes have been aptly summed up by Brian Stone as follows:

"The extraordinary formal beauty of the stanza extends to the whole poem, which achieves strict harmony between passionate grief, lofty moral vision, and mystical experience. These are the heart of the poem, and at the end they resolve their counterpoint, which proceeds always with gravity and grace, in a finale of consolation, hope and benediction."[4]

Profound faith in the Real Presence is quite clearly the sustaining mark of the Christian experience, as artistically represented in the *Pearl.* This poem contains various allusions to the Gospel: the imagery of the merchant abandoning all as worthless in comparison to the "pearl of precious price," and Jesus' words both about seeking "the one thing necessary" and the absolute need to partake of the Bread of Life, which is his flesh, etc. Thus, it moves towards the vision of the New Jerusalem where the pure Lamb of God is adored by all whose pearl-whiteness resembles that of the Host and the perfection of the Body of Christ, of which they participated on earth and which is the "consolation, hope and benediction" in the end. This perspective of genuine riches and Reality is what the eye of faith perceives, is beholden to, and looks forward to with loving hope in the Divine Presence of the Blessed Eucharist.

> Christian minds by labor light
> Can please the Prince, or to peace incline;
> For I have known him, by day and night,
> As God, as Lord, as friend most fine.
> Upon this mound I fell, so fated,
> In pity for Pearl who made me pine.
> So Pearl to God I dedicated,
> With Christ's dear blessing and with mine.

111

May He who in form of bread and wine
The priest shows daily, grant we find
Ourselves true servants to Him Divine,
And precious pearls to please his mind.[5]

Julian of Norwich (c. 1343-after 1413?)

Julian of Norwich lived as an anchorite at St. Julian's church, Norwich. The *Revelations of Divine Love* were written some twenty years after an extraordinary experience of a series of revelations which lasted over five hours during a very serious illness. The key to the problems of existence and to spiritual anxiety due to our sinfulness lies, she discovered, in the tenderness of God's love towards us rather than in our works of piety. In the following passage she describes the kindness of Christ the Redeemer manifest in the Blessed Sacrament as that of a Mother. This is the focal point of her experience and of her contemplation from the vantage point of her anchorage: "Love is his meaning." Here, "All will be well — all manner of thing will be well!"

Our Mother by nature and grace — for he would become our Mother in everything — laid the foundation of his work in the Virgin's womb with great and gentle condescension... In other words, it was in this lowly place that God most high, the supreme wisdom of all, adorned and arrayed himself with our poor flesh, ready to function and serve as Mother of all things.[6]

A mother's is the most intimate, willing, and dependable of all services, because it is the truest of all. None has been able to fulfill it properly but Christ, and he alone can. We know that our own mother's bearing of us was a bearing to pain and death, but what does Jesus, our true Mother, do? Why, he, All-love, bears us to joy and eternal life! Blessings on him! Thus he carries us within himself in love. And he is in labor until the time has fully come for him to suffer the sharpest pangs and most appalling pain possible — and in the end he dies. And not even when this is over, and we ourselves have been born to eternal bliss, is his marvellous love completely satisfied. This he shows in that overwhelming word of love, "If I could possibly have suffered more, indeed I would have done so."

He might die no more, but that does not stop him working, for he needs to feed us... it is an obligation of his dear, motherly love. The human mother will suckle her child with her own milk, but our beloved Mother, Jesus, feeds us with himself, and with the most tender courtesy, does it by means of the Blessed Sacrament, the precious food of all true life. And he keeps us going through his mercy and grace by all the sacraments. This is what he meant when he said, "It is I whom Holy Church preaches and teaches." In other words, "All the health and life of sacraments, all the virtue and grace of my word, all the goodness laid up for you in Holy Church — it is I." The human mother may put her child tenderly to her breast, but our tender Mother Jesus simply leads us into his blessed breast through his open side, and there gives us a glimpse of the Godhead and heavenly joy — the inner certainty of eternal bliss. The tenth revelation showed this, and said as much with that word, "See how I love you," as looking into his side he rejoiced.

This fine and lovely word *Mother* is so sweet and so much its own that it cannot properly be used of any but him, and of her who is his own true Mother — and ours. In essence *motherhood* means love and kindness, wisdom, knowledge, goodness....[7]

Thomas à Kempis (c. 1380-1471)

> Though the authorship of the *Imitatio Christi* has long been disputed, it is generally agreed now that Thomas Hemerken (à Kempis, near Cologne) is probably its author. He had his early education at Deventer at the hands of the Brethren of the Common Life. In 1406 he took the religious habit as a Canon Regular at Agnietenberg, where his elder brother John was prior. Apart from his work in copying manuscripts and preaching, he was a well-respected spiritual director. The *Imitation of Christ* offers a classic example of the "Devotio Moderna," that renewal movement in the latter part of the fourteenth century — the circle of Gerard de Groote. The fourth book of the *Imitation* is entirely devoted to the Blessed Sacrament.

Had you the purity of Angels, and the holiness of Saint John the Baptist, you would still be unworthy to receive or touch this Sacrament. For it is not due to any merit of his own that a man is allowed to consecrate and handle the Sacrament of Christ, and receive the Bread of Angels as his food. High the office, and great the dignity of a priest, to whom is granted what is not granted to Angels; for only a rightly ordained priest has power to celebrate the Eucharist and to hallow the Body of Christ. The priest is the minister of God, using the words of God by His own command and appointment: but God Himself is the principal agent and unseen worker, to whose will all things are subject, and whose command all creatures obey. In all that relates to this sublime Sacrament, you should have regard to God's word, rather than your own senses or any visible sign. Therefore, when you approach the Altar, let it be with awe and reverence. Consider from whom this ministry proceeds, that has been delivered to you by the imposition of the Bishop's hands. You have been made a priest, and ordained to celebrate the Sacrament: see, then, that you offer this sacrifice to God faithfully, regularly, and devoutly, and that your life is blameless. Your obligations are now greater; you are bound to exercise stricter self-discipline, and to aim at a higher degree of holiness. A priest should be adorned with all virtues, and show an example of holy life to others. His life should not be like that of worldly men, but like that of the Angels, or of perfect men on earth.

A priest clothed in sacred vestments occupies the place of Christ that he may humbly intercede with God for himself and for all men. He wears the sign of the Cross both before and behind him, that he may be ever mindful of His Lord's Passion. He wears the Cross before him on his chasuble, that he may diligently observe the footsteps of Christ, and earnestly study to follow them. His shoulders also are signed with the Cross, that he may in mercy and for the love of God bear every injury done him by others. He wears the Cross before him, that he may grieve for his own sins; behind him, that he may compassionately lament the sins of others, ever mindful that he is appointed a mediator between God and the sinner, and that he may not cease from prayer and the Holy Sacrifice until he deserve to win grace and mercy. And when a priest celebrates the Eucharist, he honors God, and gives joy to the Angels; he edifies the Church, helps the living, obtains rest for the departed, and makes himself a sharer in all good things.[8]

St. Ignatius of Loyola (1491-1556)

This Basque soldier of fortune was converted while convalescing and strove to serve God as one of the champions of the Counter-Reformation, that powerful renewal movement of the Church from within. He was an inspirer of others such as St. Francis Xavier, that promising law student who met him at the University of Paris and became one of the first of his disciples or companions in the Society of Jesus (Jesuits). Although "Jesuit" has become almost synonymous with the advance and development of everything to do with the welding together of faith, science, and culture, its founder was himself more at home with the spirit of faith pervading the Middle Ages than that of experimentation, invention, and enterprise which the Renaissance opened up.

The extract that follows is from some pages from his intimate spiritual *Diario*, pages which fortunately for us survived his attempt to burn his notes, which were not intended to be read by others. In Francis Thompson's words: "We should read it as we would the accidental revelation of a lover's intimate privacies, with the same sense of hearing what we were not intended to hear, the same sense of respectful delicacy."[9] The passage gives a sample of this man's Trinitarian and Eucharistic mysticism. It records his experience at the time of discerning God's will while drawing up the Constitutions, which he placed on the altar.

Saturday, the Fifth Mass of the Trinity [February 23, 1545]:

During my usual prayer, though there was not much at first, after the second half, my soul felt a great devotion, and was exceedingly consoled; it saw also a certain object, and a form of very bright light. While they were making the altar ready, Jesus presented Himself to my mind, and invited me to follow Him; for I am quite convinced that He is the head and guide of the Society, and that it is especially on this account that it ought to practice poverty and renunciation in the highest degree, though there are also other motives which I have considered in coming to a decision. This idea disposed my mind to fervor and to tears, but also to perseverance. So that if I had no tears at this Mass, and those of the following days, the feelings of that time sufficed to support me through all temptations and troubles. While I thought of all this, and was vesting for Mass, my emotions increased. I saw in them a confirmation of the resolve I had taken; I had no other consolations. The Holy Trinity itself seemed to confirm my decision, as the Son communicated Himself thus to me, for I recalled to mind the time when the Father deigned to place me with His Son. When I was vested, the name of Jesus impressed itself upon me more and more; I felt fortified against all attacks. I wept and sobbed afresh... When I had begun the Holy Sacrifice, I received many graces and pious emotions and gentle tears, which lasted long. As the Mass continued, many inspirations confirmed what I had resolved; and when I raised the Sacred Host, I felt as it were an inward suggestion, and a powerful impulse never to abandon Our Lord, in spite of all obstacles; and this was accompanied by a new delight, and fresh impressions. This... lasted the whole time, even after Mass, and throughout the day. Whenever I thought of Jesus this pious feeling and this fixed purpose returned to my mind.[10]

English Wills and Witnesses

Raynolds' Decree (1325)

This *Decree of Archbishop Walter Raynolds of Canterbury*
interestingly refers to a reverential fast *after* reception of Holy
Communion, a fast which Archbishop Raynolds presents as a
"modern" relaxation of the older disciplinary practice.

The Great High Priest, our Lord Jesus Christ, being about to
remove from our sight the glorious Body He had taken from His
Virgin Mother, and to place it in the heavens above, on the day of His
last supper consecrated for us the sacrament of His Body, that a
perpetual Victim, a perfect and singular Host, might be constantly
worshipped, by the mystery once for all offered for the Redemption
of our souls; and that He might live for ever in our memory, who is
ever present by His grace to bring us back to life, to mercy, to salvation
and to truth.

If, then, a faithful man should with holy fear consider the
magnificence of that Sacred Host which he receives, and with a firm
faith admire Its glory, and meditate on the too great condescension of
Its obedience even unto death, he would endeavor to prepare his soul
to receive it by a purity and sincerity almost beyond the reach of
human nature.

Among all sacrifices, the greatest is the mystical Sacrament of
the Body and Blood of Christ. This oblation surpasses every other. It
must, therefore, be offered to God with a pure conscience, and
received with true devotion, and preserved with the utmost reverence. But, alas! the sons of feasting and gluttony whose God is their
belly, long since introduced into the holy Church this abuse, that

immediately after they have received the Lord's Body on Easter Day, they have served to them unconsecrated bread and wine, and there sit down eating and drinking as in a tavern — a source of many disorders. Thus, some push forward to receive the Eucharist, that they may get sooner than others to the feasting; or if the clerks are more generous with some, the rest threaten and murmur against them; and, worse than this, some of the simpler sort, misled by the form of bread in what they have first received, and not knowing how to distinguish between material food and that of the soul, which is the Body of Christ, fall into dangerous errors against faith, as we have too much reason to fear.

Alas! in a contest for a perishable crown, men abstain from all things; while seeking the unfading crown of glory, they will not endure one hour's abstinence, but without an interval defile the Body of Christ by gluttony, and, as far as in them lies, drown it amid bodily food. Hence, since we are bid to avoid not only evil, but every appearance of evil, we hereby command all rectors, vicars and parochial priests, and other ministers in the churches, under pain of the greater excommunication, which will be incurred by the disobedient, that they prohibit for the future that, after the parishioners have received the Body of Christ according to the Catholic rite, oblation of bread or wine should be given to any of them according to the old custom, which we absolutely condemn as an abuse; and this however impudently anyone may demand them. When the solemnity of the communion is over, and they have satisfied their devotion and prayers and gone home, let the doors of God's house be shut, which delights only to receive guests for spiritual banquets.

No one ought to think this decree a hard one. The old discipline prescribed that he who had received the Body of Christ early in the morning should fast till nine; and he who had received at nine or ten, till vespers; therefore modern Christians ought to think it an easy ordinance to abstain only so long as from the time of their communion till they reach home.[1]

Henry VII (1457-1509)

Henry VII's Will offers a most interesting witness to faith and devotion regarding the Blessed Sacrament, which as it were enjoyed royal patronage. Apart from this, it raises the following questions, which lie outside the scope of this anthology to answer: Was it ever executed? And, if so, what happened to the hundreds, perhaps thousands of pyxes which were ordered to be made? Furthermore, are there any of these precious items still to be found today?

Forasmuch as we have often, to our inward regret, seen in many churches of our Realm, the Holy Sacrament of the Altar kept in full simple and inhonest pyxes, specially pyxes of copper and timber, we have appointed the Treasurer of our Chamber and Master of our Jewel House to cause to be made forthwith pyxes of silver and gilt in great number, for the keeping of the Holy Sacrament of the Altar, after the fashion of a pyx that we have caused to be delivered to them, every of the said pyxes to be of the value of four pounds, garnished with our arms and red roses, and portcullises crowned, of the which pyxes we will, that to the laud and service of God, the weal of our soul, and for a perpetual memory of us, every house of the four orders of Friars, and likewise every parish church within this our Realm, not having a pyx or some other honest vessel of silver and gilt, nor of silver ungilded, for the keeping of the said Holy Sacrament, have of our gift in our life, one of the said pyxes, as soon as goodly may be done. And if this be not performed in part, or in all, in our life, we then will that it be performed by our executors within one year at the farthest of our decease.[2]

St. Thomas More (1478-1535)

After a brilliant career in law during the reign of Henry VIII, Sir Thomas More was appointed in 1529 as Lord Chancellor of England in succession to Thomas Cardinal Wolsey. He is the epitome of the Renaissance man in England — cultured, gracious, urbane, witty — his house in Chelsea being open to friends of the highest intellectual quality such as Colet and Erasmus. His failure both to obtain or indeed agree to Henry's desire for a divorce and an annulment of marriage from Catherine of Arragon disappointed the King grievously and brought More to resign from office. He lost most of his income and gained disgrace. On refusing to take the oath on the Act of Succession as a matter of conscience, he was imprisoned in 1534 in the Tower of London. Eventually he was tried, condemned, and beheaded for high treason. When he enjoyed the king's favor (1523), he wrote, under the pseudonym of Gulielmus Rosseus (William Ross), a defense of Henry's treatise on the Seven Sacraments against Martin Luther's attack on this work. With Bishop John Fisher of Rochester, More was canonized a saint and martyr in 1935 by Pope Pius XI.

The name of Housel[3] doth not only signify unto us the blessed Body and Blood of our Lord in the sacramental form, but also — like as this English word God signifieth unto us not only the unity of the Godhead, but also the Trinity of the three Persons, and not only their super-substantial substance, but also every gracious property, as Justice, Mercy, Truth, Almightiness, Eternity, and every good thing more than we can imagine — so doth unto us English folk this English word *Housel*, though not express yet imply, and under a reverent, devout silence signify, both the sacramental signs and the sacramental things, as well the things contained as the things holily signified, with all the secret unsearchable mysteries of the same. All which holy things right many persons very little learned, but yet in grace godly minded, with heart humble and religious, not arrogant, proud and curious, under the name of holy *Housel*, with inward heavenly comfort, do full devoutly reverence. As many a good, poor, simple, unlearned soul honoureth God full devoutly under the name of God, that cannot yet tell such a tale of God as some great clerks can, that are yet for lack of like devotion, nothing near so much in God's grace and favour.[4]

St. John Fisher (1469-1535)

After a distinguished career of scholarship at Cambridge as Vice Chancellor and then Chancellor and the first Lady Margaret Professor of Divinity in the University, he was appointed Bishop of Rochester in 1504. He enjoyed such a reputation as a preacher that he was chosen to deliver the funeral orations of both Henry VII and Lady Margaret Beaufort, whose chaplain he had been. Like Sir Thomas More his conscientious objection to the Act making Henry VIII head of the English Church occasioned his arrest, trial and earned him the crown of martyrdom on June 22, 1535.

His staunch defense of Catholic doctrine was influential at the Council of Trent. In 1527 he wrote a treatise on the Real Presence and the Sacrifice of the Mass *De Veritate Corporis et Sanguinis Christi in Eucharistia* — a work which he dedicated to Richard Fox, Bishop of Winchester, who founded Corpus Christi College, Oxford:

Since to satisfy the devotion that you feel and have always felt to the Sacrament of the Eucharist, it has pleased you to call your College by Its name (for it is called the College of the Body of Christ), it has seemed fitting to me that a book which defends the truth of that Body in the Eucharist should be dedicated to your Paternity, lest you might seem to have given your College a mere empty title.[5]

Tell me, Oecolampadius,[6] do you really believe with all your heart that the Blessed Trinity is everywhere present? If so, how is it that you suffer yourself to be drawn from adoration? Why are you not day and night on your knees, and not only morning and evening, since the Blessed Trinity seeks to be adored in spirit and in truth in every place? You will find that the Blessed Trinity is invisible. True, yet He is present, as every faithful man believes. Still no one is found who remains prostrate before Him always, day and night. Why then do you find it strange that we suffer ourselves to be withdrawn from the adoration of Christ in His Sacrament, since He is neither better nor more bountiful, nor more powerful, nor indeed, as regards His sacramental presence, more visible to the eyes than the Blessed Trinity?

As to what you say to monasteries, who is there to be free from your cavils? First, you chide Catholics in general, as if they did not believe in the Eucharist, because they are not prostrate day and night before It; and then again, when you find that some strive to do this, you chide them too and call them superstitious. Had you but tasted one drop of the sweetness which inebriates the souls of those religious from their worship of this Sacrament, you would never have written as you have, nor have apostatized from the religion that you formerly professed.[7]

Mysticism and Devotion

St. Teresa of Avila (1515-1582)

This Spanish Carmelite nun began to live her evangelical vocation in earnest only after an illness at about the age of forty. Possessing a strong character, practical wisdom and deep spiritual sense, she undertook to lead a mortified life according to the primitive discipline of her Order's rule. This met with stiff opposition especially from her colleagues in the convent. She founded the convent of St. Joseph at Avila in 1562 and, with the encouragement of her spiritual director, St. John of the Cross, endeavored to reform other convents of her Order. This resulted in the distinctly separate religious family of the Discalced Carmelites which followed the primitive rule of Carmel. For the sound worth of her teaching on the spiritual life she was declared the first woman "Doctor of the Church" in 1970.

The following passage is taken from her commentary on the Lord's Prayer in a book which she wrote for her nuns at St. Joseph's, *The Way of Perfection*. In it she beautifully binds together the inner significance of the petition, "Give us this day our daily bread," with that preceding it, "Thy will be done on earth as it is in heaven."

What would be the case if the Lord had not done most of what was necessary by means of the remedy He has given us? There would have been very few who could have fulfilled this petition, which the Lord made to the Father on our behalf: "*Fiat voluntas tua.*" Seeing our need, therefore, the good Jesus has sought the admirable means whereby He has shown us the extreme love which He has for us, and in His own name and in that of His brethren He has made this petition: "Give us, Lord, this day our daily bread."

For the love of God, sisters, let us realize the meaning of our good Master's petition, for our very life depends on our not disregarding it. Set very little store by what you have given, since there is so much that you will receive. It seems to me, in the absence of a better opinion, that the good Jesus knew what He had given for us and how important it was for us to give this to God, and yet how difficult it would be for us to do so... because of our natural inclination to base things and our want of love and courage. He saw that, before we could be aroused, we needed His aid, not once but every day, and it must have been for this reason that He resolved to remain with us. As this was so weighty and important a matter, He wished it to come from the hand of the Eternal Father. Though both Father and Son are one and the same, and He knew that whatever He did on earth God would do in Heaven, and would consider it good, since His will and the Father's will were one, yet the humility of the good Jesus was such that He wanted, as it were, to ask leave of His Father, for He knew that He was His beloved Son and that He well pleased Him. He knew quite well that in this petition He was asking for more than He had asked for in the others, but He already knew what death He was to suffer and what dishonors and affronts He would have to bear.

What father could there be, Lord, who after giving us his son, and such a Son, would allow Him to remain among us day by day to suffer as He had done already? None, Lord, in truth, but Thine....

We have now reached the conclusion that the good Jesus, being ours, asks His Father to let us have Him daily — which appears to mean "for ever." *While writing this* I have been wondering why, after saying "our *daily* bread," the Lord repeated the idea in the words, "Give us this day, Lord." *I will tell you my own foolish idea: if it really is foolish, well and good — in any case, it is quite bad enough that I should interfere in such a matter at all. Still, as we are trying to understand what we are praying for, let us think carefully what this means, so that we may pray rightly, and thank Him Who is taking such care about teaching us. This bread, then,* is ours daily, it seems to me, because we have Him here on earth, *since He has remained with us here and we receive Him*; and if we profit by His company, we shall also have Him in Heaven, for the only reason He remains with us is to help and encourage and sustain us so that we shall do that will which, as we have said, is to be fulfilled in us.

In using the words "this day" he seems to me to be *thinking of a day of the length of this life.* And a day indeed it is! As for the unfortunate souls who *will* bring damnation upon themselves and will not have fruition of Him in the world to come... it is not His fault if they are vanquished. They will have no excuse to make nor will they be able to complain of the Father for taking this bread from them at the time when they most needed it. Therefore the Son prays the Father that, since this life lasts no more than a day, He will allow Him to spend it in our service. As His Majesty has already given His Son to us, by sending Him, of His will alone, into the world, so now, of that same will, He is pleased not to abandon us, but to remain here with us for the greater glory of His friends and the discomfiture of His enemies. He prays for nothing more than this "today" since He has given us this most holy Bread. He has given it to us for ever, as I have said, as the sustenance and manna of humanity. We can have it whenever we please and we shall not die of hunger save through our own fault, for in whatever way the soul desires to partake of food, it will find joy and comfort in the Most Holy Sacrament. There is no need or trial or persecution that cannot be easily borne if we begin to *partake and taste* of those which He Himself bore, *and make them the subject of our meditations....*

Join with the Lord, then, daughters, in begging the Father to let you have your Spouse today, so that, *as long as you live,* you may never find yourself in this world without Him. Let it suffice to temper your great joy that He should remain disguised beneath these accidents of bread and wine, which is a real torture to those who have nothing else to love and no other consolation. Entreat Him not to fail you but to prepare you to receive Him worthily.[1]

St. John of the Cross (1542-1591)

John of Avila was a poet and theologian of the mystical life, whose writings finely combine the fire of the Spanish character with the discipline of scholastic method. On entering the Carmelite Order and soon becoming disillusioned by the spirit of laxity that had crept in, he set about reforming the Order with the encouragement and astute advice of St. Teresa. This resulted in great opposition and imprisonment by his own friars at Toledo. With Teresa, whose spiritual director he was, he founded the reformed Order of Discalced Carmelites. The last months of his life were spent in banishment in the province of Andalusia, where he became severely ill and died at the end of the year.

St. John's experience and understanding of prayer and the mystical life were deeply rooted in contemplation within the Church, sustained by its sacraments and liturgical life. Witnesses speak of his ardent devotion while celebrating Mass. His most acute suffering while imprisoned in Toledo was to be deprived of Mass — an experience of light in darkness (his very thought of the Eucharist during imprisonment) which is reflected in the ardor of the poem cited below. The Blessed Sacrament was described as "all his glory, all his happiness, and for him far surpassed all the things of the earth." As prior at Segovia he sought the cell nearest to the reserved Sacrament. When visiting the sick in the hospital, he would always first go to pray in the chapel before the Blessed Sacrament.

How well I know that fountain's rushing flow
Although by night

Its deathless spring is hidden. Even so
Full well I guess from whence its sources flow
Though it be night.

Its origin (since it has none) none knows:
But that all origin from it arose
Although by night.

I know there is no other thing so fair
And earth and heaven drink refreshment there
Although by night.

Full well I know its depth no man can sound
And that no ford to cross it can be found
Though it be night.

126

Its clarity unclouded still shall be:
Out of it comes the light by which we see
Though it be night.

Flush with its banks the stream so proudly swells;
I know it waters nations, heavens, and hells
Though it be night.

The current that is nourished by this source
I know to be omnipotent in force
Although by night.

From source and current a new current swells
Which neither of the other twain excels
Though it be night.

The eternal source hides in the Living Bread
That we with life eternal may be fed
Though it be night.

Here to all creatures it is crying, hark!
That they should drink their fill though in the dark,
For it is night.

This living fount which is to me so dear
Within the bread of life I see it clear
Though it be night.[2]

The loftier were the words of the Son of God, the more tasteless they were to the impure, as happened when He preached the sovereign and loving doctrine of the Holy Eucharist; for many turned away (Jn 6:60-61, 67).

Those who do not relish this language God speaks within them must not think on this account that others do not taste it; St. Peter tasted it in his soul when he said to Christ: *Lord, where shall we go? You have the words of eternal life* (Jn 6:69). And the Samaritan woman forgot the water and the water pot because of the sweetness of God's words (Jn 4:28).[3]

The foundation of the friars in Cordoba was completed with greater applause and solemnity throughout the entire city than was ever given there to any other religious order. All the clergy and confraternities of Cordoba gathered, and the Most Blessed Sacrament was brought in great solemnity from the Cathedral. All the streets were beautifully decorated, and the people acted as though it were the feast of Corpus Christi. This took place on the Sunday after Ascension Thursday. The Bishop came and preached, praising us highly. The house is situated in the best district of the city, in the neighborhood of the Cathedral.[4]

St. Francis de Sales (1567-1622)

> Born of a noble family in Savoy, he was well educated in Annecy, Paris, and Padua. Renouncing brilliant prospects of worldly advancement, he followed a vocation to the priesthood and was ordained in 1593. From that time he began his mission to try to convert the Chablais from Calvinism to Catholicism. In 1599 he became Coadjutor Bishop of Geneva and succeeded to the See in 1602. He was renowned as a preacher, a teacher of catechism and a director of souls. The best known of those directed by him was St. Jane Frances de Chantal, whom he met in 1603 and with whom he had a deep spiritual friendship. Through the combination of their efforts and inspirations, the Visitation Order was founded. His teaching greatly influenced subsequent generations who, like the Salesians of St. John Bosco founded in the latter half of the nineteenth century, took their inspiration from the spirituality of St. Francis de Sales.

So far I have not mentioned the most important and sacred of all devotions, namely the sacrifice and sacrament of the Mass. The Mass lies at the very heart of the Christian religion and devotion, a most wonderful mystery, containing within itself the fountainhead of love, and is the chief means used by God in pouring out upon us his graces and favors. Prayer when united to this divine sacrifice has unspeakable power, filling the soul with the blessings of heaven. In this way *leaning upon the arm of her true love* (Sg 8:5), the soul *makes her way, erect as a column of smoke, all myrrh and incense, and those sweet scents the perfumer knows* (Sg 3:6). Do all you can to attend Mass every day so that with the priest you may offer the sacrifice of your Redeemer to God the Father for yourself and the whole Church.[5]

Our Lord himself instituted the Eucharist, which truly contains his flesh and blood, so that *if anyone eats of this bread, he shall live for ever* (Jn 6:52). Those who often receive this sacrament devoutly so strengthen their soul that it is almost impossible for them to be poisoned by any evil inclinations, for they cannot be nourished with this living flesh and at the same time be disposed towards spiritual death. In Eden, Adam and Eve were able to avoid bodily death by eating the fruit of the tree of life planted there by God. In the same way, those who eat the bread of life are able to avoid spiritual death. If we can easily preserve, for months, soft and corruptible fruits like cherries, apricots and strawberries, by conserving them in sugar and honey, it is not so strange that our hearts, no matter how frail and weak, may be preserved from the corruption of sin when conserved with the sugar and honey of the incorruptible body of the Son of God....

"I neither praise nor blame," says St. Augustine, "the daily reception of Holy Communion, but I recommend and encourage everyone to go to Communion every Sunday, so long as they are not attached to sin." I myself neither praise nor blame daily Communion without qualifications, but leave it to the discretion of your confessor, the necessary dispositions being such a delicate matter that it is not prudent to encourage it for everyone. On the other hand, it is not a good thing to discourage everyone, for some may have the right dispositions; every case must be considered individually according to that person's state of conscience. It would be imprudent to encourage frequent Communion for everyone without distinction; it would be equally imprudent to dissuade anyone, particularly if he is following the advice of his confessor.

When St. Catherine of Siena was criticized for her frequent Communion and St. Augustine's words were quoted as an objection, she answered tactfully, "Since St. Augustine does not blame, I ask you not to blame it either and I will be satisfied."

With regard to those who are married; under the Old Law, God discouraged creditors from exacting their debts on feast days, but not debtors from paying their debts when asked. To demand the payment of the marriage debt on the day of your Communion would be rather unseemly though to pay it, on the other hand, would be in no way unseemly but rather meritorious and so no hindrance to following one's devotion and going to Communion.

Certainly in the early Church, Christians used to go to Communion every day though married and blessed with many children; that is why I say that frequent Communion in no way inconveniences fathers, husbands or wives so long as prudence and discretion are observed.[6]

When the bee has gathered the dew of heaven and the earth's sweetest nectar from the flowers, it turns it into honey, then hastens to its hive. In the same way, the priest, having taken from the altar the Son of God (who is as the dew from heaven, and true son of Mary, flower of our humanity), gives him to you as delicious food. When you have received him, stir up your heart to do him homage; speak to him about your spiritual life, gazing upon him in your soul where he is present for your happiness; welcome him as warmly as possible, and behave outwardly in such a way that your actions may give proof to all of his presence. If it is impossible to go to Communion, at least unite yourself to him spiritually by a fervent desire for the life-giving flesh of your Savior. Your principal motive in going to Communion should be to advance, strengthen and console yourself in the love of God, receiving for love alone what is given for love alone. At no other time is our Lord more loving and more tender than when he, as it were, humbles himself and comes to us in the form of food that he may enter our soul and enter into intimate union with us. If you are asked why you go to Communion so often say it is to learn to love God, to be purified from your imperfections, delivered from your miseries, consoled in your troubles and strengthened in your weaknesses.

As mountain hares become white in winter because they neither see nor eat anything but snow, so by adoring and feeding on beauty, purity and goodness itself in the Eucharist you will become altogether beautiful, pure, and good.[7]

The Baroque Age

Blaise Pascal (1623-1662)

> French mathematician, theologian, savant, his contact with
> the Jansenists reinforced his religious convictions and deep
> personal faith in the reality of Jesus Christ.

On the subject of the Blessed Sacrament: We believe that the
substance of bread being changed and transubstantiated into that of
Our Lord's body, Jesus Christ is really present in it: that is one of the
truths. Another is that this sacrament also prefigures that of the Cross
and glory, and is a commemoration of both. Here we have the Catholic
faith embracing two apparently opposing truths.

Modern heresy, unable to conceive that this sacrament contains at once the presence and the figuration of Jesus Christ, and is
both a sacrifice and a commemoration of a sacrifice, believes that one
of these truths cannot be admitted without thereby excluding the
other.

They fix on the single point that the sacrament is figurative, and
in this they are not heretical. They think that we exclude this truth,
and hence raise so many objections about passages in the Fathers
which attest it. Finally they deny the Real Presence and in this they
are heretical.[1]

Jacques Benigne Bossuet (1627-1704)

> Educated by the Jesuits, he became the preacher at the court
> of Louis XIV because of his gifts for oratory. Throughout his

life and as the Bishop of Meaux he was renowned for his sense of balance and spirit of hard work, the extensive evidence of which is found in his vast literary output — sermons, meditations, letters. His dedication reflects St. Vincent de Paul's influence on him.

The flesh eaten in the Eucharist is a pledge of Jesus Christ's love for a Christian; it witnesses to the fact that he became man and that he gave himself up. Consider this pledge, this sign, this witness: you must understand this pledge, be touched by this sign, believe in this witness, otherwise what have you taken? A pledge, a sign, a witness of the immense love of your Savior. But unless you are touched by it and share in it, this precious pledge of his love would be a witness against you, and you would be among those of whom Scripture says: "He came unto his own, and his own did not receive him" (Jn 1:11). What does it mean that he came among his own unless to indicate those who are close to him. He approaches them, he is in their midst, but they have not discerned his presence, they have not respected him in a way worthy of his dignity and love.[2]

Some clever people say: nowhere do you find in the words of the Gospel that the apostles adored the body and blood of Christ when they received them. But, do we see them adoring Jesus Christ while he was constantly among them in his visible and natural human form? ... These people, who think they are refined [*subtils*] regard others as vulgar [*grossiers*]. They themselves are coarse — simply because they do not understand what true adoration is! For they cling to every word of the account of the Supper without trying to see the relation to other things reported in the Gospel. To believe in Jesus Christ since he said: "Take, eat. This is my body" (Mt 26:26); to believe him, I say, without hesitation and without disputing since he said an astonishing thing; to do what he says and to eat what looks like bread while believing with unwavering faith that it is his true body; to do likewise regarding the sacred chalice, making an act of faith so pure and sublime — is not all this to adore Jesus Christ?

Furthermore, to discern like St. Paul, the body of the Savior, to discern exactly what one understands by the body not only of a man, but of God, the true bread come down from heaven, on which one pins one's hope, finds in it one's life, focuses one's love — is this not to

adore it perfectly? And to add to this faith, the gestures of genuflec-
tions, the bowing and prostration of one's body — in a word, external
adoration — is all this not to give an outward expression to what is in
the heart? ... You ask me: why expose the Sacrament? Where does
Scripture tell us to do so? Did the ancient Church do this? O stupid and
earthly-minded man, which is greater: to expose the sacrament of the
body of the Savior in the Church, or to take it with one and reserve it
in one's home? Although the latter is described and the former not
mentioned, you do not understand what is implied or what the
Church has understood. Is not the essence identical, while its expression differs according to the Church's care in arranging its practices
for the building up of its holy people?[3]

St. Margaret Mary Alacoque (1647-1690)

> After encountering various difficulties Margaret Mary en-
> tered the convent of the Visitation at Paray-le-Monial in
> central France in 1671. In the course of eighteen months,
> beginning in December 1673, she experienced several revela-
> tions of the Sacred Heart of Jesus. The purpose of these
> visions, which took the form of devotions honoring the Sa-
> cred Heart, symbol of divine love, consisted essentially in
> promoting fervent love for the presence of Christ in the
> Eucharist. The main practices of these devotions included
> Holy Communion of the First Fridays of each month, Holy
> Hour of adoration on Thursdays, and institution of the Feast
> of the Sacred Heart (on the Friday after the octave of Corpus
> Christi). Despite the encouragement and influence of her
> confessor, St. Claude de la Colombière, S.J. (+ 1682), these
> devotions, however, were not officially sanctioned by the
> Church until seventy-five years after her death. The reason
> for this divine intervention was to counter the lukewarmness
> and, particularly, infrequency of Communion, which deprived
> most of the faithful from access to the consolation of Christ's
> presence in the Eucharist — an access which the stern and
> cold teaching of Jansenism played no little part in debarring.

One day, having a little more leisure... I was praying before the
Blessed Sacrament, when I felt myself wholly penetrated with that

Divine Presence, but to such a degree that I lost all thought of myself and of the place where I was, and abandoned myself to this Divine Spirit, yielding up my heart to the power of His love. He made me repose for a long time upon His Sacred Breast, where He disclosed to me the marvels of His love and the inexplicable secrets of His Sacred Heart, which so far He had concealed from me. Then it was that, for the first time, He opened to me His Divine Heart in a manner so real and sensible as to be beyond all doubt, by reason of the effects which this favor produced in me, fearful, as I always am, of deceiving myself in anything that I say of what passes in me. It seems to me that this is what took place: "My Divine Heart," He said, "is so inflamed with love for men, and for thee in particular that, being unable any longer to contain within Itself the flames of Its burning Charity, It must needs spread them abroad by thy means, and manifest Itself to them (mankind) in order to enrich them with the precious treasures which I discover to thee...."

On the First Friday of each month, the above-mentioned grace connected with the pain in my side was renewed in the following manner: The Sacred Heart was represented to me as a resplendent sun, the burning rays of which fell vertically upon my heart, which was inflamed with a fire so fervid that it seemed as if it would reduce me to ashes. It was at these times especially that my Divine Master taught me what He required of me and disclosed to me the secrets of His loving Heart. On one occasion, whilst the Blessed Sacrament was exposed, feeling wholly withdrawn within myself by an extraordinary recollection of all my senses and powers, Jesus Christ, my sweet Master, presented Himself to me.[4]

Brother Lawrence (c. 1605-1691)

Nicolas Herman came from Lorraine. After being a soldier, he spent a brief time as a hermit before entering the Discalced Carmelite Monastery in Paris in 1649. Here, as a laybrother in charge of the kitchen, he developed a closeness to God through the simplest of "methods" of constant prayer known as "The Practice of the Presence of God." In the following extract from one of his letters, there is perhaps a hint of faith

in the Real Presence in the imagery of the King's table and
that of the divine medicine for our spiritual ills.

I wish that you could believe that God is often nearer to us in our
times of sickness and infirmity, than when we are enjoying perfect
health. Seek no other medicine than him. To the best of my understanding, he wishes to heal us alone. Put all your trust in him. You will
soon see the results. We often delay healing by putting greater trust
in remedies than in God.

Some remedies which you use will work only so far as he shall
permit. When pains come from God, he alone can heal them. He often
leaves us maladies of the body to heal those of the soul. Find
consolation in the supreme medicine of souls and bodies too.

I foresee that you will reply that I am very comfortable, that I
drink and eat at the table of the Lord. You are right, but do you think
it would be a small distress to the greatest criminal in the world to eat
at the king's table and to be served by his hands, without, however,
being assured of his forgiveness? I think that he would feel the
greatest distress, which only confidence in the goodness of his
sovereign could assuage. Can I also assure you that whatever happiness I feel in drinking and eating at the king's table, my sins, ever
before my eyes, as also the uncertainty of my pardon, are a torment
to me — though, in truth, such distress is sweet to me.[5]

Pastoral Missions

St. Alphonsus de Liguori (1696-1787)

The founder of the Congregation of the Most Holy Redeemer (Redemptorists) is considered the Church's great moral teacher and theologian. He was the son of a Neapolitan noble who took his degree as doctor of law and practiced with great success at the bar for eight years until, on losing an important case, he became convinced of the vanity of this world. He turned to the priesthood and, after ordination in 1726, began his life's work as an evangelist. Like the Wesley brothers in Britain, whose older contemporary he was, Alphonsus preached missions especially among the poor. Having declined to accept to become Archbishop of Palermo in 1747, he was persuaded to take charge of the See of Sant'Agata dei Goti in the southern province of Beneventum. He led a simple life of austerity and preached the Gospel without show of the rhetorical pretentiousness fashionable in his age. His approach confronted the skepticism of rationalism. His ardent love and respect for the Blessed Sacrament become evidenced in many of his writings, in which he fervently encourages also devotion to the Blessed Virgin Mary — for the Son cannot be separated from the Mother, whose flesh he is.

His eucharistic teaching and deep compassion in the confessional towards those burdened by sin brought many more to conversion of heart than the rigorist, intellectualist approach of his contemporaries, whose teaching was tainted by Jansenism. According to Alphonsus (as in St. Francis de Sales in the previous century), we stand more in need of and, indeed, receive God's mercy in the sacraments, especially in the Blessed Eucharist, than the severity of his justice.

"Who the day before he suffered," etc. Here the priest, renewing the memory of the Passion of Jesus Christ, relates what the Lord did on the evening before his death, when he instituted the Sacrament and the sacrifice of his body and blood. Then the priest does the same thing, and consecrates by pronouncing the very words used by Jesus Christ, as St. Ambrose remarks: "He uses not his own words, but the very words of Jesus Christ" (*De Sacr.* 4.4).

The form of the consecration is taken from St. Matthew: "This is my body." These words need no explanation, since they themselves declare what mystery is accomplished, namely, the change of the bread into the body of Jesus Christ. The form of the consecration of the chalice is as follows: "This is the cup of my blood, the blood of the new and everlasting covenant, the mystery of faith, which shall be shed for you, and for all, so that sins may be forgiven." These words the Church has taken from different texts of the Gospel, partly from St. Luke, partly from St. Matthew... The word "everlasting" is found in St. Paul: "The blood of the everlasting covenant."

The other words, "mystery of faith," the Roman catechism declares are taught by sacred tradition, which is the guardian of Catholic truths. This divine mystery is called, "the mystery of faith," not to exclude the reality of the blood of Jesus Christ, but to show that in it the faith shines forth in a wonderful manner, and triumphs over all the difficulties that may be raised by human reason, since it is here, says Innocent III, that we see one thing and believe another. We believe, he adds, that the form that we read in the Canon was received from Jesus Christ by the Apostles, and that they transmitted it to their successors (cf. *De Alt. Myst.* 4, 36 & 5).

The Roman catechism, moreover, says that the words of consecration should be thus understood: It is my blood that is contained in the chalice of the New Covenant. This signifies that men receive no longer the figure of the blood of Jesus Christ, as was the case in the Old Law; but they really receive the true blood of the New Covenant. The words "for you and for all" are used to distinguish the virtue of the blood of Christ from its fruits; for the blood of our Savior is of sufficient value to save all, but its fruits are applicable only to a certain number and not to all, and this is their own fault... those who cooperate with grace.[1]

Our most loving Savior, knowing that his hour was now come for leaving this earth, desired, before he went to die for us, to leave us the greatest possible mark of his love; and this was the gift of the most Holy Sacrament.

St. Bernardine of Siena remarks that men remember more continually and love more tenderly the signs of love which are shown to them in the hour of death. Hence it is the custom that friends, when about to die, leave to those persons whom they have loved some gift, such as a garment or a ring, as a memorial of their affection. But what hast Thou, O my Jesus, left us, when quitting this world, in memory of Thy love? Not, indeed, a garment or a ring, but Thine own body, Thy blood, Thy soul, Thy divinity, Thy whole self, without reserve. "He gave thee all," says St. John Chrysostom; "he left nothing for himself..." St. Bernardine of Siena says that Jesus Christ, burning with love for us, and not content with being prepared to give his life for us, was constrained by the excess of his love to work a greater work before he died; and this was to give his own body for our food. This Sacrament, therefore, was rightly named by St. Thomas, "*the* Sacrament of love, the pledge of love..." St. Bernard calls this sacrament "the love of loves"; because this gift comprehends all the other gifts bestowed upon us by our Lord... The Eucharist is not only a pledge of the love of Jesus Christ, but of paradise, which he desires also to give us. "In which," says the Church, "a pledge of future glory is given us." Hence St. Philip Neri could find no other name for Jesus Christ in the Sacrament save that of "love"; and so, when the holy Viaticum was brought to him, he was heard to exclaim, "Behold my love; give me my love."[2]

St. Elizabeth Ann Seton (1774-1821)

She came from a leading Episcopalian family in New York (née Bayley) and married well. While she was accompanying her husband on a business visit to Italy, he died at Livorno. Befriended by the noble Filicchi family during her bereavement, she learned to appreciate the Catholic faith and became a convert. She records in her *Italian Journal* how shocked she was on February 10, 1804 by a young Englishman interrupting her recollection, shouting into her ear at the moment of the elevation of the Host at Mass: "This is what they call there [sic] real PRESENCE."

After returning to the United States of America, she began the foundation of the Sisters of Charity of St. Joseph at Baltimore in 1808. This Congregation devoted to education and care of the sick was properly established in Emmittsburg on July 31, 1809. She was canonized a saint by Pope Paul VI in 1975.

My sister dear [Ann], how happy would we be if we believed what these dear souls believe, that they *possess* God in the Sacrament and that he remains in their churches and is carried to them when they are sick; oh my — when they carry the Blessed Sacrament under my window while I face the full loneliness and sadness of my case, I cannot stop the tears at the thought. My God, how happy would I be even so far away from all so dear, if I could find you in the church as they do (for there is a chapel in the very house of Mr. Filicchi) how many things I would say to you of the sorrows of my heart and the sins of my life....

The other day in a moment of excessive distress I fell on my knees without thinking when the Blessed Sacrament passed by and cried in an agony to God *to bless me* if he were *there*, that my whole soul desired only him... A little prayer book of Mrs. Filiccchi's was on the table and I opened a little prayer of St. Bernard to the Blessed Virgin begging her to be *our Mother*, and I said it to her with such a certainty that God would surely refuse nothing *to his Mother*, and that she could not help loving and pitying the poor souls he died for, that I felt really I had a Mother which you know my foolish heart so often laments to have lost in early days.[3]

The Protestants admit the sacrament of the Holy Eucharist, called by themselves the Lord's Supper, but they say that the body and blood of Jesus Christ are only received by faith. It belongs to them to produce good authorities in order to prove that the words of Jesus Christ are not to be understood in their plain and obvious, but in a figurative sense. Without solid proofs the presumption will always be in favor of those who do not alter the natural sense of the words, substituting in its place a capricious one. The words of our Lord are clear enough when taking bread He blessed it, broke it, and gave it to His disciples and said: "Take (and) eat: *this is my body...*" I defy Protestants to produce the authority of any of the Fathers of the first four centuries (whom they often quote as good authorities to prove religious truth) in support of their opinion that the words of Jesus Christ in the institution of this sacrament are to be taken in a figurative sense.[4]

Thursday Morning. Corpus Christi. My dear, all I can tell you is, a carriage conveyed us to the seminary. The organ's solemn peal, then the burst of the choir... We entered without a word; prostrate in an instant. Human nature could scarcely bear it. Your imagination can never conceive the splendor — the glory of the scene....

Friday Evening. Received our all. Oh! how fervently![5]

Present as a figure *one ear of corn.* Behold the work of our Heavenly Father — what was its first beginning? Look at this separate grain — recollect the time when it was first planted in the earth and covered with the frost and snows of winter, or trampled over in mire and mud, and afterwards behold the fields covered with green and gradually adorned with these beautiful plants. They rise to the height of eight or ten feet, thousands of shocks appear at once to view in shining verdure delightful to the eye, spreading their long, broad leaves on bending stalks. On the very summit of the plant the towering plume appears, containing within it the fruitful ear, wrapt round in silken folds, which produces the multiplied grains pressed close together on every side. From whence did they proceed? from one single grain: and by what power? our Heavenly Father. What, then, must be His seed of faith, of His word, of His blood, of His cross, of His flesh in the Eucharist, deposited in our hearts through the winter of life? What must be the fruit in the harvest of eternity, whose echoing vaults and ever-verdant fields shall resound with praise and love forever! Oh, exulting, oh, delightful prospect! joyful anticipations. How endearingly should we cherish this precious *faith*, this ineffable hope, this first seed of love now shooting in our hearts during the trial of patience and winter of life which will so soon pass away and bring us to the harvest of delights in eternity!!! Oh, food of Heaven, how my soul longs for you with desire! seed of Heaven, pledge of its immortality, of that eternity it pants for. Come, come, my Jesus, bury yourself within this heart. It shall do its best to preserve that warmth which will bring forth the fruits of eternity. Oh, amen. Our Jesus.[6]

The Age of Newman

Nicholas Cardinal Wiseman (1802-1865)

After a number of years as rector of the Venerable English College, Rome, in 1840 he was appointed as coadjutor to Bishop Walsh, Vicar Apostolic of the Midland District. From 1847 to 1850 he was made Vicar Apostolic of the London District. At the restoration of the hierarchy in England (1850), he was created a cardinal and first Archbishop of Westminster. Although his first pastoral letter as Archbishop — "From the Flaminian Gate," October 7, 1850 — stirred some suspicions about "creeping Roman fever," his attitude was generally sympathetic to the Church of England and particularly to the Oxford Movement. His later policy, under Manning's influence, however, was somewhat more restrictive. Robert Browning's "Bishop Bloughram's Apology" may have been directed against Wiseman. His leanings were for an Ultramontane approach in devotional practices. In 1849, Wiseman introduced the Forty Hours' Devotion into England. The following is taken from the Pastoral Letter he wrote on this occasion.

It is now your Savior "as the hidden Manna" (Rv 2:17) of which you partake, that you have here to reverence and love: it is your Lord, your God, triumphant over death for you, yet shrouding from you His overpowering glory, to whom you have to pay your open and solemn homage; — not enshrined in His poor tabernacle, where, because unseen, He is often unhonored; but enthroned, as in heaven, above His own altar, Lord of His own sanctuary, center of all surrounding splendor, challenging with love deep adoration. Around Him shall

143

flame the hallowed tapers, by whose pure ray the Church symbolizes, however feebly, the bright spirits that shine around His heavenly throne. At His feet earth shall scatter its choicest flowers, as its grateful tribute to Him that bloomed so far from Jesse's root (Is 11:1). On all sides shall be arrayed whatever of richness and splendor our poverty can collect, to adorn the chosen abode of Him who hath said, "silver is mine and the gold is mine" (Hg 2:9), and does not disdain any manifestation of our reverence: hasten then, dearly beloved, to bring whatever may be necessary to enrich the solemnity of that happy day when your Lord, in His kingly progress, shall visit your own temple, saying, "I will fill *this* house with glory" (ibid. 8), and, whether it be splendid or lowly, shall there abide in special state. Give proof to all that come there to visit Him that you prize, that you cherish, you love this privilege which He bestows; and that, like Solomon and the people of Israel, you have "gladly offered all these things" (1 Ch 29:17) which are requisite to its becoming, and even splendid, enjoyment. And "presently the Lord whom you seek, and the Angel of the testament whom you desire, shall come to His temple" (Ml 3:1).

Oh! then, go forth with joyful hearts to meet and welcome Him; and leave Him not alone, so long as He shall condescend to dwell in the midst of you. From that lofty mercy-seat whereon He hath been placed; from that bright radiance in the midst of which, as a peerless and priceless gem, He hath been set — beauty Himself, essential Light, and matchless Splendor — there go forth on every side, not scorching rays of glory, not burning shafts of might, but a mild and constant flow of holiness and grace, which fills the entire space from roof to pavement with the very breath and air of heaven. Silent and soft, as wave impelling wave of fragrance, goes forth, and diffuses itself around, that savor of sweetness, that balm of life, that virtue which emanating from the sacred humanity of Jesus upon earth, healed all diseases (Lk 8:46). And from the threshold of this His palace now, no less than His temple, it will pass abroad and spread itself on all sides, till it reach your dwellings, and more powerful than the blessing of the Ark of the Covenant (type, whereof you now possess the reality) shed over the house of Obededom (2 S 6:12), it will impart to them peace and grace, and welfare spiritual and temporal. "I will fill this house with glory, says the Lord of hosts... and in this place I will give peace, says the Lord of hosts" (Hg 11:8, 10).

But now it is that you will practice that angelic worship, lost and unknown out of the Catholic Church — the worship of pure adoration. For beyond her pale men may praise God or address Him, or perform other religious acts, but they cannot know nor make that special homage which His presence, as we possess it, inspires; when without word spoken, or sound uttered, or act performed, the soul sinks prostrate, and annihilates itself before Him, casts all its powers, and gifts, and brightest ornaments, as worthless oblations, before His altar, and subjects its entire being as a victim to His sole adorable will. When first, then, you approach the place where He is solemnly worshipped, as you bend your knees and bow your heads, let this deep and silent adoration be your first act. Speak not in words, forget all selfish thoughts, repress even all eager longings of your hearts, and receive the benediction of your mighty Lord in solemn stillness; while you, reputing yourselves but dust and ashes at His feet, a nothingness before Him, render Him the homage of loyal vassals, humble as the clay before the potter (Is 29:16), as the creature before its God. Then raise up your eyes, those keen eyes of faith, which, through the veil of sacramental elements, see, as John did "in the midst of seven golden candlesticks, one like to the Son of man" (Rv 1:13); yes, the adorable Jesus, the King of your souls, and there feast your eyes upon that sacred humanity which love has given Him, and with it kindred and brotherhood, and ties of tenderest affection with you. And now speak to Him, but with outpoured souls, with the unrestrained familiarity of warmest friendship face to face — no longer with the awful Lord, like Moses or Elias on Horeb (Ex 33:11; 1 K 19:11), but with them, and Peter, and John on Tabor (Mt 17:1-8), where you see Him radiant with His own light, but mild and inviting love.[1]

St. Peter Julian Eymard (1811-1868)

Even before he was canonized a saint by Pope John XXIII during the Second Vatican Council (December 9, 1962), he was called the "priest of the Eucharist," for from his early ministry as a diocesan priest at Chatte and during his nineteen years as a Marist, Father Eymard found in the Blessed

145

Sacrament the source and center of his life and pastoral zeal. Struck by Christ's presence in the Blessed Sacrament, he was impelled to found two religious congregations for men and women, whose primary purpose as a community was to witness to the need and worth of prayer and adoration before the Blessed Sacrament. The apostolate flowing from such a life of dedicated service to the Sacrament of Love in Eymard's vision would fire his congregations to inspire and lead others to become adorers of Our Lord Jesus Christ in the Mystery of Faith. The first of the two texts given below is a kind of manifesto, which he published in a review he began just a few months after his long retreat of forty days in Rome. In excluding some sentences, which reflect the saint's royalist nationalism and describe the external trappings of the cult of exposition (i.e., modelled on the formalities of a royal court), we can better grasp the essential inspiration driving Eymard in his love of Jesus-Host.

The nineteenth century can be called the great age of the Eucharist, as it was first called the age of Mary. No past century is equal to our own for worship of the most Blessed Sacrament. Solemn exposition was rare, even at times when faith was most alive. In some way, it might be feared that to expose this Sacrament of love too often to the piety of the faithful would compromise its respect and majesty.

There is perhaps no need yet to have recourse to this great and ultimate means of salvation for Christian society. However, today solemn exposition of the sacramental Jesus is the grace and need of our epoch. It is the supreme grace. Exposition is the Church's powerful weapon available to the faithful....

Exposition was the saving grace of Paris and of France, just as it was of Rome... Confidence rallied about this ideal. On December 6, 1848, exposition and nocturnal adoration began at the church of Our Lady of Victories.[2] It was there really that the great work would be born of the solemn manifestation of Jesus-Host, the salvation of Paris and of France....

From Paris adoration spread quickly to the provinces; the Forty Hours have become the glory of nearly all the dioceses of France, and those who have not yet organized this royal service of the Savior are preparing to satisfy the ardent desire of noble souls and the great

146

need of the people. What is more admirable is that the most remote dioceses and poorest parishes are the first in the eucharistic movement and the most magnificent in their homage.

We are not afraid to state that the cult of exposition is the need of our times. There must be this public and solemn proclamation of the people's faith in the divinity of Jesus Christ and in the truth of his sacramental presence. This is the best of all refutations to oppose renegades, apostates, the wicked and apathetic. It towers over them like a mountain of fire — the fire of love and goodness.

The solemn cult of exposition is necessary to reawaken the faith of so many honest people who do not know Jesus Christ any more because they do not know that he is their neighbor, their friend, and their God. This cult is necessary to stimulate true piety which for so long (alas!) has been kept within the sanctuary where Jesus is always ready to bless us and to open his heart to us.

It is necessary to save society. Society is dying because it has no center of truth and charity — no more the life of family. Each one is isolated, turned inward, self-sufficient. A breakdown is imminent. But society will be reborn full of vigor when all its members come to be reunited around our Emmanuel. Quite naturally the bonds of true friendship will be strengthened as a consequence of learning to love. There will be a re-flourishing of those lovely days of the Cenacle, the family feast, the festive banquet of the great King. This is the fruit of the Forty Hours in Christian environments. A holy bishop of France used to say: "When the Forty Hours was established in my diocese, religion was reborn with it: three days of adoration is worth a powerful mission. Then, what is most consoling is that the good is lasting." This is, in effect, the most beautiful proof of the power of adoration....

The great evil of the times is that people do not go to Jesus Christ as their Savior and their God. The sole basis, law, and grace of salvation is set aside. The malaise of sterile piety is that it does not share or draw its vitality from Jesus Christ; it stops short along the way; it distracts itself with externals. But divine love has its life, its center uniquely in the sacrament of the Eucharist....

What must be done? Return to the source of life: not merely to Jesus of history in Judea or to Jesus glorified in heaven, but to Jesus in the Eucharist. He must not long be neglected but placed again at the head of Christian society, which he will direct and save... He must have faithful servants, a family of friends, an adoring people.

Thus, this is the mission and glory of our century, which will come to rank as great among the greatest ages and as holiest among the most holy. It is a fact that an age waxes or wanes in proportion to its worship of the divine Eucharist. It is there that is found the life and the measure of its faith, its charity, and its vitality. May the reign of the Eucharist come about more and more. For too long impiety and ingratitude have been allowed to hold sway over the world! *Adveniat regnum tuum.* Thy kingdom come.[3]

One day a woman, a good adorer, came to Jesus to adore him. She brought with her an alabaster box full of precious ointment which she poured upon his feet to show her love for him and to pay honor to his divinity and sacred humanity.

"To what purpose is this waste?" said the traitor Judas. "This ointment might have been sold for much, and given to the poor."

But Jesus vindicates his handmaid: "What this woman has wrought is a good work. And wheresoever this Gospel shall be preached, this also which she has done shall be told in praise of her."

This Gospel incident may be applied to the Eucharist. Our Lord is in the Blessed Sacrament to receive from men the same homage he received from those who had the happiness of coming close to him during his mortal life. He is there to give everybody the opportunity of offering a personal homage to his sacred humanity. Were this the only reason for the Eucharist it should make us very happy; for the Eucharist enables us as Christians to pay our respects to our Lord in person. This presence is the justification of public worship as well as the life of it. If you take away the Real Presence, how will you be able to pay his most sacred humanity the respect and honor which are its due? ... Without this presence, divine worship becomes an abstraction. Through this presence we go straight to God and approach him as during his mortal life. How unfortunate it would be if, in order to honor the humanity of Jesus Christ, we were obliged to go back eighteen centuries! That is all very well for the mind, but how pay an outward homage to so distant a past? We would content ourselves with giving thanks for the mysteries without actively participating in them.

But with the Eucharist we can actually come and adore him like the shepherds; we can prostrate ourselves before him like the Magi; we need no longer regret our not having been present at Bethlehem or Calvary.[4]

Matthias Joseph Scheeben (1835-1888)

Scheeben was one of the most vigorous opponents of the rationalist tendency among many theologians in the 19th century. From 1860, shortly after his studies at the Gregorian University in Rome and ordination, he became the professor of dogmatic theology at the seminary at Cologne. Until his death he held this position, applying his immense erudition to expounding the supernatural nature of the Christian life of grace. In his vision, the whole organism of Christian doctrine is a supernatural cosmos, at whose center is the Mystery of the Blessed Trinity. Within this magnificent perspective the Blessed Eucharist has a prominent part as the heart of the Church, that Communion in "Holy Things" and foretaste of the vision of God.

According to the language sanctioned by ecclesiastical usage.. the eucharistic conversion of bread into the body of Christ is to be represented along the lines of the change by which the bread which Christ ate during His earthly life was converted into His body. The latter change was effected by the natural warmth and vital energy of His body; the former is brought about by the supernatural, spiritual fire and vital energy of the divine Spirit of Christ, the *calor Verbi*, who also made ready for Him the initial existence of His body in the womb of the Virgin. By the consumption of natural bread the human body receives, so to speak, its second substance, an enlargement of its previous existence. In a similar way the body of Christ in the Eucharist receives an expanded existence, not of course in the form of material increment, but in the form of a reproduction of its original substance, insofar as its existence in the Eucharist requires an act fully as powerful as that by which its existence in heaven is sustained. For the same reason, it is not enough for the substance of the bread, if it is to be kept from augmenting Christ's body with its material content, merely to receive a different form for its matter; it must totally, matter as well as form, be consumed by the fire of the Holy Spirit, so that nothing but the body of Christ with its entire being may exist under the appearances of bread.[5]

Gerard Manley Hopkins, S.J. (1844-1889)

Educated at Balliol College, Oxford, he came under the influence of E.B. Pusey and others in the Oxford Movement and joined the Catholic Church in 1866. Two years later he entered the Jesuit novitiate and was ordained a priest in 1877. He was unknown as a poet during his lifetime except to very few close friends, particularly Robert Bridges, to whom is owed the posthumous editing of his poems (first in 1918). His intense religious personality and deep attachment to Christ the Redeemer, find expression in most of his poetry, which bears the stamp of an original mind ever striving to express in words and the rhythms of human speech a "feel" of the deepest experiences of the human heart, soul, and spirit.

After passages from his important letter to his father and to Cardinal Newman on deciding to become a Catholic, there follows *The Windhover: to Christ our Lord*, a poem which Hopkins himself rated as his finest. This poem has been seen as a symbol of the mystical experience at the elevation of the Host at Mass when all created nature "buckles" into an integral harmony.

Only one thing remains to be done: I cannot fight against God who calls me to His Church: if I were to delay and die in the meantime I should have no plea why my soul was not forfeit. I have no power in fact to stir a finger: it is God Who makes the decision and not I.

But you do not understand what is involved in asking me to delay and how little good you would get from it. I shall hold as a Catholic what I have long held as an Anglican, that literal truth of our Lord's words by which I learn that the least fragment of the conse- crated elements in the Blessed Sacrament of the Altar is the whole Body of Christ born of the Virgin Mary, before which the whole host of saints and angels as it lies on the altar trembles with adoration. This belief once got is the life of the soul and when I doubted it I should become an atheist the next day. But, as Monsignor Eyre says, it is a gross superstition unless guaranteed by infallibility. I cannot hold this doctrine confessedly except as a Tractarian or a Catholic: the Tractarian ground I have seen broken to pieces under my feet. What end then can be served by a delay in whether I should go on believing this doctrine as long as I believed in God and should be by the fact of my belief drawn by a lasting strain towards the Catholic Church?[6]

I did not know till last night the rule about *communicatio in sacris* — at least as binding catechumens, but I now see the alternative thrown open, either to live without Church and sacraments or else, in order to avoid the Catholic Church, to have to attend constantly the services of that very Church. This brings the matter to an absurdity and makes me think that any delay, whatever relief it may be to my parents, is impossible. I am asking you then whether I shall at all costs be received at once.[7]

The Windhover:
To Christ our Lord

I CAUGHT this morning morning's minion, king-
    dom of daylight's dauphin, dapple-dawn-drawn Falcon, in
      his riding
  Of the rolling level underneath him steady air, and striding
High there, how he rung upon the rein of a wimpling wing
In his ecstasy! then off, off forth on swing,
As a skate's heel sweeps smooth on a bow-bend: the hurl and
gliding
Rebuffed the big wind. My heart in hiding
Stirred for a bird, — the achieve of, the mastery of the thing!

Brute beauty and valour and act, oh, air, pride, plume, here
  Buckle! AND the fire that breaks from thee then, a billion
Times told lovelier, more dangerous, O my chevalier!

  No wonder of it: shéer plód makes plough down sillion
Shine, and blue-bleak embers, ah my dear,
  Fall, gall themselves, and gash gold-vermilion.[8]

John Henry Cardinal Newman (1801-1890)

He was brought up as an Anglican and after studies at Trinity College, Oxford, Newman became a Fellow of Oriel College. He was ordained a priest in 1824 and Vicar of the University Church of St. Mary's in 1828. After touring South Europe he became closely involved in the Oxford Movement, which led him to turn to the Catholic Church, into which he was received on October 9, 1845 by St. Dominic Barberi, C.P. Shortly afterwards, his *Essay on the Development of Christian Doctrine* was published. After being ordained in Rome, he joined the Congregation of the Oratory, which he established in Birmingham in 1849. In 1877 he was made an Honorary Fellow of Trinity College, and in 1879 was created a cardinal by Pope Leo XIII.

When he became a Catholic Newman suffered greatly by friends turning from him, by having to resign his fellowship and by losing his source of income. He described his move as "going out on open sea." He was sustained by Christ's presence in the Blessed Sacrament, in which he had believed in his Anglican days, though not always accepting the explanation of it at the time in terms of Transubstantiation: "I am writing next to the Chapel," he wrote in his first letter after leaving Littlemore. "It is such an incomprehensible blessing to have Christ in bodily presence in one's house, within one's walls, as swallows up all other privileges and destroys, or should destroy, every pain."

I betake myself to one of our altars to receive the Blessed Eucharist; I have no doubt whatever on my mind about the Gift which that Sacrament contains; I confess to myself my belief, and I go through the steps on which it is assured to me. "The Presence of Christ is here, for It follows upon Consecration; and Consecration is the prerogative of Priests; and Priests are made by Ordination; and Ordination comes in direct line from the Apostles. Whatever be our other misfortunes, every link in our chain is safe; we have the Apostolic Succession, we have a right form of Consecration; therefore we are blessed with the great Gift." Here the question rises in me, "Who told you about that Gift?" I answer, "I have learned it from the Fathers: I believe the Real Presence because they witness to it. St.

Ignatius calls it *"the medicine of immortality"*; St. Irenaeus says that *"our flesh becomes incorrupt, and partakes of life, and has the hope of the resurrection,"* as *"being nourished from the Lord's Body and Blood"*; that the Eucharist *"is made up of two things, an earthly and an heavenly"*; perhaps Origen, and perhaps Magnes, after him, say that It is not a type of our Lord's Body, but His Body; and St. Cyprian uses language as fearful as can be spoken, of those who profane it. I cast my lot with them. I believe as they.[9]

Illustration of real assent in worship/religion:

... the dogmatic sentence *"The Son is God."* What an illustration of the real assent which can be given to this proposition, and its power over our affections and emotions, is the first half of the first chapter of St. John's Gospel! or again the vision of our Lord in the first chapter of the Apocalypse! or the first chapter of St. John's first Epistle! Again, how burning are St. Paul's words when he speaks of our Lord's crucifixion and death! what is the secret of that flame, but this same dogmatic sentence, *"The Son is God"*? why should the death of the Son be more awful than any other death, except that He, though man, was God?...

The same power of the dogma may be illustrated from the Ritual. Consider the services for Christmas or Epiphany; for Easter, Ascension, and (I may say) pre-eminently Corpus Christi; what are these great Festivals but comments on the words, *"The Son is God"*? Yet who will say that they have the subtlety, the aridity, the coldness of mere scholastic science? Are they addressed to the pure intellect, or to the imagination? do they interest our logical faculty, or excite our devotion? Why is it that personally we often find ourselves so ill-fitted to take part in them, except that we are not good enough, that in our case the dogma is far too much a theological notion, far too little an image living within us?...

Religion has to do with the real, and the real is the particular; theology has to do with what is notional, and the notional is the general and systematic. Hence theology has to do with the Dogma of the Holy Trinity as a whole made up of many propositions; but Religion has to do with each of these separate propositions which compose it, and lives and thrives in the contemplation of them. In them it finds the motives for devotion and faithful obedience; while theology on the other hand forms and protects them by virtue of its function of regarding them, not merely one by one, but as a system of truth.[10]

Sermon on approaching the Great Banquet with great devotion:

The same wonderful feast is put before us in the book of Proverbs, where Wisdom stands for Christ... *"Come, eat of My Bread and drink of the Wine which I have mingled"* (cf. Pr 9:1-5), which is like saying, *"Come unto Me all you who labor and are heavy laden and I will refresh you."* Like which are the prophet Isaiah's words: *"Every one who thirsts, come to the waters, and he who has no money, come. Buy and eat. Come, buy wine and milk without money and without price"* (Is 55:1)....

God grant that we may be able to come to this Blessed Sacrament with feelings suitable to the passages which I have read concerning it! May we not regard it in a cold, heartless way, and keep at a distance from fear, when we should rejoice! May the spirit of the unprofitable servant never be ours, who looked at his lord as a hard master instead of a gracious benefactor! May we not be in the number of those who go on year after year, and never approach Him at all! May we not be of those who went, one to his farm, another his merchandise, when they were called to the wedding! Nor let us be of those who come in a formal, mechanical way, as a mere matter of obligation, without reverence, without awe, without wonder, without love. Nor let us fall into the sin of those who complained that they have nothing to gather but manna, wearying of God's gifts.

But let us come in faith and hope, and let us say to ourselves, "May this be the beginning to us of everlasting bliss! May these be the first-fruits of that banquet which is to last for ever and ever; ever new, ever transporting, inexhaustible, in the city of our God!"[11]

O most Sacred, most loving Heart of Jesus. Thou art concealed in the Holy Eucharist, and Thou beatest for us still. Now as then Thou sayest, *Desiderio desideravi,* "With desire I have desired." I worship Thee then with all my best love and awe, with my fervent affection, with my most subdued, most resolved will. O my God, when Thou doest condescend to suffer me to receive Thee, to eat and drink Thee, and Thou for a while takest up Thy abode within me, O make my heart beat with Thy Heart. Purify it of all that is earthly, all that is proud and sensual, all that is hard and cruel, of all perversity, of all disorder, of all deadness. So fill it with Thee, that neither the events of the day nor the circumstances of the time may have power to ruffle it; but that in Thy love and Thy fear it may have peace.[12]

Hymn: Praise to the Holiest in the Height

> O wisest love! that flesh and blood
>   Which did in Adam fail,
> Should strive afresh against their foe,
>   Should strive and should prevail;
>
> And that a higher gift than grace
>   Should flesh and blood refine,
> God's presence and his very self,
>   And Essence all divine.

St. Therese of Lisieux (1873-1897)

From her earliest years the youngest daughter of M. Louis Martin, a watchmaker of Alencon, was attracted to religious life. Her determination against obstacles to follow her sisters to Carmel was rewarded by special permission to enter at the age of fifteen. She was given the responsibilities of assistant novice mistress in 1893 which she most diligently fulfilled. Tuberculosis claimed her and, as for many others until comparatively recently (1946) when adequate medical treatment was discovered, proved fatal.

Her autobiography, *The Story of a Soul*, portrays a rather ordinary, perhaps even slightly spoilt, person from a middle-class French background: her secret of holiness consisted in doing the simplest little things in an extraordinary way. Her mission to pray for and sacrifice her life for priests — and her correspondence with two missionary priests in particular — witness to her great love for the Eucharist, the central Christian mystery whose ministers priests are. Her whole life is characterized by an ardent fervor for the Blessed Sacrament and desire for frequent Holy Communion, which before the epoch-making Decree of Pope St. Pius X in 1905 was not permitted or generally encouraged. Around the tabernacle of the convent inner oratory she painted a fresco with the words: "Did you but know the gift of God." Among her poems is one about the Blessed Sacrament: "My desires next to the Tabernacle."

But now our Lord wanted us to go forward side by side, so he united us by a bond closer than any ties of blood; we were to be sisters in spirit. We were like the maidens in the Canticle of St. John of the Cross, where the Bride cries out to her Lover:

> Tracking your sandal-mark,
> The maidens search the roadway for your sign,
> Yearning to catch the spark
> And taste the scented wine
> Which emanates a balm that is divine.[13]

Light of foot we followed in our Lord's footsteps: the sparks of love which he spread so generously in our souls, the strong, satisfying wine which he gave us to drink, made transitory things vanish from our sight; our lips breathed tender aspirations which he, no other, had communicated to us.

Those were wonderful conversations we had, every evening, upstairs in the room with a view... Graces like these, as you would expect, bore abundant fruit in our lives; so that the path of holiness came easy and natural to us. At first, there would sometimes be a struggle, and I would make a wry face over it; but gradually that feeling disappeared, and I could renounce my own will, from the first, without difficulty. "If a man is rich," our Lord says, "gifts will be made to him, and his riches will abound." And so it was with me; if I would only correspond faithfully with each grace that was given me, a multitude of others would follow. He gave himself to me in Communion, at the time I'm speaking of, oftener than I'd have dared to hope. I made a rule of going whenever my confessor would let me, but allowing him to judge for himself, not asking it of him as a favor.

(Nowadays, I should be more plucky, and take the opposite line; I'm quite sure that if a soul feels drawn towards frequent Communion, the confessor ought to be told about it. After all, our Lord doesn't come down from heaven every day just to wait there in a gold ciborium; he has found a much better heaven for his resting-place; a Christian soul, made in his own image, the living temple of the Blessed Trinity.)

Anyhow, our Lord, finding me so eager and so well-disposed, saw to it that my confessor should encourage me to make my Communion four times a week all through that May; and when May was over, he raised it to five times in any week when a great feast came along. It was with tears of happiness that I left the confessional; our Lord himself, I felt, was determined to be my Guest....

When a gardener takes a great deal of trouble with some fruit he wants to ripen before its time, he doesn't mean to leave it hanging on the tree; it must be served up at a banquet. And it was on the same principle that our Lord lavished his graces on such a tender plant as I was... He brought himself down to my level, and taught me, all unobserved, the lesson of love. Oh dear, those learned people who spend a whole lifetime in getting up their subjects! How surprised they'd have been to hear that there was a secret which all their scientific method couldn't discover for them, the secret of perfection! It wasn't to be understood except by the poor in spirit; and here was a girl of fourteen who was ready to tell them about it.[14]

Charles de Foucauld (1858-1916)

He was born into a French aristocratic family and after a rather dissipated life as a cavalry officer with the rank of lieutenant was filled with a sense of spiritual unrest. This led him back to the faith after his conversion by the Abbé Huvelin, an experienced spiritual director, at the church of St. Augustin in Paris. His attempts to follow a religious vocation with the Trappists proved futile. He left the order in 1897 because he sought a life of greater solitude and went to the Holy Land where, at Nazareth, he served as a gardener and general factotum at the Poor Clare Monastery until 1900. He returned to France and was ordained a priest the following year. A few months later he left for Algeria in North Africa, where a holy restlessness for God had originally stirred his heart. Here he lived as a hermit in the desert, first at the oasis of Beni Abbes, and then later in the remote Hoggar Mountains and at the oasis of Tamanrasset among the Tuaregs. Apart from applying himself to learn the difficult Tuareg language, which he mastered enough to compile dictionaries and translations, his life was mainly absorbed in simple prayer before the Blessed Sacrament, penance, and works of charity. Though greatly admired, he never made a single convert. He died most tragically, being assassinated by one of the people he befriended. The reason for this may have been because of confusion and suspicions regarding his complicity with the French army. But, the real reason must be one of the secrets which the desert keeps close to its heart.

What is it that we are asking here, O God? We are asking, both for today itself, and the whole of this life (a life that in reality is no longer than a day) for that bread which is more precious than anything else: that is, our supernatural bread, the only bread we really need, the only bread absolutely necessary to us if we are to reach our goal — the necessary bread of grace.

There is, however, another supernatural bread, which without being absolutely indispensable like grace, is indispensable to many, and which is the best of all good things. The very word bread itself reminds us of it. It is that most precious good, the paramount good, the most holy Eucharist.

One must notice, however, that in asking for these two kinds of bread, grace and the Eucharist, I do not ask for them for myself alone. I ask for *us*, that is, for all men. I ask nothing for myself alone. Everything I ask for in the *Lord's Prayer* is either for God or for all mankind.[15]

You are there, my Lord Jesus, in the Holy Eucharist! You are there only a meter from me in the tabernacle! Your body, your soul, your humanity, your divinity, your entire being is there in its double nature! You are near, my God![16]

Post-Modernism: A Reaffirmation

Maurice de la Taille, S.J. (1872-1933)

> The monumental *Mysterium Fidei* by this French Jesuit, who
> was educated in England and taught at the Gregorian Univer-
> sity in Rome, appeared in 1921. While stirring up much
> controversy, it is considered the most significant theological
> event since M.J. Scheeben's *The Mysteries of Christianity*. In
> this work he insists on the uniqueness of Christ's sacrifice,
> the Mass being a sacrament of it. His biblical, and especially
> his vast patristic, erudition provides a reliable scholarly re-
> source for a thorough historical appreciation of belief, prac-
> tice, and devotion regarding the Blessed Eucharist.

It would be frivolous to deny the constant and firm faith of the
Church in the Real Presence, even from the first century. Who
accepts today the sophisticated exegesis of the sixteenth-century
reformers? Even the Protestants, particularly those of the so-called
liberal school, have eventually come to admit that the Real Presence
is taught by the sacred writings, especially from the time of St. Paul...
For the theologian this is enough: for the real sources of theology are
the documents of divine revelation; to one who denies the authority
of these documents the theologian as such has nothing to say,
because theology is for believers... Hence we have answered adver-
saries who, though interpreting rightly St. Paul's mind, would have it
that his mind was foreign to the mind of our Lord; we have also
answered those who have maintained that, in the matter of our
sacrifice, the teaching of the Church today is other than the teaching
of the early Church... The ideal of a theologian is not to advance his
own special findings, but what he has actually gathered from the

Fathers and Doctors. His purpose is to record them honestly, coordinate and refine them, and, where necessary, set them down in detail... Hence in theology there is no place for anything which does not foster piety.[1]

Gilbert Keith Chesterton (1874-1936)

Noted for his wit, this poet and essayist began his career by training in art, which he abandoned to become a journalist. His literary reputation was established in his controversial defense of the "ordinary" man's orthodoxy and conventionality against the sophism of intellectualism. He is celebrated for his aphorisms, such as "If a thing is worth doing, it is worth doing badly." He converted from the Church of England to the Roman Catholic Church in 1922, though his interest in religious questions is traced to an earlier period with his two famous books, *Heretics* (1905) and *Orthodoxy* (1908). He is perhaps best known as the author of the stories of the sleuth, "Father Brown."

The Two Kinds
(To one who long hesitated in her conversion on this point.)

To others and of old I would have said
That dogmas deep as questioning Christendom
Sleep in the sundering of the wine and bread,
And that Incarnate Christ in every crumb.

For you I find words fewer and more human:
Content to say of him that guards the Shrine
"To drink this Wine he has lost the Love of Woman.
Yea, even such love as yours: to drink this Wine."[2]

Anscar Vonier, O.S.B. (1875-1938)

This Benedictine Abbot of Buckfast had the rare gift of being
able to render in an intelligible way the deepest theological
doctrines to the general public. The following extract is taken
from his most famous book, in which he brings out the core
of St. Thomas Aquinas' teaching regarding the *sacramental*
manner of Christ's presence in the Blessed Eucharist.

Nothing could give us a clearer insight into the eucharistic
doctrine than the position which Transubstantiation holds in the
Eucharist. We have... St. Thomas (S.T., III. q. lxxviii, art. iv) telling us
that the power which changes comes after the power of signification;
in other words, the whole external sacramental action in words and
deeds signifies one thing, and one thing only, the Body of Christ and
the Blood of Christ. This is the oldest form under which we meet the
Eucharist in Christian tradition. The Church has simply given a literal
interpretation to the words of the eucharistic rite. It was not said first
that bread was being changed into Christ's Body and that wine was
being changed into Christ's Blood; what was said first and is said at
all times, is: "This is my Body, this is my Blood"; the additional
concept of change may be truly called an afterthought.

The Church could not give the reason of her great sacramental
utterances without giving for her explanation this mysterious change
which is so near to the heart of the main mystery itself that it may truly
be called a part of it. The substance of bread is changed into Christ's
Body and the substance of wine is changed into Christ's Blood.
Transubstantiation, then, is not so much the sacrament as the divinely revealed explanation of the truth of the sacrament; Transubstantiation is not the eucharistic sacrifice, but it is the hidden power
that makes the sacrifice a reality, not a mere symbol....

The doctrine that stands in the first rank of evidence is the Body
and Blood of Christ given to us in the form of sacrifice. This is the
mystery we approach at once; we enter into it directly; nothing
prepares us for it except the authority of Christ and his Church. In
matters of the Eucharist we truly enter at once *in medias res*, so to
speak; we stumble without any preparation on the sacrament of
Christ's Body and Christ's Blood. The holiest thing is the first thing

we meet. We do not bring Christ down from heaven; we do not raise him up from the depths through the sacramental signification; he is in our hands and in our mouths before we know where we are. The sacrifice is consummated through the lightning power of the sacramental words that announce it. Overawed, as it were, by the might of the thing that has happened, we ask: How did it happen? The answer is, Transubstantiation....[3]

Transubstantiation, then, is not, and could not be, the same thing as the Eucharist, both in its aspect of sacrifice and food; but it is at the root of the sacrament, deep down in the abyss of being, where God's omnipotence is supreme.[4]

Though it be a laudable thing to teach the Catholic multitudes how to enter more deeply into the mystery of the Mass through personal devotion and attention, it could, on the other hand, be a mistaken policy to exact too intense a degree of individual piety, as if the Mass were nothing else than a good occasion for self-improvement. Mass is this and more; but above all things it is the rallying of the people of God; it is a divine act, done independently of the people; a proclamation of God's sovereignty, to which the multitudes of the faithful are expected to shout their approval. There is really nothing like the eucharistic sacrifice in the whole range of human activities, natural and spiritual... The Christian altar is the place where God does His most independent work, independent of human merit and human cooperation; it is a divine fire which burns in virtue of its own inner force and all that man can do or need do is to come within the radius of the heat of that fire.[5]

François Mauriac (1885-1970)

This distinguished member of the Academie Francaise, who was a novelist, art critic, and man of letters, turned his hand to celebrate in a prose-poem, as it were, the heart of his faith in *Le Jeudi Saint*. This little piece was, however, as he professes in its preface, the expression of his desire (even though a "simple laic"!) to share something of the beauty of the central reality of the Catholic Faith not only with fellow-believers, but also with those who do not know the joy of the gift of faith.

After nineteen centuries of unheard-of glorification, it seems that the [eucharistic] Host remains as unknown as it was when it first appeared in the Cenacle at Jerusalem — despite so many cathedrals which have soared up to heaven in its honor, despite the millions of hearts which have received it devoutly, despite being tabernacled in the most remote deserts where it has its adorers, despite the fact that it is the triumphant Host of Lourdes, and of the [International Eucharistic] Congresses of Chicago [1926] and Carthage [1930]. The light is in the world, as in the days of John the Baptist when the world did not recognize it. The disputes of philosophers, the disagreements of politics, all turn about the fulcrum of religion: it is always a question of God and those who believe in Him — of the name of Christ, which anyone wishing to get on in the world must never invoke unless he is willing to court the hatred of all because of this name....

But the very ones who speak with the greatest hate or fear do not know what they reject. They hardly suspect more of the significance of this enigma than did the chief priests who left the first little church of Galilee. To be understood by the whole world, the secret of Holy Thursday remains impenetrable to those outside. One must be within the Church; one must be incorporated into it; one must become a part of the vine — one of its branches and tendrils. Why do young women join the crucified life of Carmel or the Poor Clares? Why does youth in its full vigor choose to wear garments which bring on them ridicule because they signify chastity and solitude? What inspires such a decision? Why do men and women suddenly turn from the midst of a life of sin? ... Sometimes even their appearance is transformed — their look, their laugh....

In Paris there are certain Masses where priest, servers, faithful in the nave, and, within the enclosure, nuns, who are fused into a unity. This is certainly not because of their equality in love or grace. Yet, it reigns over them — from the most holy to the most wretched — as a pre-established harmony. The Spirit conducts this concert like a miraculous symphony, in which the unbeliever cannot have a part. Mystery of joy! We cannot convince you of what is evident to us unless you would have already entered. Do you think that it is impossible to escape from this circle? No, because it depends on you to seek it. God draws the hearts of those who seek him. He who seeks finds. He who knocks at the door, has the door opened for him. How many wish precisely not to seek, to focus their gaze elsewhere, to turn away their attention!

Mystery of Holy Thursday! Mystery, as vulnerable as is all love! Mystery that is ready to give itself up, to open itself, to be the strength of each soul which insists for much or little: it does not remain impenetrable except to human indifference.

The secret of Holy Thursday was borne by Christ during the three years of his public life: being a man like us, of flesh and blood, but being also God, he knew his destiny and towards what it led... From his first miracle, at Cana, the secret of the Eucharist was doubtless in his heart. He could change water into wine; he brought about this change before the eyes of all. Water became wine; wine will become blood. From that time he prepares the minds of those who at the same time were turning to him with their hearts.

This secret would be difficult to express, if he were not God! Not only the bread and wine become his flesh and his blood, but this food must be capable of being distributed to all those who are hungry and thirsty. It is important that this nourishment is never lacking and that all are fully satisfied. Thus, the two instances which followed one another when he multiplied bread witness to this and manifest the omnipotence of Christ. Having multiplied bread, he will go on to dare pronounce the first words concerning the mystery of Holy Thursday.

Jesus bears the burden of his secret, for each time that he confides in his friends, they are scandalized and do not understand. Nothing in the Gospel disturbs us more than these confidences which seem almost natural, than these sudden glimpses regarding what he was preparing. Christ sometimes goes no further than begin to speak, as if the silence of his friends discouraged him to go on: their questions, their slowness to understand, prevented him from proceeding....

What solitude enveloped the living Christ!... But he does not vow himself to solitude; he does not embrace it like so many men of genius. He does not flee from the crowd, but gives himself to them. Humanly speaking, Christ's uniqueness among the world's great men consisted primarily in his gift of self — this complete abandonment of himself to others. Before being handed over, he delivers himself into their hands. He did not belong to himself! He came not to be served, but to serve, as the servant of servants. Nothing belonged to him: he lived on the road, in the fields, in villages. The poor and bodies of lepers pressed against him. They suffocated him so that he took refuge in a boat in order to breathe. Soiled hands clutched at his clothes; his strength was drained.

No one has ever been less protected, defenseless, more available — such as he still remains in the tabernacle: entirely for all.[6]

Ronald Knox (1888-1957)

Ronald Knox was the son of Bishop Edmund Arbuthnott Knox of Manchester, who in his time was one of the most prominent evangelicals in the Church of England. During his studies at Balliol College, Oxford, he became a leading light in the Anglo-Catholic Movement in the years before the First World War. He was received into the Church of Rome in 1917 and ordained a priest two years later. After teaching a few years at St. Edmund's College, Ware, he became chaplain to Catholic undergraduates at Oxford in 1926. Having resigned this appointment in 1939, he devoted himself during the war years and afterwards to translating the Bible into modern English — a remarkable achievement, which has been unsurpassed even by the best modern renderings. The passage below is taken from his best known sermon for the Feast of Corpus Christi, which he preached at the "artists' church" in Maiden Lane. Knox's great devotion to the Blessed Eucharist perhaps goes back to 1909, when he visited the Cistercian monastery at Caldey Island, where reservation of and devotions to the Blessed Sacrament deeply impressed him. What he witnessed of the Catholic practices and devotions, frequent communion, Benediction, and so on, during his visits to Belgium in the following years made him yearn for similar things to be taken up and spread in the Anglican Church.

The voice of the beloved — everywhere, in the mystical interpretation of the poem (Sg 2), the voice of the Beloved is understood of Christ speaking to the faithful soul. And that voice at the window brings to my own mind a fancy which I have often had, which I suppose many of us have had before now, in looking at the sacred

Host enthroned in the monstrance. The fancy, I mean, that the glittering Disc of whiteness which we see occupying that round opening is not reflecting the light of the candles in front of it, but is penetrated with a light of its own, a light not of this world, shining through it from behind, as if through a window, outdazzling gold and candle-flame with a more intense radiance. Such a visual impression you may have just for a moment; then you reflect that it is only an illusion; and then on further thought you question, Is it an illusion? Is it not rather the truth, but a truth hidden from our eyes that the Host in the monstrance, or rather those accidents of it which make themselves known to our senses, are a kind of window through which a heavenly light streams into our world; a window giving access on a spiritual world outside our human experience?

Behold, he stands behind "our wall"; the wall of our corrupt nature, which shuts us off from breathing, as man breathed in the days of his innocence, the airs of heaven; the wall of sense, which cheats us when we try even to imagine eternity; the wall of unmortified affection, which shuts us in with creatures and allows them to dominate our desires; the wall of pride, which makes us feel, except when death or tragedy is very close to us, so independent and self-sufficient. Our wall — we raised it against God, not he against us; we raise it, when Adam sinned, and when each of us took up again, by deliberate choice, that legacy of sinfulness in his own life. And through that wall the Incarnation and the Passion of Jesus Christ have made a great window; St. Paul tells us so; "he made both one, breaking down the wall that was a barrier between us," as the Temple veil was torn in two on the day when he suffered. He "made both one"; made our world of sin and sight and sense one with the spiritual world; made a breach in our citadel, let light into our prison.

Not for a moment, amid the confusion of an historical situation; the window is there for all time, if we would only recognize it. He himself, in his risen and glorified Body, is the window between the two worlds. As the window belongs both to the room inside and to the open air outside, so his glorified Body belongs at once to time and to eternity; belongs to time, because he took it upon himself, when he was born in time of his Blessed Mother, belongs to eternity, because it is now transfigured with the light of glory which is part of our future inheritance... now that he reigns in heaven, he will make himself manifest on earth still; but his glory will be veiled, more jealously than ever, as he confronts, now, the gaze of the sinner and the doubter, as he gives himself into the hands of the unworthy.

We all know what veil it is that covers him now; it is the mystery which occupies our thoughts... In this mystery of Transubstantiation, he has broken into the very heart of nature, and has separated from one another in reality two elements which we find it difficult to separate even in thought, the inner substance of things from those outward manifestations of it which make it known to our senses... A veil, that is what we look at, a curtain drawn over the window, as you may curtain the windows of a sick-room, because the patient's eyes are not strong enough to face the full glare of daylight. But behind that curtain, all the time, is the window which lets our world communicate with the world of the supernatural. As the angels ascended and descended on Jacob's ladder, so here our prayers go out into the unseen, so here grace comes flooding through, like a rushing mighty wind, into the stagnant air of our earthly experience.

And at the window, behind the wall of partition that is a wall of partition no longer, stands the Beloved himself, calling us out into the open... Arise (he says), make haste and come. Come away from the blind pursuit of creatures, from all the plans your busy brain revolves for your present and future pleasures, from the frivolous distractions it clings to. Come away from the pettiness and the meanness of your everyday life, from the grudges, the jealousies, the unhealed enmities that set your imagination throbbing. Come away from the cares and solicitudes about the morrow that seem so urgent, your heavy anxieties about the world's future and your own, so short either of them and so uncertain. Come away into the wilderness of prayer, where my love will follow you and my hand hold you; learn to live, with the innermost part of your soul, with all your secret aspirations, with all the center of your hopes and cares, in that supernatural world which can be yours now, which must be yours hereafter.[7]

Emile Mersch, S.J. (1890-1940)

Throughout his teaching and writing his aim was to present
a synthesis of faith from the perspective of the Mystical Body
of Christ, in which we discern the "whole Christ."

The Eucharist is preeminently the sacrament of grace, as it is
preeminently the sacrament of the Church and the mystical body, the
sacrament of the Christian and of Christian life. Every sacrament is a
sacrament of grace, of the Church, and of the Christian; but the
Eucharist is the sacrament par excellence, *the* sacrament, the Blessed
Sacrament.

If Christ assimilates us and transforms us into Himself in this
sacrament by making us members of His body, the reason is that He
has a higher life than our natural life. This is the life of divinization and
grace; in a sense it is infinite; it is the life which Christ's human nature
receives because of its union with the Son.

"As the living Father has sent Me, and I live by the Father, so he
who eats Me shall also live by Me" (Jn 6:35, 48, 51). The Eucharist
divinizes us by uniting us to Christ. The grace it confers is divinization,
divine adoption, and union with the whole Trinity....

We can be somewhat more specific. In this sacrament, Christ
assimilates us to Himself such as He is in the moment of His supreme
act, that is, His redemptive death. In other words, He assimilates us
formally and directly, not to His transfiguration and heavenly glory,
but to His conflict against sin. The sacrament was instituted, not for
the saints in heaven, but for poor sinners who are struggling against
sin that is always oppressing them. Its effect is not the instantaneous
production of fervor in its highest pitch, as we should expect if we
thought only of Christ and His holiness, but the launching of redeemed sinners, still burdened with their weakness and sluggish
minds, on their journey to God. The effect is not immediate admittance to eternal triumph, but persistent progress along the road that
leads to victory; for the Eucharist is our viaticum, our Pasch, our
passage; it is our glory also, but in hope and pledge, not yet in
actuality....

Christ the Redeemer, who assimilates Christians to Himself, is
Christ in the greatest act of His love. His love impels Him to perfect

obedience to the Father and to the offering of Himself as a holocaust for men. This love permeates Christians and transforms them into itself.

Therefore the Eucharist gives us charity; it is the sacrament of charity, no less than the sacrament of grace. We honor it more by devotedness to our fellow men than by an ornate ceremonial, although the latter is also indispensable. The love it engenders for God and our neighbor, by assimilating us to Christ's integral love and incorporating us into Him, is in turn integral love, the love that cannot stop short of the complete gift of self....

We perceive that the Eucharist manifests Christ more than it hides Him. It conceals only His external features, which remain inaccessibly remote from us, however close He may draw to us. Yet it gives us Him who wishes to do away with remoteness, who wishes to dwell within those whom He loves. Christ comes among us to be taken and eaten by us; and there are some who would say that this has no meaning!...

The consecrated host, reclining on the paten, is motionless and silent; it seems to be the perfect ideal of calm recollection and reposeful intimacy. Yet the truth is far different; this living bread represents humanity's supreme effort to leave its lower self behind and, in its head, mount up to God. In this same effort the strong embrace of infinite love clasps all the children of adoption to itself in God's well-beloved Son, to make them enter somehow into one another as divine love itself enters into them to transform them and their love into the image of itself. This is the perfect human act, and it is diffused through the whole Christ.[8]

Julien Green (1900-)

This American-French novelist describes the "irregular" way his father, who was an American business agent in Paris, came to be converted through receiving the Blessed Eucharist. In this account he also indicates that he is a believer. He himself became a convert on reading those pages on the Real Presence in Cardinal Gibbons' book, *The Faith of our Fathers* (1876). His *Journals* describe his sense of a twofold obligation: to himself and to God. He served in the U.S. army during World War II (1942-1945). His novels, mostly written in French, deal with rather neurotic characters who are obsessed by trivia. He was the first American to be elected to the Academie Francaise (1971).

He [my father] used to go very often to the church of Notre Dame des Victoires, a stone's throw away [from his office]. What drove him there? He couldn't say. This church simply drew him as it still attracts those who are searching. One day while Mass was being celebrated, my father joined the line of people going up for communion in good faith, and received the Holy Eucharist. This was utterly irregular. But he didn't know better. Sometimes, it pleases God to overlook all our rules. Like me, my father instantly believed and got in touch with our friend Roselys, who gave him the address of a religious. The rest followed without difficulty.[9]

Visionaries

Paul Claudel (1868-1955)

A stone on the pavement near the Blessed Virgin Mary's statue in Notre Dame, Paris, marks the spot of Claudel's conversion from a worldly life to one of fervent faith on Christmas Day, 1886, at the age of eighteen. Even while following a distinguished career in the French diplomatic service, which took him to the United States and the Far East, he devoted his considerable literary talents to writing plays which centered on the theme of the world's consecration to God in Christ. The beauty of generosity in suffering, which is elevated and transformed through religious faith, is illustrated in such plays as *L'Announce faite à Marie* and *Le Soulier du satin*. He also contributed richly to French poetry by reinstating the vitalizing importance of religious sentiment in the rhythms and imagery of language. Thus, in the following extract he ridicules the emptiness to which poetry was reduced by poets like Rimbaud or Mallarmé in their endeavor to endow human language with a power it can never possess by itself. He shows the transforming power of words pronounced by a priest at the Consecration of the Mass: by God's power human words accomplish and realize what they point to or signify.

Rimbaud, why do you flee, and yet stay, as in picture books,
The boy who runs away from home and heads for the pines into
    the storm?
You were seeking so remote an Eternity in self-indulgence amid
    ephemeral sensations.

Raise your sights and look ahead; gaze at the Unleavened Bread in
the monstrance — for that's where life is.
Your anguished mind dashes itself against your cage,
screaming out blasphemies,
But another road leads us to turn our steps toward Jerusalem.
You were not deceived in desiring to devour things, poet devoid of
the priest's power.
This is, are words which can instantly serve to unveil Being.
This thing adorned by paper flowers truly is Supreme Beauty.
These words, which though so hackneyed that no one heeds them
any more, — they were the abode of Truth.
Yet, can words which restored the dead to life become exhausted
or die?
Whenever the priest pronounces them, this bread sustains their
substance.
For us to take in the Word that is the wholly human — fully God
and man, we have only to open our mouth,
At length I behold with my own eyes it is possible to hold the
sublime!
Grasp the One who became flesh of our flesh, take possession of
the
First Cause present in a body offered to me and within reach.
Not only my soul, but also my body can attain contact with this
truth!
Even during this life the whole man can realize his power to
conquer death!
The veil, concealing things has become transparent to me at this
point.
I comprehend Substance through the Accident at last.[1]

Pierre Teilhard de Chardin, S.J. (1881-1955)

This Jesuit priest's studies in anthropology, which took him
to the Far East, led him to a profound sense of theological
awareness in faith regarding the mystical reality of the divine
presence permeating and bringing the evolutionary process
of creation to its eventual fulfillment under Christ's sover-

eignty, which he called the "Omega Point." He faithfully submitted to the judgment of the Church in not publishing his writings — a ban which was lifted only after his death.

In spite of the strength of St. Paul's expressions (formulated, it should be remembered, for the *ordinary run* of the first Christians), some readers may feel that we have been led to strain, in too realist a direction, the meaning of "Mystical Body" — or at least that we have allowed ourselves to seek esoteric perspectives in it. But if we look a little more closely, we shall see that we have simply taken another path in order to rejoin the great highway opened up in the Church by the onrush of the cult of the Holy Eucharist.

When the priest says the words *Hoc est enim Corpus meum*, his words fall directly onto the bread and directly transform it into the individual reality of Christ. But the great sacramental operation does not cease at that local and momentary event. Even children are taught that, throughout the life of each man and the life of the Church and history of the world, there is only one Mass and one Communion. Christ died once in agony. Peter and Paul receive communion on such and such a day at a particular hour. But these different acts are only the diversely central points in which the continuity of a unique act is split up and fixed, in space and time, for our experience. In fact, from the beginning of the Messianic preparation, up till the Parousia, passing through the historic manifestation of Jesus and the phases of growth of his Church, a single event has been developing in the world: the Incarnation, realized, in each individual, through the Eucharist....

But how can we avoid going further and believing that the sacramental action of Christ, *precisely because it sanctifies matter*, extends its influence beyond the pure supernatural, over all that makes up the internal and external ambience of the faithful, that is to say that it sets its mark in *everything* which we call "our providence"?

If this is the case, then we find ourselves (by simply having followed the "extensions" of the Eucharist) plunged once again precisely into our *divine milieu*. Christ — for whom and in whom we are formed, each with his own individuality and his own vocation — Christ reveals himself in each reality around us, and shines like an ultimate determinant, like a center, one might almost say like a universal element. As our humanity assimilates the material world, and as the Host assimilates our humanity, the eucharistic transformation goes beyond and completes the transubstantiation of the bread on the altar. It is the fire that sweeps over the heath; the stroke that vibrates through the bronze. In a secondary and generalized sense, but in a true sense, the sacramental Species are formed by the totality of the world, and the duration of the creation is the time needed for its consecration. *In Christo vivimus, movemur et sumus* (In Christ we live and move and have our being).

Grant, O God, that when I draw near to the altar to communicate, I may henceforth discern the infinite perspectives hidden beneath the smallness and the nearness of the Host in which you are concealed. I have already accustomed myself to seeing, beneath the stillness of that piece of bread, a devouring power which, in the words of the greatest doctors of your Church, far from being consumed by me, consumes me. Give me the strength to rise above the remaining illusions which tend to make me think of your touch as circumscribed and momentary.

I am beginning to understand: under the sacramental Species it is primarily through the "accidents" of matter that you touch me, but, as a consequence, it is also through the whole universe in proportion as this ebbs and flows over me under your primary influence. In a true sense the arms and the heart which you open to me are nothing less than all the united powers of the world which, penetrated and permeated to their depths by your will, your tastes and your temperament, converge upon my being to form it, nourish it and bear it along towards the center of your fire. In the Host it is my life that you are offering me, O Jesus....

To adore... means to lose oneself in the unfathomable, to plunge into the inexhaustible, to find peace in the incorruptible, to be absorbed in defined immensity, to offer oneself to the fire and the transparency, to annihilate oneself in proportion as one becomes more deliberately conscious of oneself, and to give of one's deepest to that whose depth has no end. Whom, then, can we adore?

The more man becomes man, the more will he become prey to a need, a need that is always more explicit, more subtle and more magnificent, the need to adore....[2]

In the Light of the Monstrance:

The light was fading. I pressed a switch, and the lamp on my desk lit up... My friend gave a start; and I noticed that his gaze remained fixed on the lamp, as though to draw from it his memories of the past, as he began again to confide in me.

"On one occasion," he said, "I was again in a church and had just knelt down before the Blessed Sacrament exposed in a monstrance when I experienced a very strange impression.

"You must, I feel sure, have observed that optical illusion which makes a bright spot against a dark background seem to expand and grow bigger? It was something of this sort that I experienced as I gazed at the host, its white shape standing out sharply, despite the candles on the altar, against the darkness of the choir. At least, that is what happened to begin with; later on, as you shall hear, my experience assumed proportions which no physical analogy could express.

"I had then the impression as I gazed at the host that its surface was gradually spreading out like a spot of oil but of course much more swiftly and luminously. At the beginning it seemed to me that I alone had noticed any change, and that it was taking place without awakening any desire or encountering any obstacle. But little by little, as the white orb grew and grew in space till it seemed to be drawing quite close to me, I heard a subdued sound, and immeasurable murmur, as when the rising tide extends its silver waves over the world of the algae which tremble and dilate at its approach, or when the burning heather crackles as fire spreads over the heath.

"Thus in the midst of a great sigh suggestive both of an awakening and of a plaint the flow of whiteness enveloped me, passed beyond me, overran everything. At the same time everything, though drowned in this whiteness, preserved its own proper shape, its own autonomous movement; for the whiteness did not efface the features or change the nature of anything, but penetrated objects at the core of their being, at a level more profound even than their own life. It was as though a milky brightness were illuminating the universe from within, and everything were fashioned of the same kind of translucent flesh.

"You see, when you switched on the lamp just now and the glass which had been dark became bright and fluorescent, I recalled how the world had appeared to me then; and indeed it was this association of images which prompted me to tell you this story."[3]

Caryll Houselander (1901-1954)

This Catholic writer began her education in a Jewish kindergarten before being sent to various schools. She was baptized in the Church of England and became a Catholic at 6! Her training in art took her through a number of occupations, including work in an advertising office and the censorship office during World War II. Her writings focus mainly on spiritual and mystical themes related to Christ's sufferings in the world, e.g. *This War is the Passion* (1941).

Benediction was at four. At half past three the church was full, the benches crowded, the people kneeling in the aisles... It is in Benediction that hundreds find the only visible beauty that shines out on the drabness of their lives, like stars burning into a grey twilight. It is an easy and sweet ceremony, with the singing of hymns, and the relief of prayers spoken out loud, a sweetness, a gentleness, a goodnight to the little flock....

Father Smith... unlocked the Tabernacle door and lifted out the Sacred Host. Walking carefully and slowly, as St. Joseph might have done when Our Lady put the Divine Child into his arms to carry, he went behind the Altar, up the tiny steps, and set the great Monstrance on its throne.

Again there was a lurching forward, a rattling and creaking and dropping as the congregation plunged and dived down into adoration. The heads of the children went down, the rows of the boys' heads, like round knobs of unpolished wood. One tiny little girl, a First Communicant of the year, squinted through her locked fingers, and screwed up her eyes, to see the gilded rays of the Monstrance blurred as if they were real glory....

Again the bell rang out, loud and sweet and solemn, the bell of Benediction. It shivered into silence. Silence possessed the people. Silence possessed the whole of Riverside. Not the silence of emptiness, but of fullness, of a crescendo of expectation, like a towering wave, gathered to the whole of its strength, lifted up to its full height, pausing in the moment of its utmost integrity, before rolling on, to fling itself forward and break upon the rocks.

Father Smith lifted the great Monstrance above the bowed heads, held it up for a moment before his plain face, suffused with love, as if he held the sun up, burning in his hands. Slowly he made the Sign of the Cross with it, lowered it onto the Altar and knelt before it.

The flowers on the Altar breathed the shimmering breath of the candle flame. The incense rose in straight blue lines through the haze of gold.

"Blessed be God," said the priest, and the wave broke, surging, tumbling, rushing forward in a torrent of praise.

"Blessed be God," roared the people....

Now the "Adoremus" rose, gentle as a caress and flowing over the Sacred Host, as Father Smith lifted It from the Monstrance, put It back into the Tabernacle and locked the door.[4]

Gerald Vann, O.P. (1906-1963)

Renowned as a retreat master and preacher, Gerald Vann's prolific writings witness to the efficacy of St. Thomas Aquinas' dictum: "*Contemplata aliis tradere*" ("Hand on to others what you have contemplated" — S.T. IIa IIae, q. 188, a. 6). He himself lived this maxim fully. He understood better than most that the mystery of the "heart of man" involves a transformation and integration of human mind, emotions, imagination, and spirit — all of which are challenged to respond fully to God, the mystery of whose presence empowers a person with the newness of being human.

Gestures often convey a depth of meaning and conviction denied to mere words. We are not spirits but body-spirits; often we can see reality most clearly, not in the dry bones of reasoned statement, but in the living rhythm of movement or other material symbol: the handclasp of friendship, the kiss of peace, the open arms of welcome, the head bent in shame or grief. Constantly we use that sort of symbolism; and God, who does not do violence to the nature he has created, teaches us to do likewise in our approach to him; for our worship is fully a self-dedication when by means of such symbolism every level, bodily and spiritual alike, of our nature is engaged and offered and sanctified....

But some of these symbols are of a special kind and a special power: they are the sacraments, and they are said to "effect what they signify," unless positively impeded... as all the lesser symbols are grouped about the sacraments, so the other sacraments are grouped about the greatest of all symbols, the Eucharist. This is the focal point of the whole Christian life because here all other offerings are gathered into the immensity of the self-offering in Christ, and all the upward strivings of sin-laden humanity are fulfilled in and answered by the acceptance of that self-offering and the outpouring of divine life upon the world which it calls forth. It has been truly said, giving the word "sign" its fullest meaning, that the Mass is the *Sign* of the Cross.

This is shown very clearly in a mime called *Stones into Bread*. A mime is itself a prolonged symbol: teaching the heart through bodily movements. *Stones into Bread* shows the story of humanity: the happiness of creative work in a sinless world; the coming of sin and evil through the agency of Satan, and so the loss of purpose and community; then the saving from sin, the calling back to life and love through Christ the Redeemer. And here the Mass is represented; but it is Christ who stands before the altar and takes the cup; and when the human offerings of bread and wine are to be changed into the divine Victim he walks slowly backward to the cross which stands behind, and extends his arms upon it as in crucifixion — for the Mass... is "the same sacrifice as that of the Cross" — and then, the self-offering made and accepted, he returns to the altar, and gives mankind in Communion the divine life which as Victim he had called down for them. The Mass is the Sign of the Cross.[5]

Adrienne von Speyr (1902-1967)

Wife, mother and medical doctor from a Protestant background, Adrienne von Speyr was received into the Catholic
Church at the age of 38 through the ministry of Father Hans
Urs von Balthasar, the great European theologian. In the
course of her life she authored more than 60 works of which
the following meditation on Jn 14:19, "Yet a short while and
the world will no longer see me; but you see me, for I live, and
you also will live," provides a sense of her deep faith in the Real
Presence of Christ in the Eucharist.

His life, which moves between life and death, leads down
beyond death into hell, and then returns to the world and leads up to
the Father: that is the life of the Lord that they [his disciples] see. But
beyond this personal path of his life that they can somehow see,
survey and follow, whose direction they can give and whose seg-
ments they can describe, there stands his life in the Father, which he
lives from primal beginnings and which the Son puts into the Eucharist for mankind. Believers see him because they themselves will live.
The Eucharist is his divine form of life on earth and at the same time
his form of life that has been made accessible to men, in which he lives
and in which we likewise live. For himself he sees a direct continuity
between his temporal life and the Eucharist, which in reality is
beyond time. He lives perpetually whether he is in the world in the
shape we acknowledge as the human life form, or whether he abides
in the Eucharist, of which we know in faith that it is his assumed and
yet eternal form of life.

But he also sees a continuity between his life and our life. Both
flow into each other and a real separation is no longer thinkable.
When he establishes this community between his and our life in the
Eucharist, he not only gives us a share in his divine life, but also in the
mysteries of his temporal life. Every aspect of his life — Cross,
Descent, Resurrection or Ascension — becomes definitive for our
life. Which mystery will apply to us lies wholly in his judgment. There
is no rule prescribing which of the Lord's mysteries will be the sign
of a Christian life. Thus, for example, little Therese remains fixed at
the very beginning of the Passion, while other destinies roll through
the whole suffering.

The Lord can communicate his life in totally different ways: to one he mediates it very suddenly, without transition, as if from heaven; to others gradually, through their seeking; to one on the occasion of a very particular experience; to another in a meditation or a Holy Communion. Perhaps such a person has communicated for years, but this time he receives the Lord in the mode of a sharing in his divine life. But he can also give his life in the Eucharist differently every day, so that each day's work is defined and colored by the particular character of the Communion that one has received. Or perhaps he gives a person only a participation in his first thirty years of life, in which nothing conspicuous, nothing extraordinary happens.

In the Eucharist, too, there is the space of time in which one sees the Lord, and the space of time in which one does not see him. For the person whose faith is not really alive, the time in which one does not see him is that during which he is hidden in the Tabernacle. He becomes visible in the host during Mass, at Holy Communion and in Exposition. In the Tabernacle he is not visible, and the visibility of the host is replaced by faith alone. But those who truly believe will see him even then. They should be so permeated by their faith that they see him only within their faith, whether or not the visible form of his presence is to be seen. For the visibility of the host in the Exposition and its invisibility in the Tabernacle, this alternation of the Eucharist's conditions, is a mystery within faith itself, showing that most of the Lord always remains hidden. The host is shown in Exposition, but it is shown in the sign of not-being-shown. What is shown is the hiddenness. The hidden and the shown host reciprocally contain each other: each of the two mysteries embraces the other and reveals it as well: the Hidden is the Shown, and the Shown is the Hidden.

Therefore, too, neither is to be ranked above the other or set up as the only admissible or desirable one in the Church. For precisely this alternation shows the impenetrability of the whole mystery: on neither of the two conditions can a system of the Eucharist be constructed. In one church there can be Exposition, in another not; both are correct, and each presupposes the other. This possible simultaneity of the two conditions is disturbing, for it shows how much the mystery of the hiddenness and openness of the Eucharist always transcends us. It will not satisfy our urge for total understanding.

But whether shown or not shown, both forms flow into the common mystery of his life and our life. This creates in our life a place for his life, which is hidden as well as apparent; he causes our life, too, to become both veiled and visible. Thus he also places our life in a rhythm of contemplation and action, and in the Eucharist he shows how both conditions, grasped at their roots, encourage and penetrate each other. For not only hiddenness is contemplation, and not only exposition is action. The Eucharist is at work also in the Tabernacle; there is also vision in Exposition. Contemplation and action are, so to speak, different isotopes of a single and transcending reality of the life of the Lord and our life in him, which can appear under different aspects. Thus, too, there is no division between action and contemplation, no equipoise to be established between them.

Exposition of the host may not be preferred to the host's hiddenness. It may not become a religious sensation. It is not an exhibition. Prayer before the exposed Most Holy Sacrament is not better or more effective than that before the hidden Lord. Certainly, when the host is shown, it is done so that people may look at it; it is not the sign for the faithful to look away or at the floor at that moment. "You will see me," says the Lord. Therefore, one should really look at him. To look away here would be just as wrong as if, out of humility, one were not to listen when he speaks to us.[6]

Theologians of Vatican II

Charles Journet (1891-1975)

> The scholarly life of Cardinal Journet was entirely devoted in pastoral charity to the service of the Church as university and seminary professor and as the Archbishop of Fribourg in Switzerland. The following text is the conclusion of a conference which he gave during the Second Vatican Council at St. Louis of France in Rome in 1965. This conference was intended as an introduction to the study of Pope Paul VI's Encyclical Letter, *Mysterium Fidei*.

"The Lord," says St. Francis of Assisi in his *Testament*, "gave me such faith in churches that I would pray simply in this way: *We adore you, Lord Jesus Christ, in all your churches throughout the whole world, and we bless you because you have redeemed the world by your most holy Cross.*"

Even more than being the house of the Christian people, a church is Christ's house. A mystery, a presence, fills the poorest Catholic church. It is dwelt in. Its life does not primarily stem from the fact that there is movement within it of the crowds that come and go. Before this, it is itself a source of life and purity for those who cross its threshold. It houses the Real Presence, the presence of Christ's Body: it is the "place" where Love supreme has touched our human nature in order to involve it in an eternal marriage; it is the radiant focal point empowered to illumine the whole drama of time and our human adventure.

On entering it, everyone can meet there in personal and silent intimacy Jesus of the Gospels. Everyone — no matter how ignorant, how burdened with sins, or how deeply anguished — may dare to approach him, just as the sinful woman once did in the house of Simon the Pharisee. Everyone can cry out to him like the blind beggar of Jericho: "Lord, that I may see!"

When a person earnestly asks you what he must do to find the Truth, tell him to go and sit in a church for a while each day with the Gospels in his hand at a time when there is no one about. Ask him to do this even perhaps before explaining to him the catechism and the Christian mysteries, before plunging him into the midst of the crowd of believers, among whom he might feel like a fish out of water and where he might get the impression that the Church is no different from any other communal gathering or group. Later he will be able to grasp that the Real Presence is the underlying reason for the Church's permanent quality in space and time until the Parousia.[1]

Karl Rahner, S.J. (1904-1984)

The name of this Jesuit theologian, who first taught at Innsbruck and later as professor at Munster, has sometimes become synonymous with "incomprehensibility" — because of his profundity of insight often expressed in a most complex style. Nevertheless, the addresses of this peritus of the Second Vatican Council to students and mixed audiences possess a directness and incisiveness which relate faith to contemporary problems. His essays on the pastoral importance of visits to the Blessed Sacrament leave no doubt as to his appreciation of this devotional practice in the Western Church.

The practice of "visits" [to the Blessed Sacrament] is in fact simply a legitimate, intensified continuation of [an] early Christian altar devotion... If anyone tries to reject "tabernacle devotion" by appealing to the fact that it did not exist in early Christian times, he must allow one to point out to him that, if he really does regard the devotional manners of the early Church as providing a standard for himself, then he must at least practice "altar devotion." But how is he going to be able to do this today, with the *sacramentum permanens* there resting on the altar, without finding his altar devotion turning into "tabernacle devotion," as it has in fact done, rightly, throughout the Church?...

The most private kind of tabernacle devotion is a realization of membership in the Church, of responsibility to her; an apostolate of prayer, we might say, in a very genuine and profound sense... In and with the wish to receive the sacrament later there is *now* a true eating of the heavenly bread... We can surely say that the most appropriate context for spiritual communion is when a person is kneeling before the altar of Christ, with the Bread of Life lying upon it... the visible surety of that to which he clings by faith....

It is not medieval, but biblical for a Christian to realize when considering the sacrament, that we are given the bodily Self of the Lord... that we are given the possibility of addressing ourselves in faith and love, in adoration and acceptance, to that Lord bodily present to us... It is actually plain heresy to say (in theory and hence in practice) that Jesus Christ in the Sacrament of the altar is not to be honored with an external cult of adoration... that exposition is to be rejected.[2]

What Christ gives us is quite *explicit* in his own words if interpreted according to their Aramaic meaning. The expression *"This is my body"* means *"This is MY-SELF"*; for this reason John 6:57 has replaced the words "body" and "blood" simply by the phrase "whoever eats ME." Indeed, He gives himself as nourishment as a whole. This is the reason adoration is utterly legitimate, because one finds oneself before not any kind of food, which one takes as a thing, but face to face with Him, himself. Also that manner of treating the Eucharist as a thing — such as is found in antiquity — cannot pretend to be an authentic and complete interpretation of the biblical data. The "Medieval" attitude of discovering in the Sacrament the living person of Jesus Christ is perfectly in accord with the Bible. Thus, this is the reason all endeavors to meet a person, or rather *this* Person are entirely legitimate.[3]

Hans Urs von Balthasar (1905-1988)

In 1929 this Swiss intellectual entered the Society of Jesus, whose Ignatian spirituality influenced the existential approach in his copious writings. He was the spiritual director and friend of the mystic Adrienne von Speyr. After her death in 1967 he stated that she had exercised a great influence on him, including his decision to leave the Jesuits in 1948. With some others he began the international periodical *Communio*. Until his death he was a member of the International Theological Commission set up by Pope John Paul II, who declared him a cardinal "*in pectore*" a few days after his death.

The Eucharistic Cult

The mystery of the Church is born when Jesus freely exercises the power he has to "lay down his life and take it up again" (Jn 10:8), when he exercises this power by giving to this surrender "for his friends" (Jn 15:13) the form of a meal, of eating and drinking his Flesh and Blood (Jn 6:55), an act whereby he fills his friends with his own substance — body and soul, divinity and humanity. Granted the mystery of Jesus' inseparably divine and human reality, this act of love that "loves to the end" (Jn 13:1) exhibits a compelling and transparent logic. It is the fulfillment of his own love not as a merely personal and extravagant outpouring of self; rather, the power he has to give his life for others is bestowed on him by the Father that he may achieve this giving of self as a mandate from the Father (Jn 10:17). In this surrender of himself the Son is the substantiated love of God given to the world, a love which in this handing over of self becomes "glorified" and "gives thanks" to itself (is Eucharist); the Father to the Son and, in visible and audible form (Jn 17), the Son to the Father.

For Christ the meal is the sealing of his corporeal death; flesh that is consumed, blood that is spilled. The supper and the Cross together constitute the "hour" for which he had come (Jn 12:27 ff.). The insertion of the content of the Cross into the form of the supper is at the same time a sign of the sovereign freedom of his self-surrender... and a sign of the permanent validity of this form for the

Church, since the form — the meal — is a social act intended to constitute the interior form itself of the Church.

In the eucharistic surrender of Jesus' humanity the point is reached where, through this flesh, the triune God has been put at man's disposal in this final readiness on God's part to be taken and incorporated into men. Applied to the Church this means that, in the end, every exercise of the ecclesial reality is a realization (in Newman's sense) of this event, which had occurred before the Church had come to be: the ecclesial cult is, in essence, a *memoriale passionis Domini.* This cult is a meditation in retrospect on the event which in the first place constitutes the Church, the outpouring of the bodily-spiritual reality of Jesus as Son of the Father, his release from the confinement of his earthly individuality into the social reality of the Church, which arises only from Jesus' outpouring of self. Hence, the memory of the event of Jesus' self-surrender is a remembering (*anamnesis,* 1 Cor 11:24 ff.) that recalls the birth of the Church. In other words, it is a memorial that consciously establishes contemporaneity with the act whereby the Church becomes herself.

Insofar as this birth occurred once and for all, it is a remembering of a past event and, thus, a true memorial meal commemorating a death. But since this man who died is no longer dead, but lives (Ac 25:19) and has promised to come again, it is a memorial meal that looks to the future, when he will return (1 Cor 11:26; Lk 22:18) to transform the memorial meal of the death definitively in the eternal banquet of joy (Mt 26:29; Lk 22:30). Finally, however, insofar as all Jesus' earthly activity has been taken up and made present in the risen Savior, what had occurred once and for all can and must become present here and now. The meal of the Church whereby the Church comes to be, is the very same as the meal of suffering whereby Jesus surrendered himself unto death; but it is also the same as the eschatological meal, only sacramentally veiled.

The presentation of the event of the Church's coming-to-be is the center that gives meaning and legitimacy to the memorial meal of hope, and this actualization, since it is accomplished in obedience to Christ's charge, is the encounter between a primary act of Christ himself (he comes to be, makes himself present) and a secondary act of the Church, which is taken up into this act of Christ's; in its remembering, celebrating, and obeying, the Church recalls and presents to itself the Lord Christ made present in her midst. The power of any human community as it celebrates the memory of a great dead person, already has about it a certain power to call them back to life. Many religions, and even large portions of the Old Testament itself, know of no other kind of immortality. And we should not underestimate the community-building power of such remembering: it is one of the human realities that carry a general power of conviction and which Jesus in a wonderful way fulfills and more than fulfills.

The Beloved who died for us becomes alive and present for us in the midst of our remembering *(in meam commemorationem)*. And this to the end not only that he may stand in our midst in order to let himself be seen and touched; not only that he may eat a fish and a honeycomb before our very eyes; but in order to partake with us a common meal (Rv 3:20) in which he is himself both the host and the food that is served. The accent that renders the Eucharist comprehensible falls on the Real Presence, in which the living Christ makes himself present to the Church by meals of his deed of power; but this deed of power by no means neglects the realization of the community which, as it realizes him by remembering him, also realizes itself. *Anamnesis* is always a breakthrough to objective truth by virtue of a subjective truthfulness whereby we overcome and transcend ourselves. In her confession of her fallenness and alienation *(Confiteor!)*, the Church breaks through and discovers her own true reality as she obeys Christ ("Do this...") and encounters Christ and herself in Christ, and in Christ the Father and the Holy Spirit.[4]

Yves Congar, O.P. (1904-)

This Dominican theologian has been one of the great architects whose work prepared the climate for reception of the "New Theology" espoused by the Second Vatican Council. From 1947-1956, however, his teaching was considered dangerous to Catholic Faith by the Holy Office and he was "exiled" to Jerusalem by pressure from Rome. He likes to refer to these difficult years of trial by recalling Rilke's words: "One must bear patiently with what is difficult until it becomes absolutely intolerable; only at this point does one change, and if it continues to be difficult at this stage, it means it is true."

Under John XXIII he was reinstated and became greatly acclaimed in the years that followed. Paul VI recognized his great influence on him personally. His work in ecumenical theology and regarding the role of the laity in the Church illustrates the depth and vision of his creative thinking, while reflecting his vast erudition and sense of the Church's tradition.

Eucharistic Christ — Lord of the Cosmos:

In the Eucharist there is no annihilation; there is a change or conversion of the bread into the body and of the wine into the blood.

I believe that the importance of this point of doctrine, its religious significance, is very significant... How can man, earthbound and sinful as he is, succeed in reaching the throne of God? And then the miracle occurs, God himself takes our place and fulfills the sacrifice. Even before this happened we could offer him only what we had already received from him, somewhat in the way children can only celebrate their parents' birthdays by offering flowers gathered from their father's garden, or a present bought with money from their mother's purse. But what we are now considering is something much greater than this. Through transubstantiation, our humble offering is transformed into that of Christ, whilst still remaining our own, or rather that of the Church; this is why after the consecration, the liturgy continues to speak of the elements on the altar as *our* gifts and also as the offered body and blood of Christ. Ultimately it is always a question of that *admirabile commercium*, that wonderful exchange and intercourse, hymned in the Christmas liturgy, and of that principle in which the Fathers sum up God's whole purpose: He became man in order that we might become God! Our offering, and ourselves in and through it, can travel all the distance to God, because it has been transformed into the supremely holy and effective offering of Jesus Christ, which, in this way, retains its autonomy and yet is extended to his mystical Body.[5]

François-Xavier Durrwell, C.SS.R. (1912-)

François-Xavier Durrwell was born in Alsace in 1912. On joining the Redemptorists he was sent to the Biblical Institute in Rome for special studies. His first book, *The Resurrection: a Biblical Study* (1950) was welcomed as throwing new light on the path of theology.

Gift and Work of the Spirit:

The Eucharist is eminently the sacrament of the Holy Spirit. For it is, more than any other, the sacrament of Christ's passover, from which flow rivers of living water. It is the bread of life (cf. Jn 6:48-51), the life which is that of the Spirit. It belongs to the realities of spirit and life (cf. Jn 6:65) which constitute the domain of the Spirit. St. Paul calls it "spiritual food" (1 Cor 10:3). It is in the power of the Spirit that the Eucharist is celebrated and in this same power it spreads in the Church. In this sacrament, as in everything, the Spirit is at the beginning and at the end; he is the soul of its celebration.

He is at the beginning. It is his prerogative to transform the bread and wine into real symbols of the paschal presence of Christ in the midst of the Church. For it is through him that Christ rises again; moreover the Eucharist is what we can see in this world of the resurrection of Jesus. The Spirit is creative. It is he who gives meaning to things; it falls to him to bring the bread and wine and the meal to their most intense fulfillment, by making them the bread of eternal life and the wine of the Kingdom. He is creator of all things by attracting them to Christ because "all things were created through him and for him" (cf. Col 1:16 ff.). He influences the bread and wine and incorporates them into Christ, making them subsist entirely in him. In the Eucharist, the Spirit manifests clearly that he is at the service of the Son's presence in the world and that he has the power to incorporate into Christ.

It is therefore the Spirit that the Church invokes so that the Eucharist may take place: "Let your Spirit come upon these gifts to make them holy, so that they may become for us the body and blood of our Lord, Jesus Christ" (Eucharistic Prayer II). Then "the Spirit comes down on the gifts, *making the mystery of the resurrection of our Lord from the dead a present reality...* This Spirit, who has raised him from the dead, now comes down to celebrate the mysteries of the resurrection of his body" (*Narsai [d. 502], Hom. 17, On the Expounding of the Mysteries. Cf. A. Hamman, Lettres chretiennes 7, p. 236*).

The Spirit transforms the bread and wine *by the very power which raises Christ to life,* for he always acts in the Church as the power of the resurrection of Jesus. The changing of the bread and wine into the sacrament of the presence of Christ is derived from the mystery of the resurrection, from the mystery of God who, in the Spirit, begets his son in the world.

The transforming action of the Spirit is thus connected with the mission which devolves on him to glorify Christ, to testify in his favor, by manifesting him to the Church (cf. Jn 16:14). The Eucharist is an excellent witness: it attests, by achieving, the resurrection of Jesus in the Church.

It is the risen Christ that the Spirit makes present in the Church — nothing is added to Christ's glorification, which is complete — the Spirit makes him present as in the resurrection itself, so that the faithful enter into communion with him in the passover of salvation....

Nor does Christ come *after* his death, but in the moment of death in which the Spirit glorifies him. Jesus was offered through an eternal Spirit (cf. Heb 9:14); his offering was "made eternal" in this Spirit. Jesus retains his glory at the summit of his ascent to the Father whither the Spirit led him, that is, in his death: submitting to the Spirit even to death, he gives complete acceptance to the Father. The Eucharist is the Easter sacrament, the sacrament of Christ risen to life in death. It is the extension to our space and time of the passover of salvation, so that the Church may take part in it.

To make him present, the Spirit does not destroy the bread, which earth has given and human hands have made, in such a way that we should have to say: "On the altar there is no longer any bread, there is only the misleading appearance of it." The Spirit does not put an end to the first creation; he brings it to its final fulfillment. Sin alone breaks with creation, whereas the Spirit transforms it by enriching it and by going beyond the act of creation. He changes the bread and wine by making the best bread and wine imaginable, the sacrament of the eschatological banquet.

191

But the Spirit does not work alone; he works in conjunction with Christ as well as for himself. It is Jesus who says over the bread: "This is my body." His words are said in the omnipotence of the Spirit through whom Christ is the Kyrios: what it decrees it causes to exist. It is thus that the Lord will transfigure our wretched bodies "into copies of his glorious body." He will do this "by the same power (that of the Spirit) with which he can subdue the whole universe" (Ph 3:21).

Latin theology has tended to attribute the eucharistic transformation to the words of Jesus alone, pronounced by the minister of the Church; Greek theology has been inclined to reserve this role of consecration to the Spirit. In the Old Testament God created by Breath *and* by Word; in the New, every salvific action is the concern both of the Spirit and of Christ in complete unity of action. From this we must conclude that the Eucharist is the common work of them both. Christ is the mediator of all sanctification, but through the power of the Spirit. The words: "This is my body, this is my blood," pronounced by the Church, form part of the apostolic proclamation; these are the very words of Christ (cf. Rm 10:14; 2 Cor 2:17; 13:3), but they are made effective by the power of the Spirit who conveys them. In sacramental realities — in the Church, in the Eucharist — the action of the Spirit assumes concrete forms: in the Eucharist it is exercised through the ministry of the Church, through which Christ's action is expressed.

If the Church begs the Spirit to come down on the gifts, so that he may transform them, it is not that the Eucharist is one of the graces that the Church obtains by asking for them and according to the degree of her confidence. This descent is of the essence of the institution. The transformation of the bread and wine is part of the memorial established by Jesus and celebrated according to his command. Similarly, the sanctifying power of baptism is inherent in the rite that the Church is commissioned to carry out. The Church therefore pronounces with assurance the words of Jesus: "This is my body...," but she accompanies them with a humble prayer to the Spirit, for she is totally the receiver, even in the accomplishment of her mission. Her attitude is one of welcoming, her ministry is exercised in humility and prayer. Jesus himself receives power from the Spirit, who is, however, at his service. The Church, therefore, presents the bread and wine to the Spirit that he may make the resurrection of Christ visible through the ministry of the priest who says: "This is my body."[6]

Francis Clark (19??-)

> While professor of dogmatic theology at the Gregorian University, Rome, Dr. Clark was invited to give a public lecture on an appraisal of the controversy in the 1960's concerning the Real Presence. This lecture, from which the text below is taken, was held, under the presidency of Cardinal Heenan of Westminster, before an audience of many Fathers of the Second Vatican Council and others.

The truth of the Real Presence is one aspect of the whole rich eucharistic mystery, and we must never lose sight of its integral connection with the other aspects — especially sacrifice and communion — and with the whole. The deep meaning of Our Lord's words at the Last Supper has been unfolded to us first through the inspired interpretation of St. Paul and St. John, and then progressively through the believing, praying and teaching Church down the ages. Namely, *this* which we take and eat, *this* which is the mysterious center of the Church's worship, *is* Jesus Christ himself, present in the very flesh in which he was born of the Virgin Mary, in which he died on the Cross, in which he is now victoriously glorified. The sacrifice of salvation is daily celebrated at our altars and the work of our redemption thereby made operative, because *what* is offered in the consecrated Host and chalice, he *who* offers himself there, is the High Priest and Victim Himself. We truly participate of the sacrificial banquet because we receive there the same Victim of the unique sacrifice. *Dominus est*: this *is* Christ, not anything less. Whatever speculative theology may say further about the Real Presence must start and finish at that central truth.

Both historically and theologically, the defense and guarantee of that primary revealed truth is the complementary doctrine, implicit in the life of the Church, which we call transubstantiation. That long process of doctrinal unfolding from the patristic age to Trent has to be traced and pondered theologically in order to appreciate the essential content of the eventually defined dogma.

The authentic witness of tradition is to a real conversion of the very constitutive being of the bread and wine into Christ's natural body and blood. Substance in this dogmatic tradition is not tied to the technicalities of Aristotelian philosophy, but means in general the concrete reality of created things — as, for instance, in the celebrated fifth-century homily *Magnitudo*, which had a considerable influence in the later crystalizing of the doctrine. In the basic realism of this change of the terrestrial substance into Christ's, the Church finds the perennial safeguard of her belief in the realism of Christ's corporal presence.

Faith seeks understanding of why this is the way to the Real Presence; and the most profound speculative answer, though obscured in post-Tridentine scholasticism and seldom fully grasped by present-day critics, is still that of St. Thomas Aquinas. His further theological explanation is not of faith, but the Church has approved it as helping to illumine what is of faith.[7]

Adorers in Spirit and Truth

James Alberione, S.S.P. (1884-1971)

Called an Apostle for our times on account of the extent and significance of his many works, Father James Alberione was born at San Lorenzo di Fossano in the Italian province of Cuneo on April 4, 1884. When he died in Rome on November 26, 1971, comforted by the visit of Pope Paul VI, he had founded six religious congregations and three secular institutes (one more came into being after his death but had been on the drawing boards even earlier), all of which make up the Pauline Family, one of the most modern means for the propagation of the faith in all the world through the mass media of social communications. The heart of his work and his spirituality was Christ, the Divine Master, Way, Truth and Life, but it was from the Eucharist that the Pauline Family was born and continues to nourish itself to this day.

First and foremost, our piety is eucharistic. From this vital source, the eucharistic Master, everything is given life. This is how the Pauline Family was born, from the tabernacle. And from here it is sustained in life, work and holiness. Our sanctity and apostolate spring from the Mass, Communion, and the Eucharistic Visit.

Imitate the great eucharistic silence. Live in silence; avoid useless and frivolous words. The less talkative you are with men, the more sensitive you will be to divine conversation. And the more your soul is shut off from external things, the more readily will it enter into intimate, friendly conversation with Jesus. To be interior souls, there must be silence.

How useful it is every so often to remain in contemplation before the tabernacle — without forcing ourselves to think of lofty things! To be able to tell Jesus simply: "You are my Master. You have given me an example. I want to do as You did."

The eucharistic Visit for the apostle is like an audience, or a school, where the disciple engages in conversation with the Divine Master. Many methods are proposed for obtaining the maximum fruit from this practice. But especially suitable is the one which honors Jesus Master, Way, Truth and Life. First of all, the Visit is not a complex of prayers. It is precisely a "visit," something you'd make to a dear person, your mother, for example. There is an exchange of greetings, an exchange of news, of gifts, promises, etc. The Visit has the scope of establishing our lives in Jesus Christ, that is, to live in Jesus, for Jesus, with Jesus.

The ways of making the eucharistic Visit are many. Because it is easy at times to put it off, the first way is determination to make it. The second way is the same. And the third, likewise: to make it. As St. Francis de Sales says: if you ask me how to walk, I must reply, first move one foot, then the other, and then the first again.

In making the Visit, consider yourselves as representatives of humanity before the tabernacle, gathering the hearts of all men and women and children everywhere in your own, presenting all their needs to God, asking Him to give them strength in weakness, and light in obscurity. Do this so that they may be kept far from sin, so that Jesus may conquer the resistance of sinners, so that those who are consecrated to God may be granted holiness and zeal. Jesus has given us this ministry: to represent humanity before the tabernacle. This is your vocation: a ministry of love![1]

Carlo Carretto (1910-1988)

This prophetic figure of Catholic Action arose from a Piedmontese peasant background, the third of six children. After years as Pope Pius XII's trusted leader of the Catholic Action Movement in Italy, he felt the call of Christ to the desert and set off to join the Little Brothers of the Gospel in the Sahara, where Charles de Foucauld had given his life to Jesus in the Eucharist. Carlo's witness to the joy of serving

Christ came into its own through his conferences, spiritual writings, and conversations with all and sundry (especially the youth) who came to the well-loved fraternity which he returned from Africa to found at Spello, near the city of his beloved Francis of Assisi, on whose feastday he died (October 4, 1988). The following description of his novitiate experience reveals the heart of Carretto's vitality, once he learned to read what pure Love communicates to those who faithfully adore the silent presence of Christ in the Holy Eucharist.

The great joy of the Saharan novitiate is the solitude, and the joy of solitude — silence, true silence, which penetrates everywhere and invades one's whole being, speaking to the soul with wonderful new strength unknown to men to whom this silence means nothing.

Here, living in perpetual silence, one learns to distinguish its different shades: silence of the church, silence in one's cell, silence of work, interior silence, silence of the soul, God's silence.

To learn to live these silences, the novice-master lets us go away for a few days' "desert."

A hamper of bread, a few dates, some water, the Bible. A day's march: a cave.

A priest celebrates Mass: then goes away, leaving in the cave on an altar of stones, the Eucharist. Thus, for a week one remains alone with the Eucharist exposed day and night. Silence in the desert, silence in the cave, silence in the Eucharist. No prayer is so difficult as the adoration of the Eucharist. One's whole natural strength rebels against it.

One would prefer to carry stones in the sun. The senses, memory, imagination, all are repressed. Faith alone triumphs, and faith is hard, dark, stark.

To place oneself before what seems to be bread and to say, "Christ is there living and true," is pure faith.

But nothing is more nourishing than pure faith, and prayer in faith is real prayer.

"There's no pleasure in adoring the Eucharist," one novice used to say to me. But it is precisely this renunciation of all desire to satisfy the senses that makes prayer strong and real. One meets God beyond the senses, beyond the imagination, beyond nature.

This is crucial: as long as we pray only when and how we want to, our life of prayer is bound to be unreal. It will run in fits and starts. The slightest upset — even a toothache — will be enough to destroy the whole edifice of our prayer life.

"You must strip your prayers," the novice master told me. You must simplify, deintellectualize. Put yourself in front of Jesus as a poor man: not with any big ideas, but with living faith. Remain motionless in an act of love before the Father. Don't try to reach God with your understanding; that is impossible. Reach him in love; that is possible.

The struggle is not easy, because nature will try to get back her own, get her dose of enjoyment; but union with Christ Crucified is something quite different.

After some hours — or some days — of this exercise, the body relaxes. As the will refuses to let it have its own way it gives up the struggle. It becomes passive. The senses go to sleep. Or rather, as St. John of the Cross says, the night of senses is beginning. Then prayer becomes something serious, even if it is painful and dry. So serious that one can no longer do without it. The soul begins to share the redemptive work of Jesus.

Kneeling down on the sand before the simple monstrance which contained Jesus, I used to think of the evils of the world: hate, violence, depravity, impurity, egoism, betrayal, idolatry. Around me the cave had become as large as the world, and inwardly I contemplated Jesus oppressed under the weight of so much wickedness.

Is not the Host in its own form like bread crushed, pounded, baked? And does it not contain the Man of Sorrows, Christ the Victim, the Lamb slain for our sins?[2]

René Voillaume (1905-)

Although Charles de Foucauld wrote rules for "Little Brothers" and "Little Sisters," these religious communities did not come into existence until Father René Voillaume and four other French priests began to live at El Abiodh Sidi Cheikh, on the fringes of the Sahara. They adopted a life of adoration and prayer inspired by de Foucauld's original rule. Scattered by the Second World War, the communities or "fraternities" regrouped after 1945 and live a simple lifestyle, supporting themselves in the midst of working class situations. But, at the heart of their lives they are sustained by adoration of the presence of Jesus in the Holy Eucharist. Father Voillaume, the first Superior of this Congregation of "Little Brothers," has written much on the need for prayerful response to Christ's presence as the unique "Bread of Life," which is uniquely capable of satisfying the hungers of the human family.

The Eucharist is a baffling mystery for human reason. When we consider that uninterruptedly, throughout the entire Christian Church, for the last two thousand years, bread and wine have been consecrated and offered as the Savior commanded in memory of him, we are not faced with an abstraction, but with a prodigiously concrete reality: the reality of bread and wine. What Christ intended, by founding, by creating, the Eucharist, he and he alone can tell us....

There are indeed a number of different aspects to be grasped. Besides the relationship with the Passion and death of Jesus, introducing the idea of the sacrifice of the New Covenant, there is also the idea of food, wonderfully expressed by Jesus himself in his discourse on the bread of life (Cf. Jn 6:26-59). Then again there is that aspect of the Eucharist as being given to the Church, as principle and expression of the Church's unity.

All these aspects were affirmed by Christ himself, as also by Saint Paul. But these various functions of the Eucharist, as sacrifice, as food and as sacrament of unity, together presuppose that Christ is truly though mysteriously present with his body and with his blood in the consecrated bread and wine. It seems best therefore to begin with this notion of the presence of Christ in the Eucharist, which has given rise in time past as also today, to so many controversies, debates and efforts to explain what this really means.

You remember Christ's words over the bread: "This is my body." They are simple words, words that could not be simpler. There is a subject, a verb of affirmation and a complement.

If we now turn to the discourse on the bread of life recorded by Saint John, we cannot help being struck by the force and realism used by Jesus there too. It is one of his most remarkable discourses.

In it, Christ offers himself to mankind as food, as bread come down from heaven, as the bread given by God himself. At the outset, we understand Christ to be the bread of life because he is the Word of God: he feeds us with his truth and with his teaching. But by an imperceptible transition, Jesus then passes on to the Eucharist. And here his discourse acquires a nearly shocking realism: "He who eats my flesh and drinks my blood has eternal life." And he repeats the same statement several times, as though afraid of not being understood — so often indeed that the listening Jews were horrified. To understand their sense of outrage and how at the same time their sense of outrage underlines the objective, realistic character of the Lord's words, we have to put ourselves in those Jews' place as they listened to him talking of eating the flesh of the Son of Man, and above all of drinking his blood.

For, be it not forgotten, according to Jewish law, blood was regarded as the symbol of life and was categorically forbidden as food. Even now, Jews never eat meat that has not previously been drained of blood. The very idea of drinking blood was abhorrent. It was out of the question to drink the life-principle.

For people who had been brought up from childhood to think of drinking blood as something absolutely forbidden and abominable, their reaction on hearing Jesus' words was physical nausea. They were appalled, and we can see why. "This is intolerable language! How could anyone accept it?" (Jn 6:60). They left Jesus and went away. But, we observe, Jesus did not retract one word of what he had been saying; the Jews had understood him perfectly. All he said to the Apostles was: "What about you, do you want to go away too?" And then it was that Simon Peter made his famous reply: "Lord, who shall we go to? You have the message of eternal life" (Jn 6:67).

If we compare this discourse on the eucharistic bread with the account of the institution of the Lord's Supper, we realize that Jesus' words: "This is my Body" have to be understood in their ordinary, concrete sense: they mean the body of Christ, the blood of Christ.

Furthermore, this is the sense in which Christians interpreted the words in the earliest times (cf. 1 Cor 10 & 11)... According to Christian faith, Christ's body is really — I do not say physically — present in the bread, and his blood really present in the wine. We have, at once, to believe in this presence and also to believe that this presence is not like other presences. There is no word to express it, since there is no other example of this mode of presence in nature. The mode may be called spiritual, but it is none the less real as, if not more real than, the presence of a being of flesh and blood. And Christ himself suggests as much, without modifying any of the brutal realism of his discourse, by concluding with these words: "The spirit is what gives life, the flesh has nothing to offer" (Jn 6:63). And this is the Christian faith, simple and strong.[3]

You will always be right in imitating the attitude of soul —which is so simple, so logical, so full of love — of Frère Charles of Jesus towards the Blessed Sacrament. Our devotion to the Eucharist must be profound, honest, totally embraced as essential. When one has acquired the disposition of receiving this gift of God with the soul of a child, one is upset by the reasoning of certain people, especially priests and religious, who dispute the devotion towards the Eucharist and sometimes question its legitimacy on liturgical or historical grounds... Why not, in the simple logic of faith, love the Eucharist with all the love with which we love Jesus himself? This is what filled Father de Foucauld with the spontaneity of a child.[4]

Bishop Fulton J. Sheen (1895-1979)

> Bishop Sheen's teaching, preaching and writing informed, enlightened and inspired millions of people during his full and active life. His success sprang from a combination of deep intellectual knowledge and a profound spirituality formed before the Blessed Sacrament where he spent at least an hour each day in prayer. Steeped in the teaching and traditions of the Church, he was gifted with an ability to reach people of all religious backgrounds. He was a pioneer and a master in the use of the mass media, especially television, to convey the truths of the Gospel. People responded to the certainty of his convictions and the authenticity of his concern and love for them. At his death in 1979, there was a tremendous outpouring of love and respect from all over the world for this man who never ceased to credit whatever success he may have had to his daily visit with the Lord.

The Hour of His exaltation having come, for within less than twenty-four hours He would surrender Himself, He gathered His twelve Apostles about Him. In one sublime act He interpreted the meaning of His death. He declared that He was marking the beginning of the New Testament or Covenant ratified by His sacrificial death. The whole Mosaic and pre-Messianic system of sacrifice was thus superseded and fulfilled. No created fire came down to devour the life that was offered to the Father, as it did in the Old Testament, for the fire would be the glory of His Resurrection and the flames of Pentecost.

Since His death was the reason of His coming, He now instituted for His Apostles and posterity a Memorial Action of His Redemption, which He promised when He said that He was the Bread of Life.

> He took bread and blessed and broke it,
> And gave it to them, saying,
> This is My Body, given for you. (*Lk 22:19*)

He did not say, "This represents or symbolizes My Body," but He said, "This *is* My Body" — a Body that would be broken in His Passion.

> Then taking wine into His Hands, He said:
> Drink, all of you, of this;
> For this is My Blood of the New Testament,
> Shed for many, to the remission of sins. (*Mt 26:28*)

His coming death on the following afternoon was set before them in a symbolic or unbloody manner. On the Cross, He would die by the separation of His Blood from His Body. Hence He did not consecrate the bread and wine together, but separately, to show forth the manner of His death by the separation of Body and Blood. In this act, Our Lord was what He would be on the Cross the next day: both Priest and Victim. In the Old Testament and among pagans, the victim, such as a goat or a sheep, was apart from the priest who offered it. In this eucharistic action and on the Cross, He, the Priest, offered Himself; therefore He was also the Victim. Thus would be fulfilled the words of the prophet Malachi:

No corner of the world, from sun's rise to sun's setting,
Where the renown of Me is not heard among the Gentiles,
Where sacrifice is not done, and pure offering
Made in My honor; so revered is My name,
Says the Lord of hosts, there among the Gentiles

(Ml 1:11)

Next came the Divine command to prolong the Memorial of His death:

Do this for a commemoration of Me. *(Lk 22:19)*

Repeat! Renew! Prolong through the centuries the sacrifice offered for the sins of the world!

Why did Our Blessed Lord use bread and wine as the elements of this Memorial? First of all, because no two substances in nature better symbolize unity than bread and wine. As bread is made from a multiplicity of grains of wheat, and wine is made from a multiplicity of grapes, so the many who believe are one in Christ. Second, no two substances in nature have to suffer more to become what they are than bread and wine. Wheat has to pass through the rigors of winter, be ground beneath the Calvary of a mill, and then subjected to purging fire before it can become bread. Grapes in their turn must be subjected to the Gethsemane of a wine press and have their life crushed from them to become wine. Thus do they symbolize the Passion and Sufferings of Christ, and the condition of Salvation, for Our Lord said unless we die to ourselves we cannot live in Him. A third reason is that there are no two substances in nature which have more traditionally nourished man than bread and wine. In bringing these elements to the altar, men are equivalently bringing themselves. When bread and wine are taken or consumed, they are changed into man's body and blood. But when He took bread and wine, He changed them into Himself.[5]

Mother Teresa of Calcutta (1910-)

This living "saint" of our times needs no introduction! Malcolm Muggeridge's interview with her for BBC television, which has occasionally been repeated, has brought her story into our homes; and it has become a lovely book, *Something Beautiful for God* on our coffee tables! This woman, who was born in Albania and went out to India, has won the hearts of everyone. For her inspired sensitivity to Christ's presence "in the distressing disguises of the poor" impelled her to leave the cosy comfort of her convent in Bangalore to take to the streets, where she and those who joined her in new religious congregations (for men and women) reach out and lift up literally millions from the indignity of human misery. Her energy and loving compassion, she confesses, derive from the tenderness of love shown in the Blessed Eucharist.

Jesus says time and again that we have to love one another. He had to come for that one purpose: to tell us that God loves us, that we are precious to him, that we have been created to love and to be loved, and that we must love one another as he loves us, as the Father has loved him... When we look at the cross we know how he loved us. And when we look at the Tabernacle we know how he loves us still. That is why he made himself the Bread of Life: we just forget this tenderness of love. And he made himself this Bread of Life to satisfy our hunger for his love. And as if that were not enough for him, he made himself the hungry one, the naked one, the humblest one so that you and I can satisfy his hunger for our human love. This is something so wonderful — the sick, the poor, the unwanted, the unloved, the lepers, the drug addicts, the alcoholics, the prostitutes — Christ in the distressing disguises. And they are — I always feel — the privileged: to be in his presence twenty-four hours!...

Sacrifice is necessary in our lives if we want to realize the tenderness of God's love. Sacrifice is his love in action. God sent Jesus to teach us this love. And you will find out in your own life. Have you ever experienced the joy of loving? Have you ever shared something with the sick, with the lonely, together making something beautiful for God. This is something that has to come from within us. That is why Jesus made himself the Bread of Life — to create that in our life.

If it is not there it is good to examine our heart: is our heart clean? Jesus said: "Blessed are the clean of heart, for they shall see God." Now unless we see God in each other we cannot love each other. And so it is important for us to have a clean heart. With a clean heart we will be able to be only all for Jesus and to give Jesus to others. That is why Jesus made himself the Bread of Life. That is why he is there twenty-four hours. That is why he is longing for you and for me to share the joy of loving. And he says: "As I have loved you." If I can give you any advice, I beg you to get closer to the Eucharist and to Jesus... We must pray to Jesus to give us that tenderness of the Eucharist. Parish priest, ask your people to have adoration in your churches wherever you can. Make it even once a week, so that the tenderness of love may grow in your heart to share it with others... The cross is the proof that he loved us and the Tabernacle is the proof that he loves us now with tender compassion.[6]

Sister Briege McKenna (19??-)

> Born in County Armagh, Ireland, Sister Briege McKenna is a member of the religious Congregation of St. Clare. Her ministry of healing and evangelism have taken her to all parts of the world, including Latin America and the Far East. Her special contribution to the Movement of Christian Renewal has been to reawaken an appreciation of traditional Catholic devotion to the Blessed Virgin Mary and the Blessed Sacrament.

Jesus said, "Blessed are those who do not see and yet believe." This is a great challenge to us as Catholics. We can't explain the Eucharist because it is a miracle and a mystery. What counts is not understanding in the head, but believing in the heart. Feelings do not make Christ present in the Eucharist. It's the power of the Holy Spirit working through the ordained priest that makes him present to us in the Eucharist. I may feel nothing, but Jesus is still there.

On the other hand, I could go to a prayer service and take a piece of bread and try everything to make Jesus present, but that will not make him present. It requires the power of ordination.

Sometimes I ask myself if I really believe that Jesus is present in the Eucharist. Do I believe that this is the gift that Jesus spoke about in John 6? Remember that many of Jesus' disciples and followers couldn't believe him when he said that to be saved they must eat his body and drink his blood.

It was easy to accept Jesus when he was performing miracles and when he was doing all kinds of signs and wonders, but it's hard to believe when you can't understand and when you can't see things with your own eyes. But that is the challenge for the Christian. We are called to believe that Jesus is there in the Eucharist and that he loves us.

The very same challenge that is given to us was given to the first disciples. It was even harder for them. They did not have our advantage: knowledge that Jesus rose from the dead, the witness of the apostles after Pentecost, two thousand years of tradition... He's the same Jesus yesterday, today, and forever. He is the Jesus who healed in the Gospel. So he must be fulfilling his promises of answering his people's needs.

We can't blame the priest for our lack of faith when we say the priest is boring or not charismatic or too ioud or too timid, but the priest is not really the issue. The real issue is our own faith. It's true that if the priest has great faith, it is a great step toward meaningful worship. That's why, in my ministry to priests, I always challenge the priests to greater faith... The Church obliges us to attend Mass, not because Jesus needs us, but, like all good mothers, the Church knows we need the Bread of Life... to be strengthened for our journey.[7]

Epilogue

Towards the Love Banquet[1]

In the ante-chamber of the great love-feast
there are many,
many moving about,
moving restlessly uncertain
awkwardly hesitant — asking
directions about where's
the opening — when's
the beginning — how
it'll be inside:
we see through a glass darkly.

In the ante-chamber, dimly, but not badly, lit
in the half-light
through tinted glasses
in a blur of cigarette smoke
sight is strained for myriad
weary eyes, bleary eyes,
eyes frightened in the dark —
yet hopeful eyes that wait
longingly for the light:
eye has not seen.

In the ante-chamber distant honey-music
can barely be caught
if you listen hard above
the din of gossip and hoarse
laughter, ignoring the plaguy

coarse medley of roaring
dance-band and plangent voice
lone-sighing for the Word-
filled silence of deepest soul:
nor has ear heard.

In the ante-chamber all is still, now —
movement arrested,
voices quietened,
music seeming more gentle —
as eyes turn to look at
a stranger — just another
waiter — yet One who's vaguely familiar
in his kindly tone, his calming gaze,
his gesture of pouring out the wine:
which God has prepared for those who love.

Notes

Foreword

[1] *Letters from a Traveller*, Collins, Fontana 1967, p. 60 ff.
[2] Cf. *Evangelii Nuntiandi*, n. 22.

Introduction

[1] *Religio Medici*, 1, 16.
[2] Cf. Is 9:2; 42:6; Lk 1:79; 2:32; Jn 1:4 ff.; 8:12; 9:5; Rv 21:23 ff.; etc.
[3] Taymans d'Eypernon, S.J. (*The Blessed Trinity and the Sacraments*, Newman Press, Westminster, MD, 1961, p. 131) cites S.T. III, q. 75, a. 1, contra. Cf. *Eccles. Hist.* III.
[4] Cf. Joseph Ratzinger, *Introduction to Christianity*, Burns & Oates, London, 1969, p. 257 ff.
[5] The Constitution on the Sacred Liturgy (*Sacrosanctum Concilium* [S.C.], n. 6 [end]) cites Trent, Session 13: Decree on the Holy Eucharist, ch. 5 (DS 1644). N.B. Trent's use of the word *"repraesentatur."*
[6] Ph 4:6; cf. Col 3:15-17.
[7] *Letters to Malcolm: Chiefly on Prayer*, Geoffrey Bles, 1964 (Harcourt, Brace & World, 1964; Fount Paperbacks, 1977), ch. 19.
[8] *The Diary of a Country Priest*, Collins, pp. 12-20.
[9] In a discussion with Romain Rolland on the "oceanic feeling" of at-onement with the universe in certain moments of enthrallment with its grandeur and beauty, etc., Sigmund Freud compared this experience with that of being "in love," although he reduces it to a sense of the physical forces involved in sexual attraction:
"At the height of being in love the boundary between ego and object threatens to melt away. Against all the evidence of his senses, a man who is in love declares that "I" and "you" are one and is prepared to behave as if it were a fact" (*Civilization and Its Discontents* [ed. James Strachey, vol. xxi, London, 1961, p. 65] cited by Anthony Storr, *Solitude* [Fontana Paperbacks, Flamingo, 1989, p. 187]).
[10] Cf. St. Ambrose, *Apol. Prophetae David*, 12, 58: "You have shown yourself to me, Christ, face to face. I find you in your sacraments"; cf. also, St. Leo, Serm 74 (Second Sermon on the Ascension - PL 54, 398): "What our Lord did visibly has passed into the sacraments."
[11] Cf. St. Augustine, *De Civitate Dei*, XIV, 15, 2; cf. Gn 3; Rm 5:12 ff.
[12] *Confessions*, VII, 10 (tr. by R.S. Pine-Coffin in Penguin Classics, 1970, p. 147).
[13] Cf. Dogmatic Constitution on the Church, *Lumen Gentium* [L.G.], n.3.
[14] St. Thomas Aquinas, *Summa Theologiae*, IIa IIae, q. 180, art. 1 in corpore.

[15] Cf. *Eucharisticum mysterium*, n. 3.

[16] Cf. S.C., 7.

[17] Encyclical Letter (3 September 1965), *Mysterium Fidei*, 38-39 (citing St. Thomas Aquinas, *Sum. Theol.*, IIIa, 1. 73, art. 3c); transl. in CTS Publ., London, 1965, p. 18 ff.

[18] Cf. S.C., 10; Dogmatic Constitution on the Church, *Lumen Gentium*, 11; Decree on the Ministry and Life of Priests, *Presbyterorum Ordinis*, 5 & 6; Decree on the Bishops' Pastoral Office in the Church, *Christus Dominus*, 30; Decree on the Missionary Activity of the Church, *Ad Gentes*, 9; also Pope John Paul II, Letter on the Mystery and Worship of the Holy Eucharist (24 February 1980), 4.

[19] Loc. cit.

[20] *The Rich Man's Salvation*, 29; Loeb Classics 92, p. 331.

[21] *Didache*, ix, 1-2; cited in Loeb, ibid.

[22] Cf. St. Augustine, *Confessions*, X, 27, 38; any believer would be spiritually tone deaf not to catch the eucharistic overtones in the cluster of images in this hymn to Beauty especially in the concluding couplet:

> *Gustavi et esurio et sitio;*
> *tetigisti me, et exarsi in pacem tuam.*
> I tasted and I hunger and thirst;
> you touched me, and I have been set on fire
> for your peace.

[23] Encyclical Letter on the 20th anniversary of *Populorum Progressio* (Paul VI, 30 December 1987), *Sollicitudo Rei Socialis*, 48; transl. in *Briefing 88*, Vol. 18, No. 5, p. 113 ff.

[24] *Insegnamenti*, Vol. VI (1968), p. 372; cited by F. Pratzner in *I Congressi Eucaristici Internazionali: Breve Storia*, p. 15 (Ms).

[25] Address at the 43rd International Eucharistic Congress, Nairobi, August 1985.

[26] 1 Cor 11:23-26 (R.S.V. translation). This text complements those in the Synoptics in recording the Institution Narrative. Cf. Mt 26:26-28; Mk 14:22-24; Lk 22:19-20. These texts suggest two sources of preaching and celebration: Mt and Mk associated with Jerusalem on the one hand; Lk and 1 Cor with Antioch on the other. They existed in the living tradition of Christian worship prior to becoming woven into the respective Gospels or letter of Paul.

[27] Ac 2:42, 46-47 (vv. 43-45 are generally recognized by scholars to be a later addition) is a most ancient descriptive summary of the pattern of the primitive Church's essential religious practices. The phrase "breaking of bread" had a definite eucharistic connotation, irrespective of whether or not every example of its use referred to the celebration of the Eucharist, e.g. Lk 24:35 at the end of the encounter at Emmaus.

[28] After the destruction of the Temple (70 A.D.), when the gradual separation from Judaism moved on apace.

[29] Cf. 1 Cor 10:14-17; Rm 12:5; Ep 1:22-23; Col 1:18-22.

[30] Cf. John Paul II, Encyclical Letter *Redemptor Hominis* (4 March 1979), 20; also Letter (24 February 1980), 4. The lapidary adage: "*The Church makes the Eucharist and the Eucharist makes the Church*," is traceable to Henri De Lubac, SJ, *The Splendour of the Church*, Sheed & Ward, London, 1956, pp. 92, 106.

[31] Jn 6:57. Cf. *Geist und Leben* 32 (1959), p. 263.

[32] Readers are referred to the works of Piolenti & Solano, which regrettably do not exist in English translation.

33 One tradition of the legend is mentioned in *Tess of the d'Urbervilles*; another, more detailed, is preserved in his poem *The Lost Pyx*.

34 The original title of this poem, written in 1801, was "The Wine-god" and is perhaps more suited to it. The suggestion of "Night and Wine" for its title seems quite appropriate for this poem whose unity is more emotional than logical. Cf. *Friedrich Hölderlin: Selected Poems*, tr. J.B. Leishman, The Hogarth Press, London, 1944, pp. 98-101.

35 *Poems*, ed. Walter Hooper, Geoffrey Bles, 1964 (Harcourt, Brace & World, 1965).

36 Encyclical Letter *Populorum Progressio*, 26 March 1967; (AAS 59).

37 "Modern man listens more willingly to witnesses than to teachers, and if he does listen to teachers, it is because they are witnesses" (Pope Paul VI, *Evangelii Nuntiandi*, n. 41 [CTS S312, p. 52]).

38 Cf. Cardinal Joseph Ratzinger re the failure of modern catechetics and the need of a lived faith:
"It is interesting to recall that the early Church did not develop any highly specialized missionary activity. In fact it did not have any particular strategies for announcing the faith to the pagans, and yet it became a time of great missionary success. The conversion of the pagan world to Christianity was not the result of a carefully planned activity but rather the fruit of the faith that was made visible through the life of the early Christians and the community of the Church. It was this real invitation to live this experience which was the only missionary force of the early Church. This community of life of the early Church was an invitation to others to share in it and discover its source. Instead the apostasy of the modern era derives from the lack of witness of a lived faith among Christians. Today there is an urgent need for a new evangelization but we will not achieve it with carefully thought-out theories. The catastrophic failure of modern catechesis is all too evident. It is only if faith is lived that it can attract others and offer them what their hearts are looking for. The living out of Christian faith is the door through which the Holy Spirit enters the world" (*Auf Christus Schauen*).

39 Cf. Prosper of Acquitaine, *Indiculus*, pp. 6-9: "legem credendi lex statuit supplicandi"; cf. also First Notebook of St. Vincent of Lerins, ch. 23; H. Schmidt, "Lex orandi, lex credendi in recentioribus documentis pontificiis" in *Periodica* 40 (1951) 5-28.

40 *Lettres aux Fraternités*, Paris, p. 581.

The Heart of the Church's Proclamation of the Mystery of Faith

1 Cf. Constitution on the Sacred Liturgy (*Sacrosanctum Concilium*), n. 56.

2 Cf. Dogmatic Constitution on the Church (*Lumen Gentium*), n. 11.

3 Cf. Raymond Maloney, *The Eucharistic Prayers*, Dominican Publ., Dublin, 1985, cf. p. 156 ff. Words in italics are in Eucharistic Prayer II.

4 The anaphora seems held in parenthesis between this richly evocative expression, repeated at the end.

5 Note that there is no *Sanctus* breaking the flow of the anaphora.

6 The Institution Narrative in all recently revised texts of the Eucharistic Prayers of the Western Catholic liturgies (apart from minor variations) is the same. It is structured on the accounts in the New Testament.

7 Original meaning of "logikos." Cf. E. Mazza, *The Eucharistic Prayers of the Roman Rite*, op. cit., p. 72.

"The Rock Was Christ"

1 Cf. Michael O'Carroll, C.S.Sp., *Corpus Christi*, op. cit., p. 1; also Herbert A. Musurillo, *The Fathers of the Primitive Church*, Mentor-Omega, The New American Library, Inc., New York, 1966, p 260 ff.
2 The symbol of the Fish is well represented in the primitive Christian art of the catacombs. It is referred to in Christian literature at the end of the second century. Cf. Tertullian, *De Baptismo*, 1; Clement of Alexandria, *Paedagogus*, III, 12, 101 (end). It is generally thought to be an acrostic signifying "Jesus Christ Son of God Savior," made from the Greek letters for "Fish." It became properly a eucharistic symbol in the fourth/fifth centuries (cf. St. Augustine, *De Civitate Dei*, XVIII, 23).
3 Cf. O'Carroll, ibid., p. 157; Musurillo, ibid., p. 262.

Early Witnesses

1 One of the earliest names for the eucharistic celebration. Ignatius also speaks of the "Agape," which was a meal shared by Christians in apostolic times (cf. *Letter to the Smyrnians, viii*). The Eucharist, which was later separated from it, was originally celebrated within the context of this feast as indicated by St. Paul's First Letter to the Corinthians and the Acts of the Apostles.
2 *Letter to the Ephesians, iv-v*. Tr. in *The Divine Office*, Collins, 1974, vol. I, p. 410; pp. 168 & 624.
3 Literally, "my *eros* is crucified," which led to Origen's celebrated mistranslation in mystically commenting on the Canticle of Canticles (cf. *Prol. in Can.*, 3 [end]).
4 *Letter to the Romans, vi-vii*. Tr. in D.O., vol. III, op. cit., p. 168.
5 This is the first know usage of the word as a substantive for the sacrament. Ignatius pleads for unity among those who celebrate the unique sacrament of the Lord's Body and warns against those who deny its visible reality, such as the Docetists, who cut themselves off from the "catholic" [from the Greek meaning "whole"] Church (cf. *Smyrnians, vi-viii*).
6 *Letter to the Philadelphians, iii-iv*. Tr. in D.O., vol. III, op. cit., p. 624.
7 *Didache*, N. 9, 1 - 10, 6; 14, 1-3; Funk 2, 19-22, 26. Tr. in D.O., op. cit., vol. III, p. 283 ff.
8 *Apol.* I, lxvi-lxvii. Tr. in D.O., op. cit., Vol. II, p. 530 ff.
9 Homily on the Passover, cc. 2-7, 100-105; Tr. *The Paschal Mystery* (Edited by A. Hamman), Alba Patristic Library, Vol. 3, Alba House, Staten Island, NY, 1969, pp 26 ff.
10 "Epiclesis" is the technical term for the prayer of invoking the Holy Spirit at the consecration.
11 *Adversus Haereses*, IV, xviii, 4-6; Tr. in D.O., op. cit., Vol. I, p. 434.
12 The common faith of Christians has constantly seen the direct link between the Eucharist and sharing in the life of the Risen Lord, as members of his body (cf. supra, St. Ignatius: "medicine of immortality" and also 1 Cor 10, 11, 15; Jn 6:51). Later, St. Thomas Aquinas would thus call the Blessed Eucharist: "the pledge of future glory" (*pignus futurae gloriae*). The words of St. Alphonsus Liguori's hymn have strengthened many: "For how can he deny me heaven / Who here on earth himself hath given."
13 Ibid., V, 2, 2-3; Tr. in D.O., op. cit., Vol. II, p. 543.

Notes

Alexandrian Catechists

[1] *Paedagogus*, I, vi, 37-38, 42, 43; cited in F.C., *Clement of Alexandria: Christ the Educator*, CUA, Washington, DC, 1954, p. 36 ff.

[2] *Paedagogus*, II, ii, 19-20; Ibid., p. 110 ff.

[3] *Hom. in Exod.*, xiii, 3; translation of these texts in Henry Bettenson, (Ed.), *The Early Christian Fathers*, Oxford University Press, 1969, p. 249 ff.

[4] *Comm. in Matthaeum*, xi, 14; ibid.

[5] *Comm. in Ioannem*, 32, 24, 16; ibid.

Church of Martyrs

[1] *De Pudicitia*, 9. These and the following texts of Tertullian translated from *Corpus Christianorum*, Vol. I, with recourse to Bettenson, op. cit., p. 147 ff.

[2] *De Resurrectione Carnis*, 8; ibid.

[3] *De Corona*, 3; ibid.

[4] *Ad Uxorem*, ii, 5; ibid.

[5] Tertullian's quotation from Jn 6:33 is not in accord either with the Vulgate (which did not exist in his day) or the Vetus Afra (African Latin version); he has "sermo," which is not in either of these versions.

[6] See the original Latin: "*perpetuitatem postulamus in Christo, et individuitates a corpore ejus*"; "individuitatem" is better rendered by "indivisibility" rather than literally as "individuality." The original meaning of "individuality" is clearly seen thus as pertaining to integrity and wholeness of a person in himself and in relation to the community. Here, this sense is further enhanced by being a member of Christ's body, by means of which a person becomes his true self in relation to the reality of God and his family. This phrase is also pregnant with the allusion of inseparability from the eternal life of God contained and signified in participating in the sacrament of Christ.

[7] *De Oratione*, 6, 2; ibid.

[8] *Adv. Marc.*, IV. 40; ibid.

[9] *Epistle 63*; Translated from *Corpus Scriptorum Christianorum Latinorum*, Vol. 3, op. cit., 2, 701-717.

[10] *De Orat. Dom.*, 18, 22; cf. ibid., 280-281, 283-284.

A Golden Age of Catechesis

[1] *Sermon* 3, 2, 4-5; ed. Lamy 3, 216-222; translated in D.O. op. cit., Vol. III, p. 45* ff.

[2] *Mystagogical Catecheses*, 4, I, 3-6, 9; cf. ibid., Vol. II, p. 427 ff.

[3] *Epistle 93* (To the Lady Caesaria); PG 32, 484-485; tr. from FC, revised in Daniel J. Sheerin, *The Eucharist* (Message of the Fathers of the Church, 7), Michael Glazier, Wilmington, DE, 1986, pp. 304 ff.

[4] *The Shorter Rules*, No. 172; PG 31, 1196; tr. W.K.L. Clarke, cited in Sheerin, p. 286 ff.

[5] *The Great Catechetical Oration* 37; Tr. by J.H. Strawley, revised in Sheerin, op. cit., p. 60 ff.

[6] *Catechesis* 3, 13-19; SC 50, 174-177; tr. in D.O., op. cit., Vol. II, p. 297 ff.

[7] *Hom. in Matt.* 50, 3-4; PG 58, 508-509; Tr. in D.O., op. cit., Vol. III, p. 480 ff.

[8] *De Trinitate*, VIII, 13-16; PL 10, 246-249; in D.O., op. cit., Vol. II, pp. 565 ff.

[9] *De Sacramentis*, IV, 5-16; Tr. from CSEL, 73, 46 ff.

[10] *Tr. II on Exodus*; Tr. from Latin text in CSEL 68, 26, op. cit., pp. 29 ff.

[11] *Confessions* (c. 400), VII, 10, 16; tr. from the critical Latin text by M. Skutella (1934), *Bibliotheca Scriptorum Graecorum et Romanorum Teubneriana* (Verlag von B.G. Teubner, Leipzig).

[12] *Sermon 272* (c. 405-411); tr. from PL 38, 1247-1248.

[13] *Enarratio in Ps. 98:9* (Carthage, c. 411-412); Tr. from ed. CC, op. cit., 39, 1385-6.

[14] *Sermon 12 on the Passion*, 3, 6-7; Tr. from PL 54, 355-357.

[15] *Sermon 2 on the Ascension*, 1-4 (PL 54, 397-399); Tr. from D.O., op. cit., Vol. II, p. 642 (slightly amended).

Byzantine Mystagogy

[1] Note the typical Dionysian word play throughout this section on the technical Greek name for the rite (*synaxis*), "to draw together."

[2] This theme is frequently expressed at the Second Vatican Council; cf. Constitution on the Sacred Liturgy (*Sacrosanctum Concilium*), n. 10; Const. on the Church (*Lumen Gentium*), n. 11.

[3] *Eccles. Hist.*, c. III, i (PG 3, 247C); Tr. by Colm Luibheid & Paul Rorem in *Pseudo Dionysius*, CWS, Paulist Press, Mahwah, NJ, 1987, p. 209 ff.

[4] The mystery of the Incarnation is seen as extended in the eucharistic mystery. PG 3, 441A ff., loc. cit., pp. 220 ff.

[5] *The Church's Mystagogy*, cc. xv-xvi, xxi in *Maximus the Confessor*, CWS, Paulist Press, Mahwah, NJ, 1985, p. 201 ff.

[6] This image was earlier employed by Theodore of Mopsuestia in his Baptismal Homily V, 36; cf. E. Yarnold, S.J., *The Awe Inspiring Rites of Initiation*, St. Paul, 1973, pp. 258 ff.

[7] *De fide orthodoxa,* IV, 13; Tr. FC 37, pp. 354-361 (revised); cf. PG 94, 1136 ff.; cf. also Solano, op. cit., p. 766.

Gregorian Counsel

[1] *In Eccles.*, Bk. viii, 6; tr. in D.O., op. cit., Vol. I, p. 565 ff.

[2] *Sermo 36 on Lk 14:16-24*; PL 76, 1266-1267; tr. by M.F. Toal in *The Sunday Sermons of the Great Fathers*, vol. III, Longmans, Green, p. 180 ff.

Celtic and Anglo-Saxon Faith

[1] *Instructions* 13, 1-3; Tr. in D.O., op. cit., Vol. III, pp. 469 ff. and 473 ff.

[2] *Bede: A History of the English Church and People*, Vol. I, 27; Tr. by Leo Sherley-Price, Penguin Classics, 1986, p. 78 ff.

[3] IV, 24, op. cit., p. 252 ff.

[4] *Sancti Venite: Analecta Hymnica Medii Aevii* 51, 298-299. Tr. by Father James Good, an Irish missionary in Lodwar, Kenya.

Controversy, But Firm in Faith

[1] Like many of the Fathers, Paschasius attributes the Letter to the Hebrews to St. Paul.

[2] *De corpore et sanguine Domini*, IV; PL 120, col. 1277-1278.

[3] Probably a reference to Paschasius.

Notes

[4] *De corpore et sanguine Domini*, lxix (PL 121, col. 154-156); ix (ibid., col 131); xcvi (ibid., col 168-169); ci (ibid., col 170).

The Carolingian Renaissance

[1] Cited in Nathan Mitchell, OSB, *Cult and Controversy: The Worship of the Eucharist Outside Mass*, Pueblo Publishing Co., New York, 1982, p. 104.
[2] Ibid., p. 105.
[3] Ibid., p. 105.
[4] Ibid., p. 105 ff. Italics refer to rubrics.

Faith Seeking Understanding

[1] *Monastic Constitutions*, c. I sect. iv; PL 150, cols. 456-457.
[2] *The Prayers and Meditations of Saint Anselm*, Collins, Penguin Classics, 1988, p. 100 ff.

Monastic Mystical Theology

[1] The imagery of the kiss is based on the spiritual interpretation of the Song of Songs (cf. 5:13; 7:8, etc.) as in some of the Fathers, e.g., Origen, Gregory of Nyssa, and so on. Medieval Cistercians made much of this in describing the mystical union between Christ and the soul (cf. Bernard's commentary on the Song of Songs; also Aelred of Rievaulx, *De amicitia spirit.*, 2:21-26). William's words recall the romantic adventure depicted in a secular Greek novel by Achilles Tatius, *Clitophon and Leucippe* (II, 37), which however was probably unknown to the monks since interest in it was not aroused until its appearance in Latin in 1554. The traditional Christological interpretation of the Song of Songs was in keeping with the Fathers' insight in reviewing the whole of the Old Testament in the light of Christ. The Song of Songs thus provided them with a biblical model of communion between God and mankind, a model based on belief in the intrinsic goodness and worth of human relations and sexuality which God created in the beginning in his own image and likeness (cf. Gn 1 - 2).
[2] *Meditativae Orationes*, VIII, 7-8; PL 180. Tr. from the critical Latin text in SC, n. 324 (Jacques Hourlier).
[3] *The Golden Epistle*, X, 30. Sheed and Ward, 1980, p. 55 ff. Tr. of Walter Shewring revised in modern English.
[4] *In Coena Domini*; PL 183, 271-273; *St. Bernard On the Christian Year*. Selections from his sermons, tr. and ed. by a Religious of C.S.M.V., A.R. Mobray & Co., Ltd., London, 1954, p. 84 ff.
[5] *Saint Bernard: The Nativity*, tr. by Leo Hickey, Scepter Ltd., Dublin, 1959, p. 6 ff.
[6] Cf. Leviticus 23 and 25. Hence the reference to Moses, who was thought to be the author of the Pentateuch. The imagery links the table of the word with that of the Sacrament.
[7] This and the following passage are cited because they imply the necessity for deep reverence for all that pertains to the Holy Sacrament of the Lord's Body, a reverence which Aelred characteristically situates in the context of tender love.
[8] *The Mirror of Charity*, tr. by Geoffrey Webb and Adrian Walker, The Catholic Book Club, London, 1962, pp. 80 f., 90 f., 118, 126.

215

[9] *Hildegard of Bingen: Scivias*, Bk. II, Vision 6: "Christ's Sacrifice and the Church," nn. 15-16, 24; tr. by Mother Columba Hart and Jane Bishop, CWS, Paulist Press, Mahwah, NJ, 1990, pp. 246 and 252.

[10] *Transubstantion* was a neologism. Its first known use was by Rolando Bandinelli (later Alexander III) in *De Sententiis Rolandi*, published c. 1140.

[11] *De Sacramento Altaris*, II, 1; Tr. from the critical Latin text in SC, n. 93 (Editions du Cerf, 1963), p. 142 ff.

The Renewal of the Church

[1] *The Ancrene Riwle*, Rendered into modern English and edited by M.B. Salu, London, 1955, p. 7.

[2] "Letter to the Faithful" (2nd Version) in *Francis and Clare: The Complete Works*, tr. by Regis J. Armstrong and Ignatius C. Brady, CWS, Paulist Press, Mahwah, NJ, 1982, pp. 67 ff.

[3] "The Testament"; ibid., p. 154. J.R.R. Tolkien expressed a similar view in writing to his son Michael, who was disturbed by the shortcomings of priests. Cf. *The Letters of J.R.R. Tolkien*, edited by Humphrey Carpenter with the assistance of Christopher Tolkien, Houghton Mifflin Company, Boston, 1981, p. 337 ff.

Schooled in Faith

[1] *Commentary on St. Luke's Gospel*, 22, 19; Tr. in D.O., op. cit., Vol. III, p. 397* ff.

[2] *Thomas Aquinas: Selected Writings*, Selected and Edited by M.C. D'Arcy, S.J., Everyman: Dent, London, p. 24 ff. (tr. slightly modernized).

[3] Translated by Gerard Manley Hopkins, S.J.

[4] *A Mirror for Simple Souls*, Edited and translated by Charles Crawford, Gill's Spiritual Classics, Gill & MacMillan, 1981, pp. 51-54.

[5] German Works: *Counsels on Discernment*, ch. 20: *Meister Eckhart: The Essential Sermons, etc.* Translated by Edmund Colledge and Bernard McGinn, CWS, Paulist Press, NY, 1981, pp. 270-272.

Medieval Gems

[1] Cf. the hymn *Lauda Sion* of the Office of Corpus Christi: "Sumit unus, sumunt mille... nec sumptus consumitur" ("Though one or a thousand eat, it would not be consumed").

[2] Cf. the hymn *Adoro Te*: "Visus, gustus, tactus in te fallitur, sed auditu solo tuto creditur" ("Sight, taste, touch in thee are deceived; hearing alone is safely believed").

[3] *Catherine of Siena: The Dialogue*, 110-111; tr. by Suzanne Noffke, CWS, Paulist Press, New York/Mahwah, 1980, pp. 206 ff., 209 ff.

[4] In *Medieval English Verse*, Penguin, 1968, p. 137.

[5] The stanza quoted here is the last of the poem, n. 101; ibid., p. 173 ff.

[6] The imagery of motherhood as applied to God/Christ nourishing his little ones can be traced to Jesus' own figure of the hen gathering its chicks under his wing and to St. Paul's analogy of milk as spiritual food (cf. 1 Cor 3:2). This teaching is taken up in the Fathers (cf. Clement of Alexandria [*Paedogogus* I, 35 ff., etc.] who refers also to Homer [*Iliad* 13, 6] to justify the use of such a manner of speaking.

[7] *Revelations of Divine Love*, c. 60; Translated into modern English by Clifton Wolters, Penguin, 1966, p. 169 ff.

[8] *The Imitation of Christ*, IV, 5; translated by Leo Sherley-Price, Penguin, 1986, p. 194 ff.

[9] *St. Ignatius Loyola*, Burns & Oates, London, 1962, p. 95 ff.

[10] Cf. *The Spiritual Journal of St. Ignatius of Loyola: Feb. 2, 1544 to Feb. 27, 1545*, translated by William J. Young (Roma Centrum Ignatianum Spiritualitatis, 1979). Reprinted from Woodstock Letters (1958).

English Wills and Witnesses

[1] T.E. Bridgett, CSSR, *A History of the Holy Eucharist in Great Britain*, Burns & Oates, London, 1908, pp. 161 ff. and 168.

[2] *Testamenta Vetusta*, p. 33, cited in T.E. Bridgett, CSSR, Ibid., pp. 247 and 224.

[3] Etymologically this word for Holy Communion and the Blessed Eucharist means sacrifice, victim. It was frequently used before the Reformation for the Sacrament of the altar received by the faithful (cf. John Lingard, *The History and Antiquities of the Anglo-Saxon Church*, pp. 235 & 236).

[4] *Treatise on the Passion*, cited in *The Wisdom and Wit of Blessed Thomas More*, edited by T.E. Bridgett, CSSR, Sheed & Ward, London, 1977, p. 140 ff.

[5] Cited by T.E. Bridgett, CSSR, *A History of the Holy Eucharist in Great Britain*, op. cit., p. 247.

[6] John Oecolampadius was a German Reformer who in general followed Zwingli's teachings.

[7] *De Veritate Corporis et Sanguinis*, I, cap. 21; cited in Bridgett, op. cit., p. 224.

Mysticism and Devotion

[1] *The Way of Perfection*, cc. 33 & 34; tr. by E. Alison Peers, Doubleday, NY, 1977, pp. 140 ff.

[2] "Song of the soul that is glad to know God by faith," *Poems of St. John of the Cross*; tr. by Roy Campbell, Collins, 1979, p. 45 ff.

[3] "The Living Flame of Love," Commentary: 5-6 in *The Collected Works of St. John of the Cross*, Tr. by Kieran Kavanaugh and Otilio Rodriguez, ICS, Washington, DC, 1979, p. 581.

[4] "Letter to Madre Ana de San Alberto, Prioress of Caravaca, Seville, June 1586"; ibid., p. 686.

[5] *Introduction to the Devout Life*, tr. by Michael Day, Cong. Orat., Burns & Oates, London, 1956, p. 71 ff.

[6] St. Francis de Sales' teaching on frequent Communion is remarkable as a firm stand against the Jansenistic tendency prevailing at the time.

[7] Op. cit., pp. 81 ff.

The Baroque Age

[1] *Pensées* 733, Penguin, 1966, p. 253 ff.

[2] *Oeuvres completes de Bossuet*, t. III, Outhenin-Chalandre Fils, Besancon, 1836, p. 346.

[3] Ibid., p. 353.

[4] *The Autobiography of Saint Margaret Mary*, Tr. by the Sisters of the Visitation, Tan, Rockford, IL, 1986, p. 67 ff.

[5] Letter to Reverend Mother Prioress, Nov. 17, 1690 in *The Practice of the Presence of God*, Tr. by E.M. Blaiklock, Hodder & Stoughton, 1986, p. 54.

Pastoral Missions

1 *The Holy Eucharist*, edited by Rev. Eugene Grimm in *The Complete Works*, Vol. VI, Redemptorist Fathers, Brooklyn, NY, 1934, pp 42-44.
2 Ibid., pp. 275-277.
3 *Italian Journal*: Feb. 24, 1804, in *Elizabeth Seton: Selected Writings*, edited by Ellin Kelly and Annabelle Melville, Paulist Press, New York, 1987, p. 233 ff.
4 *Memoirs, Letters and Journal of Elizabeth Seton*, Vol. I, edited by Robert Seton, P. O'Shea Publisher, New York, 1870, pp. 165 and 167.
5 Ibid., Vol. II, p. 18 [Letter to Celia Seton, June 9, 1808].
6 Ibid., p. 142 ff.

The Age of Newman

1 Archives, Archdiocese of Westminster.
2 Eymard links the political turmoil throughout Europe in 1848 with the terrible days of the French Revolution; for him social order and religious respect go hand in hand.
3 *Le Très Saint Sacrement*, Juin 1864, pp. 5-13.
4 *The Real Presence*, Eymard League, New York, 1938.
5 *The Mysteries of Christianity*, translated by Cyril Vollert, SJ, B. Herder Book Co., St. Louis & London, 1947, p. 498 ff.
6 Letter of October 16/17, 1866, *Selected Prose*, edited by Gerald Roberts, Oxford University Press, p. 30 ff.
7 Ibid., p. 28 (feast of St. Theresa, 1866).
8 *The Poems of Gerard Manley Hopkins*, Fourth edition, edited by W.H. Gardner and N.H. MacKenzie, Oxford University Press Paperback, 1970, p. 69.
9 *An Essay on the Development of Christian Doctrine*, Longmans, Green & Co., London, 1914, p. 23.
10 *Grammar of Assent*, Image Books, Doubleday & Co., Inc., Garden City, New York, 1955, p. 121 ff.
11 *Parochial and Plain Sermons*, Vol. VII — The Gospel Feast — Longmans, Green & Co., London, 1896, p. 176 ff.
12 From *Meditations and Devotions*, Pt. I, xvi; Burns & Oates, London, 1964, p. 87.
13 Stanza 25 (translated by Roy Campbell, op. cit., p. 21).
14 *Autobiography of St. Therese of Lisieux*, translated by Ronald Knox, P.J. Kenedy & Sons, New York, 1958, pp. 133 ff.
15 *Oeuvres spirituelles. Anthologie*, Editions du Seuil, Paris, 1958. This passage was written in Rome on January 23, 1897, on leaving the Trappists to go to Nazareth.
16 Retreat notes written in Nazareth in 1897 and cited by René Voillaume in *Les fraternités du Père de Foucauld. Mission et Esprit*, Paris, 1946, p. 85.

Post-Modernism: A Reaffirmation

1 *The Mystery of Faith: Regarding the Most August Sacrament and Sacrifice of the Body and Blood of Christ*, I, Sheed & Ward, London, 1941, Preface.
2 *GK's Weekly*, Sept. 7, 1933.

Notes

[3] Cf. Pope Paul VI in *Mysterium Fidei*, n. 46 regarding this term as the most "suitable and accurate" name for the mysterious change at Mass (Cf. ARCIC *Windsor Statement* 1971, n. 6 concerning the common agreement and comment on "Transubstantiation").

[4] *A Key to the Doctrine of the Eucharist*, Burns Oates & Washbourne Ltd., London, 1925, pp. 176 ff.

[5] *The People of God*, Burns Oates & Washbourne Ltd., London, 1937, pp. 156 ff.

[6] *Le Jeudi-Saint*, Flammarion, 1931, pp. 78-80, 82-86.

[7] *The Window in the Wall And Other Sermons on the Holy Eucharist*, Burns & Oates, London, 1956, pp. 2 ff.

[8] *The Theology of the Mystical Body*, B. Herder Book Co., 1952, p. 591 ff.

[9] Translated from the column in *Le Monde*, February 3, 1978.

Visionaries

[1] From *La Messe Là-bas*.

[2] *Le Milieu Divin*, Collins Fontana, 1964, p. 123 ff.

[3] *Hymn of the Universe*, Collins, London, 1965, pp. 47-48.

[4] *The Dry Wood*, Sheed & Ward, London, 1947, p. 79 ff.

[5] *The High Green Hill*, The Catholic Book Club, London, 1951, pp. 127-129.

[6] *The Farewell Discourses*, Meditations on John 13-17, translated by E.A. Nelson, Ignatius Press, San Francisco, 1987, pp. 124-127.

Theologians of Vatican II

[1] *Le Mystère de L'Eucharistie*, Tèqui, Paris, 1980, p. 27 ff.

[2] *The Christian Commitment*, Sheed and Ward, 1963, p. 195 ff.

[3] "Über die Besuchung des Allerheiligsten" in *Geist und Leben* 32 (1959), p. 263.

[4] *The Glory of the Lord: A Theological Aesthetics*, Vol. 1, Ignatius Press, San Francisco, 1982, pp. 571 ff.

[5] *The Revelation of God*, DLT, 1968, pp. 189 ff.

[6] *Holy Spirit of God*, Geoffrey Chapman, London, 1966, pp. 96 ff.

[7] Cf. *Emmanuel* (publication of the Priests' Eucharistic League, USA), New York, September 1966, p. 249 ff. A fuller account of the argument of this lecture is contained in the author's Notes for students at the Gregorian University — cf. *Adiumenta ad tractatum de SS. Eucharistiae sacramento* (Pont. Univ. Greg., Rome 1966), pp. 108-184.

Adorers in Spirit and Truth

[1] *Thoughts: Fragments of apostolic spirituality from his writings and talks*, St. Paul Editions, Boston, 1974, pp. 141 ff.

[2] *Letters from the Desert*, Darton, Longman & Todd, London, 1972, pp. 11 ff.

[3] *Faith and Contemplation*, translated by Bishop Victor Shearburn, C.R., Darton, Longman & Todd, 1974, pp. 70 ff.

[4] *Lettres aux Fraternités...*, Paris, 1974, pp. 58 ff.

[5] *Life of Christ*, McGraw Hill Book Co., Inc., New York, 1958, pp. 324 ff.

[6] Talk at the International Eucharistic Congress, Nairobi, 1985.

[7] *Miracles Do Happen*, Pan Books, London, 1987, pp. 62 & 68.

Epilogue

[1] In retrospect this poem, written over twenty years ago, applies to the life of my brother, who delighted so many in pouring out the wine of his music until he was called on Ash Wednesday, 1990, to higher service at Love's Banquet. R.I.P.

Index of Entries

A

Abercius   7
Aelred of Rievaulx, St.   85
Alacoque, St. Margaret Mary   133
Alberione, James, SSP   195
Albert the Great, St.   97
Alphonsus de Liguori, St.   137
Ambrose, St.   44
Ancrene Riwle   93
Anselm, St.   78
Aquinas, St. Thomas   98
Augustine of Hippo, St.   49

B

Baldwin of Ford   90
Balthasar, Hans Urs von   186
Basil the Great, St.   36
Bede the Venerable, St.   66
Bernard of Clairvaux, St.   83
Bossuet, Jacques Benigne   131

C

Carolingian Texts   75
Carretto, Carlo   196
Catherine of Siena, St.   109
Chesterton, Gilbert Keith   160
Chrysostom, St. John   40
Clark, Francis   193
Claudel, Paul   171
Clement of Alexandria   21
Columbanus, St.   65
Congar, Yves, OP   188
Cyprian, St.   29
Cyril of Jerusalem, St.   34

D

de Foucauld, Charles   157
de la Taille, Maurice, SJ   159
Didache   13
Dionysius the Areopagite   55
Durwell, François-Xavier, CSSR   190

E

Eckhart, Meister   104
Ephraem, St.   33
Eymard, St. Peter Julian   145

F

Fisher, St. John   121
Francis de Sales, St.   128
Francis of Assisi, St.   94

G

Gaudentius of Brescia, St.   47
Green, Julien   169
Gregory Agrigentinus, St.   61
Gregory of Nyssa, St.   38
Gregory the Great, St.   62

H

Henry VII's Will   119
Hilary of Poitiers, St.   43
Hildegard of Bingen, St.   88
Hippolytus   3
Hopkins, Gerard Manley, SJ   150
Houselander, Caryll   176
Hymn, Oldest Eucharistic   69

I

Ignatius of Antioch, St.   11
Ignatius of Loyola, St.   115
Imitation of Christ   113
Irenaeus of Lyons, St.   18

J

John Damascene, St.   59
John of the Cross, St.   125
Journet, Charles   183
Julian of Norwich   112
Justin Martyr, St.   14

K

Knox, Ronald   165

L

Lanfranc of Canterbury   77
Lawrence, Brother   134
Leo the Great, St.   53

M

Mauriac, François   162
Maximus the Confessor, St.   57
McKenna, Sr. Briege   205
Melito of Sardis, St.   16
Mersch, Emile, SJ   168
Mirror for Simple Souls   102
More, St. Thomas   119

N

Newman, John Henry Card.   152

O

Origen of Alexandria   24

P

Pascal, Blaise   131
Paschasius Radbertus, St.   71
Pearl, The   111
Pectorius   9

R

Rahner, Karl, SJ   184
Ratramnus   73
Raynolds, Archbp.   117

S

Scheeben, Matthias Joseph   149
Seton, St. Elizabeth Ann   139
Sheen, Bp. Fulton J.   201

T

Teilhard de Chardin, Pierre   172
Teresa of Avila, St.   123
Teresa of Calcutta, Mother   204
Tertullian   27
Therese of Lisieux, St.   155
Thomas à Kempis   113

V

Vann, Gerald, OP   177
Voillaume, René   198
von Speyr, Adrienne   179
Vonier, Anscar   161

W

William of St. Thierry   81
Wiseman, Nicholas Card.   143